THE
FALL
OF
Boris
Johnson

Also by Sebastian Payne
Broken Heartlands

THE FALL OF Boris Johnson THE FULL STORY

SEBASTIAN PAYNE

MACMILLAN

First published 2022 by Macmillan
an imprint of Pan Macmillan
The Smithson, 6 Briset Street, London EC1M 5NR
EU representative: Macmillan Publishers Ireland Ltd, 1st Floor,
The Liffey Trust Centre, 117–126 Sheriff Street Upper,
Dublin 1, D01 YC43
Associated companies throughout the world
www.panmacmillan.com

ISBN 978-1-0350-1655-6

3 5 7 9 8 6 4

A CIP catalogue record for this book is available from the British Library.

Typeset by Typo•glyphix, Burton-on-Trent, DE14 3HE
Printed and bound by CPI Group (UK) Ltd, Croydon, CR0 4YY

Visit **www.panmacmillan.com** to read more about all our books
and to buy them. You will also find features, author interviews and
news of any author events, and you can sign up for e-newsletters
so that you're always first to hear about our new releases.

For Bronwen,
who was and remains a slight Boris fan

Contents

'When a regime has been in power too long, when it has fatally exhausted the patience of the people, and when oblivion finally beckons – I am afraid that across the world you can rely on the leaders of that regime to act solely in the interests of self-preservation, and not in the interests of the electorate.'

– BORIS JOHNSON

Introduction –
Drinks at the Garrick Club

Boris Johnson shuffled into the mahogany and red dining room of the Garrick Club one cold November evening with a relaxed grin on his face. Scooping up a drink as the dinner was about to begin, he beamed at his former journalist colleagues. Rumours had been circulating that he would attend, but many were stunned not only that the prime minister had just walked in, but that he had done so on time (unlike the filing of his newspaper articles). Johnson had returned to a gathering to celebrate his spiritual home: among the comment writers of *The Daily Telegraph*. Fresh from the success of the COP26 climate conference in Glasgow, he could finally let his guard down.

Since 1831, the Garrick has wined and dined the great of London's cultural scene. From A. A. Milne to Stephen Fry, the institution inspires improbable passions among its members – with its garish salmon club ties and sumptuous Covent Garden surroundings (Johnson was not a member when he arrived for supper in late 2021). His choice of transport had been criticised; the optics were poor, jetting back from a conference about climate change. But he could not care less, he was among friends. After two years of the Covid pandemic he was the global statesman and at the centre of everyone's attention, something that he had craved since childhood.

In the private room, a broad table was set for around thirty

Fleet Street veterans who had worked with a colleague later to become the most powerful man in the country. The occasion was a reunion of columnists and leader writers whose careers stretched back to the 1960s. The dominant era represented was Charles Moore's, editor from 1995 to 2003; the occasion convened by Stephen Glover and Neil Darbyshire, both senior figures at the *Daily Mail* who had stints at the *Telegraph* in the 1980s and 90s when Johnson was becoming the paper's star political columnist.

The assembled diners – including editor of *The Oldie* magazine Harry Mount, former *Today* programme editor Sarah Sands and editor of ConservativeHome website Paul Goodman – were surprised and delighted to see Johnson was present. Guzzling roast pheasant[1] with Grand Marnier soufflé, washed down with hefty bottles of claret, the collected journalists celebrated what seemed to be the very best of times. Glover noted in his speech that the attendees were 'responsible for millions of words over the decade' and 'it would be impossible to calculate the damage we've done'.

At the prime minister's end of the table Dean Godson, the *Telegraph*'s former chief leader writer, impersonated his old proprietor Conrad Black attempting French; Johnson laughed so hard his friends feared he might crack a rib. One attendee said, 'The extraordinary thing is that I've known Boris in passing for thirty-odd years, but I've never seen him happier and laugh harder than that evening.' Another remarked, 'It was a triumphant homecoming, he had proven himself beyond doubt at having beaten us all.'

When Johnson spoke at the supper, after much wine had been consumed, he delivered a typically comic and self-deprecating speech where one attendee said he (improbably) claimed to have only penned two leaders for the *Telegraph*, the second of which was about the row between author Salman Rushdie and Ayatollah

Khomeini, then the supreme leader of Iran. After his editorial came down on the side of the Ayatollah, the paper's then proprietor Conrad Black informed Johnson he didn't need to write any more, so the yarn went. The hacks lapped it up.

The prime minister's 'very infectious' tone adding to the gaiety of the evening. He rapidly moved on to his favourite topic: his achievements. He paid tribute to the success points of his own government – delivering Brexit and the world-leading Covid vaccine rollout. Then came a heckle: one *Telegraph* writer shouted out that he had not been especially conservative. With his well-worn hangdog expression, an artful ruffle of his thatched hair, Johnson admitted they had a point. There was no malice, it was not an evening for serious policy debate, but to celebrate one of their own.

Johnson later stumbled out of the Garrick Club after the supper had concluded, wearing the same grey suit with blue tie he had donned hours earlier in Glasgow. Moore was photographed at his side, in a double-breasted suit with red tie. The wide grins on both their faces spoke not only to an enjoyable evening, but the decades of warm professional and personal relations. Repaying his early career patronage, Moore had been ennobled[2] by Johnson in 2020.

Moore's demeanour may have been jolly, but his concern for a close friend weighed heavily on his mind. Three days before the Garrick supper, he wrote a *Telegraph* column[3] on the case of Owen Paterson, the Conservative MP and former environment secretary who was facing a suspension from the House of Commons having been found guilty of 'paid advocacy', misconduct that would end his political career. During the investigation, Paterson's wife Rose had committed suicide and Moore made the case that Paterson was being hounded. Moore insisted he did not discuss the matter with the prime minister that night.

But weeks before the Garrick supper, Johnson's closest allies had voiced similar misgivings and had begun plotting a ruse to try and stave off the end of Paterson's career. In the Cabinet and the whips' office, those responsible for Tory party management were crafting a scheme that would disastrously backfire and create a fissure between Conservative MPs that would expose the flaws in Johnson's premiership and see the man feted by his former colleagues as a great leader heaved out of power within the year, rather than his stated desire of serving for at least a decade.

The botched plan to save Paterson was not cooked up at the Garrick alongside the pheasant, but one *Telegraph* alumni reflected on that supper later, 'He palpably felt so powerful and so popular that he thought "I can save Owen Paterson, I'm untouchable at the moment." He was certainly giving off that air. He looked like someone very much enjoying being prime minister at their peak of their powers.'

***

That Garrick supper took place thirty turbulent months after Johnson entered 10 Downing Street in July 2019, amid the Brexit wars and one of the Conservative party's deepest ever crises. The UK's febrile divisions had been tearing apart its politics and social fabric. Three years after 17.4 million Britons had voted to leave the EU, Westminster had failed to fulfil the result. The Tories were hurting: David Cameron had been turfed out as leader after his campaign to remain in the EU failed. Theresa May, his successor, failed and failed again to see through the UK's exit from the bloc. The nadir of her time as prime minister came in May 2019, when the Conservatives came fifth in the ludicrous set of European Parliament elections that took place while the UK's exit from the bloc was in progress. The party faced extinction.

Johnson had long been the bookmakers' favourite to be the next prime minister. From the day he announced[4] 'of course I'm going to go for it', there was an inevitability he would succeed May as the only contender who could reinvent and save the Tories. During the MPs' shortlisting process, where the Conservative parliamentary party selected the final two contenders to be voted on by the 150,000-odd members, he topped[5] each round with clear majorities. His rival, the subdued foreign secretary Jeremy Hunt, stood from the centre left of the party and made little impact. Nearly two decades after he first became an MP, three years since his first bid for prime minister failed, and the countless times he had been written off, Johnson garnered two-thirds of the party's vote. He finally rolled into Downing Street on 24 July 2019.

From the off, the drama and chaos scarcely let up. Outside Number 10 for the first time, Johnson pledged that the UK would exit the EU 'do or die' on 31 October that year. Members of Johnson's first Cabinet had a markedly more right-leaning bent than what had come before, with many of Johnson's long-time supporters handed prime secretary of state portfolios. A few days into power, the prime minister spoke[6] at the Science and Industry Museum in Manchester to pledge a new high-speed rail route from Leeds to Manchester, later known as Northern Powerhouse Rail (he has a lifelong devotion to infrastructure, as part of his quest to leave his physical mark on the country).

A few weeks before Johnson became prime minister, a meeting had taken place with a cabal of his friends and acolytes to figure out how prime minister Johnson would break the Brexit deadlock: without a majority in parliament to deliver a 'no deal' Brexit, or a plan to negotiate a new withdrawal agreement with the EU, he faced being the shortest-lived prime minister in history. Also present at the meeting was his young partner Carrie Symonds, a Conservative party activist who he began dating the previous year and would go on to become his most crucial sounding board. After an inconclusive discussion, one of Johnson's closest allies told him, 'You're going to need to send for Dom.' He duly visited the north London home of Dominic Cummings, the mercurial strategist behind the Vote Leave campaign.

After some persuasion Cummings agreed to come with him to Number 10, but the terms were onerous. He would report directly to Johnson; he would be de facto chief of staff without the title; he would exercise total authority over all politically appointed special advisors. With no alternative, Johnson acquiesced. The relationship was uneasy from the start. Each man felt innately superior and different to the other: Cummings the nerdish strategist and thinker, Johnson the charismatic politician and national figure. Cummings saw Johnson as his useful tool to smash the British state and rebuild it in his image, the prime minister saw Cummings as someone with the force of personality to break the Brexit deadlock.

Throughout his first summer in office, the Brexit deadlock remained and rumours abounded that Johnson would prorogue parliament to ensure it could not further delay the UK's departure. On 28 August, he duly asked the Queen to end the parliamentary session. This was later overturned by the Supreme Court as 'unlawful'[7] but the outrage prompted by suspending parliamentary scrutiny soon deprived Johnson of his working majority when twenty-one Tory MPs were expelled[8] for defying his orders to vote against leaving the EU without a deal – including the former chancellor Ken Clarke and Nicholas Soames, grandson of Johnson's hero Winston Churchill. These expulsions were a defining moment in his rise, a signal of Johnson's intent to break conventions, reshape the Tory party in his image, and do whatever it takes for Brexit.

In October Johnson struck a new agreement[9] with Brussels, albeit one that essentially raised a trade border between Northern

Ireland and the rest of the UK. Instead of approving the new deal, the House of Commons forced Johnson into yet another Brexit delay.

Johnson's calls for a general election to resolve the deadlock and to 'get Brexit done' ramped up. The country at last went to the polls on 12 December. With Tory MPs refusing to back his deal, only one option remained: a new parliamentary party in his own image. The result was the greatest electoral feat of his career. His status as the most compelling political campaigner of his generation was proven by winning the Tories their largest major-ity[10] since 1987. Jeremy Corbyn, the opposition's left-wing leader, stood no chance. When Johnson arrived in Sedgefield, the County Durham seat represented by Tony Blair for twenty-four years, he was greeted by crowds chanting his name. Working-class England buried reservations about the party and its leader to put him back in Downing Street. Once again, he had defied the consensus. By collapsing the so-called 'red wall' of former heartlands, Johnson was handed a generational chance to reshape the country. The UK finally left the EU on 31 January 2020.

The early days of Johnson's second term were marked by triumphalism. His Downing Street aides, led by Cummings, declared a war on the established media, the civil service and many of the country's respected institutions. In his quest to repay the trust of those first-time voters, Johnson pressed ahead with the High Speed 2 (HS2) railway in February,[11] followed by a Cabinet reshuffle that booted out those outside his inner circle. The most critical change, however, was the forced resignation of Sajid Javid. Johnson and Cummings ordered the chancellor to sack his team of advisors and replace them with Number 10's picks. Javid refused[12] and he was replaced by Rishi Sunak, the young chief secretary to the Treasury. This marked another inflection point of his premiership: had Javid remained chancellor, the most critical power nexus of his government could have been remarkably different.

The country's palpable relief of a stable government after the chaos of the Brexit years was soon shattered when Covid-19 was found in every nation of the UK by the start of March 2020. Johnson was initially slow to act, as the government bickered about the best way to tackle the pandemic. The first lockdown came[13] on 23 March, when Johnson ordered citizens to stay at home. All shops, schools and nonessential businesses closed; normal life ceased. Days later, Johnson himself was diagnosed with Covid. The prime minister was admitted to St Thomas' Hospital on 5 April and moved to intensive care two days later.[14] He recovered but the long fatigue and his brush with death left a deep mark on his premiership.

As the first wave of Covid abated, the first true scandal of his premiership arrived when it was revealed that Cummings had driven to the market town of Barnard Castle in the north-east of England when nonessential travel was forbidden. In a bizarre press conference in the Number 10 garden, Cummings claimed[15] he had travelled thirty miles from his family home to test his eyesight.

Johnson's one-year anniversary of entering Downing Street was marked by a gradual easing of Covid restrictions, albeit with rising fears that another coronavirus wave would hit the country. In September, the so-called 'rule of six' was introduced,[16] restricting how many people could gather indoors, followed by a convoluted system of tiered restrictions later that month. In late October, Johnson announced a month-long 'circuit breaker' lockdown[17] that largely mirrored the draconian restrictions of March. While society was shut down, Cummings left Downing Street after an acrimonious falling out[18] that neither would soon forget. The nation reopened with some restrictions still in place, on the same day Pfizer's Covid-19 vaccine was approved[19] by medical authorities, the first green-lighted jab in the world.

As Christmas dawned, Britons were advised not to travel and the third and final Covid lockdown came into force[20] on 4 January as the Delta variant of Covid spread rapidly. While the prime minister's legacy on Covid is mixed, the vaccine rollout of 2021 was an unadulterated success. His habit of claiming something British was world-beating was proven to be accurate for once. Lockdown ended on 29 March and life gradually returned to a semblance of normality as Covid abated. Riding off the success of the jabs, Johnson delivered a remarkable set of local election results for the Tories in April, including winning the northern seat of Hartlepool for the first time – proving that his electoral potency went beyond the events of 2019. In May, Johnson married Carrie in a small ceremony at Westminster Cathedral; they celebrated afterwards in the Downing Street garden.

Ominous signs, however, began to emerge that the glory of 2019 was fading, that Johnson's coalition stretching the breadth of England was beginning to collapse under the contradictions of governing. In June 2021, the Tories lost the leafy Buckinghamshire constituency of Chesham and Amersham to the Liberal Democrats – the first time the seat had not been represented by a Conservative – prompting party fears that his populist governing style was turning off the traditional Tory base. In July, all remaining Covid restrictions were abolished on 'Freedom Day' – a decision Johnson privately vacillated over for weeks. August brought the withdrawal of UK troops from Afghanistan and the fall of Kabul to the Taliban, a shambolic and shameful moment for all Western countries. Dominic Raab, his foreign secretary, was widely mocked for claiming 'the sea was closed'[21] when asked if he was paddleboarding as British troops were being evacuated.

Ignoring the growing warnings about his premiership, Johnson began the autumn political season with a bang by reshuffling his Cabinet again, promoting Liz Truss to foreign secretary, demoting Raab to justice secretary, creating a new ministry for the levelling-up agenda to tackle regional inequalities and tasking long-time minister Michael Gove to head it. The Cabinet shake-up had been planned for months, according to those involved, and was initially due to take place at the end of July. Several struggling ministers left government while devoted loyalists such as Nadine Dorries were handed new briefs, hers as culture secretary. A week later, Johnson announced a defence pact with America and Australia to counter the dominance of China, known as Aukus. As the economy geared up after the pandemic, however, a crisis in the UK's fuel supplies – triggered by the rise in energy prices – led to supply chain disruptions, soaring wages and thousands of job vacancies.

Johnson's post-pandemic zenith came at that year's Conservative party conference in Manchester, where his allies observed that he was 'pretty chipper'. The prime minister adopted the slogan of 'Build Back Better' from the pandemic and leaned into[22] rising wages, claiming that he wanted a highly productive, highly paid economy that would no longer rest on 'mainlining' cheap labour from abroad. It was typically ideologically and culturally diverse: invoking his political lodestars Churchill and Margaret Thatcher, channelling tennis star Emma Raducanu and praising the Dunkirk spirit for the Afghanistan evacuation. And there were plenty of jokes: Gove was nicknamed 'Jon Bon Govey'[23] after the Cabinet minister was videoed dancing at an Aberdeen nightclub. The prime minister seemed almost bored, hubristically so, by the lack of controversy. When he ran into veteran rebel David Davis in the conference hall, Johnson asked him,[24] 'Why aren't you causing me more trouble?' As they left Manchester, his advisors privately acknowledged 'this is as good as it gets'.

Across the media, journalists lauded Johnson as a phenomenon. Tim Shipman of *The Sunday Times* expressed the feelings of many when he observed,[25] 'Boris Johnson now squats like a giant toad across British politics. He has expanded the Overton window in both directions. Praising bankers and drug companies, while tight on immigration and woke history. Cheered for lauding the NHS and pro LGBT. Where does Labour find a gap?'

And a year later, he was gone. From that high point, the fall of Boris Johnson is the most remarkable political defenestration in modern British political history because so few believed it would ever actually happen. The so-called 'Teflon politician' had defied conventions and odds so many times few thought it could ever end. The parallel to Johnson is Thatcher, who similarly proved herself an election winner that transformed the political scene but eventually lost the confidence of her MPs. Like Johnson, her end was long in the making. It was a similar alchemy of policy and personality that ended her reign as the longest-serving prime minister of the twentieth century.

Was it always going to end this way? Could a better team, a stronger Cabinet, improved structures have resulted in better decisions, fewer mistakes, and a longer stint in power? Or did Johnson's personality and governing style, with its benefits but many flaws, mean his government was always going to come to an almighty smash ending? The answer lies in the story of what took place between the dinner on 2 November 2021 to his announcement on 6 July 2022 that he would resign as Conservative party leader. Although few were aware at the time, the Garrick Club supper marked one of the last true bright spots of Johnson's time in power. As Johnson laughed that night at the jokes and scrapes of his life as a journalist, some further successes lay ahead, especially abroad, but his gradual exit had almost imperceptibly begun.

***

Owen Paterson was not a close friend or ally of Boris Johnson's. The sixty-six-year-old's temperament was one of an unyielding hardliner: he entered parliament in 1997 as MP for North Shropshire – an archetypal rural constituency with a vast Conservative majority. Paterson rose to become shadow secretary of state for Northern Ireland and he clashed with Cameron's modernising agenda, voting against same-sex marriage legislation.

His second and last role in government as environment secretary was even more jarring, underscoring his reputation as an anachronism that the party seemingly had left behind. Paterson's scepticism of climate change again clashed with Cameron's agenda, as did his brittle persona. During a failed badger cull in 2013, Paterson was ridiculed for claiming[26] 'the badgers have moved the goalposts'. It was no shock when he was booted out of the Cabinet as Cameron prepared to reorientate for the next election. On the backbenches, Paterson's campaigning efforts were focused on promoting Brexit.

Most of his time, however, was focused on promoting his bank balance. Paterson took up a part-time role in 2015 as a consultant for Randox, a health care company based in Northern Ireland for which he was initially paid £49,000, a sum that was to later double. During the Covid pandemic, Randox was awarded a £133 million contract for testing kits (no other company was offered the work). Paterson represented Randox in a call with James Bethell, the health minister then responsible for private sector contracts. Randox was awarded a further £347 million contract for testing work. Such lobbying was not enough for Paterson: in December 2016, he took up another role with Lynn's Country Foods, also based in Northern Ireland. Emails showed Paterson lobbied the Food Standards Agency about their 'naked bacon' produce.

To the casual voter, and those closely watching his outside interests, Paterson appeared to be a lobbyist first and an MP second. An inquiry by Kathryn Stone, the independent standards commissioner, was opened into Paterson's outside roles in October 2019 but as the investigation progressed, tragedy struck when Paterson's wife, Rose, committed suicide in June 2020. There was no definitive link between the investigation and her death, but the *Mail On Sunday* published emails[27] between Rose and a friend that included links to articles about Paterson and Randox. The investigation rumbled on throughout 2021.

The report, published on 26 October, was damning. It found that Paterson had breached rules on paid advocacy with his approaches to government ministries and agencies on behalf of Randox and Lynn's Country Foods. It recommended a thirty-day suspension from the House of Commons – a move that would have likely led to a recall petition and the end of his parliamentary career. Three days after Stone's report, Charles Moore published his *Telegraph* article defending Paterson. And three days later, Johnson dined with Moore at the Garrick Club.

The conduct of one backbench Tory would normally be a matter purely for the chief whip: Mark Spencer, a jolly rotund Nottinghamshire farmer liked, if not feared, by MPs.

Yet when Johnson met his Downing Street aides the following morning after the Garrick supper, dealing with the Owen Paterson affair had risen to the top of the agenda. Before the Garrick Club dinner, those around him said he was sceptical of intervening. One close aide recalled, 'I can remember in a couple of conversations with him after the dinner he definitely changed.

It was like this seed about Owen Paterson and the need to defend him had been planted.'

Johnson's inner circle of aides and ministers was split between those who felt Paterson should be assisted, and those who could see the pitfalls of trying to save an MP who had blatantly broken parliamentary rules. Two Johnson loyalists, Jacob Rees-Mogg, the patrician leader of the House of Commons, and Mark Spencer plus Declan Lyons, Johnson's political secretary and his critical link with the parliamentary party who was drafted in to facilitate their plans, had already begun plotting how the Paterson situation could best be handled with scant consultation among the wider party machine.

The Spencer–Rees-Mogg–Lyons trio presented their plan to Johnson: they had considered rejecting the report outright but suggested instead that the government would put forward a motion in the House of Commons that would delay a vote on the report and punishment, followed by forming a new nine-strong committee that would explore parliamentary standards and whether there should be a recourse mechanism. It was to be proposed by Andrea Leadsom, the former business secretary. The new committee would (peculiarly) be chaired by former minister John Whittingdale, who had been sacked by Johnson in the last reshuffle. 'God knows why John got involved,' one MP said.

Two individuals close to the Spencer–Rees-Mogg–Lyons trio said the cabal also looked at reducing Paterson's suspension to below ten days, which would have meant no automatic recall petition – a ploy that would have been fraught with the same image problem. 'It would have still created a row because it would have been transparently gerrymandering,' an official said.

Those involved with the plot insist the trio fully grasped that Paterson had broken parliamentary rules but ran two counter-arguments to merely accepting Stone's findings. First was that there was no appeal mechanism for the punishment (had it existed, it is unlikely Paterson would have won given the weight of evidence about his behaviour). Second was an argument from the heart, which found the most traction with Johnson. Spencer, Rees-Mogg and Lyons keenly felt that Paterson had paid a high enough price with the death of his wife and did not deserve to lose his political career too.

This debate took place while Johnson was abroad, physically absent from Downing Street – a theme that was to emerge in other later scandals. 'He was always away when stuff went wrong,' one colleague recalled. 'When you're travelling as PM, it's bizarrely impossible to get people on the phone and things run out of control very quickly.' Some in Number 10 blamed Dan Rosenfield, his chief of staff, for not ensuring he received proper written advice whether home or away. 'It was a fundamental process flaw,' one said. Another government insider said, 'It was the classic case of the PM not realising the significance of how big a problem it was because no one was really telling him.' Decision-making had shrunk to a fatally small clique.

Upon his return to Downing Street, the Paterson plot found favour with Johnson not just because of its supposed compassion but also because of its focus on reforming parliamentary standards. Johnson had been previously investigated[28] over his declarations for a holiday to Mustique paid for by a Tory donor and he had little time for such pettifogging rules; to reshape them was his prerogative.

Johnson, the plotting trio and pro-Paterson MPs were all hopelessly naive. Throughout these weeks of discussions, they missed the obvious problem with the whole endeavour: the average voter could see that Paterson had been through a horrific personal situation, but they could also grasp that he had blatantly breached parliamentary rules. His significant sums of earnings were unlikely to garner much sympathy with the public. With the discussions taking place among no more than half a dozen aides and ministers, Johnson was isolated from further advice that may have persuaded him that saving Paterson and changing the parliamentary standards rules to do so was a terrible idea.

Before the scheme went public on 3 November, his chief of staff Dan Rosenfield and communications chief Jack Doyle instructed Johnson to actually read and contemplate the report, after it became apparent he had not bothered to do so. He also raised an obvious problem in his discussions with Spencer–Rees-Mogg–Lyons: would the Labour party play ball? If they opted out of working with the new committee to examine standards, its legitimacy would collapse. One official recalls Rosenfield asking, 'Why would Labour play ball with this? And what happens when Labour say, "Fuck off, I'm not putting anyone on the committee."' Rosenfield was assured by Spencer that the opposition were fully on side.

Among the wider Downing Street staff, knowledge of the plot to save Paterson was limited until that morning of 3 November. To the civil servants, it was presented as a fait accompli. One said, 'It was like "everyone's going to row in behind it, everyone's on board. It will be rough, but we'll push through".' A WhatsApp was sent to lobby journalists at 11.12 a.m. announcing what would happen. 'This isn't about one case but providing Members of Parliament from all political parties with the right to a fair hearing,' it said. 'Therefore the Commons should seek cross-party agreement on a new appeals process whereby the conclusions of the standards committee and the commissioner can be looked at. This could include judicial and lay member representation on the appeals panel.' The announcement of the plot shocked many at Conservative party HQ and the whips' office.

Motions on parliamentary standards are typically voted

through without objections or amendments so what happened that evening was unprecedented. In the Commons debate Rees-Mogg told MPs that concerns about the Paterson situation had become 'too numerous to ignore'.[29] He reiterated the point that it was not about the individual case but the system. 'It is not for me to judge him, others have done that, but was the process a fair one?' Tory MPs and opposition MPs saw the Paterson plot for exactly what it was: a Tory ruse to save one of their own.

During the vote that evening, senior MPs could scarcely believe what they were being ordered to do. Christian Wakeford, one of the more outspoken newly elected Tories who won Bury South for the first time since 1997, walked up to Paterson in the voting lobbies to call him a 'fucking selfish cunt'. The result showed the mess Johnson had waded into: thirteen Tory MPs voted against and ninety-eight abstained. As it was announced, opposition MPs heckled 'shame' and shouted at the government benches, 'What have you done to this place?'

Number 10's insistence that the motion was not about Paterson's case was moot. Hannah White, from the Institute for Government think tank, said, 'The decision to redesign the system and allow Paterson to appeal his case against whatever new rules are put in place vindicates the public view that there is one rule for MPs and another for the rest of us.' Or, as one Johnson ally put it retrospectively, 'It was patently obvious that Labour were not going to miss the chance to say, "The Tories are reforming the regime to protect themselves."'

Immediately after the amendment passed, Dan Rosenfield's prediction came true. Angela Rayner, Labour's deputy leader, announced her party would 'not be taking any part in this sham process or any corrupt committee'. The Liberal Democrats and Scottish National party followed suit. Following the vote, Rosenfield was in the prime minister's outer office with Lyons and Simone Finn, deputy chief of staff. Someone asked what would happen, Rosenfield responded, 'We're going to scrap it straight away because we have lost this fight.'

Johnson was stuck in the worst of all situations: a lame duck parliamentary committee and Paterson still on the hook. Either he would have to press ahead alone to try and reform standards with a committee of only Conservative MPs, or he would need to rapidly accept he had messed up. Spencer and Rees-Mogg spoke to him, ashen-faced, and admitted they had no plan. Lyons, who was chiefly drafted in to enact their instructions and marshall different sides of the arguments, awaited instructions. Johnson consulted with his aides overnight. One person he spoke to recalls the sentiment was, 'Look, we are clearly in a corner here, we've cocked this up and we need to change it.'

The final straw came in an interview Paterson gave to Sky News[30] where he showed no contrition at all, despite reassurances to Spencer. 'I wouldn't hesitate to do it again tomorrow,' the disgraced MP said. One ministerial aide watched him in horror: 'Owen was not behaving brilliantly at this time and that made it a lot harder.' Another government official recalled Johnson was 'totally furious' both at Paterson's behaviour and the whole ruse.

The next morning, the U-turn came – just one in a long history of rapid strategic or policy reversals that became a hallmark of Johnson's government. Rees-Mogg told the Commons on 4 November, 'I fear last night's debate conflated the individual case with general concern, this link needs to be broken,' and the changes to the standards committee would not go ahead. Those involved saw no alternative: 'We backed ourselves into a corner, there was no way that the committee could ever work.' Paterson soon announced he was off and quit politics – forcing a parliamentary by-election in his traditionally safe North Shropshire constituency that the Tories went on to lose to the Liberal Democrats.

Johnson was castigated. Friday's *Daily Mail* headline read 'On day of farce, Tories U-turn on disgraced MP Paterson after public fury . . . he quits . . . and a nation aghast at Boris's misjudgement asks . . . IS ANYBODY IN CHARGE AT No 10?' On Saturday, the former prime minister John Major, a long-time Johnson critic, told the BBC that the way the government had handled the affair was 'shameful'.

But it was not over. The Paterson scandal blew into a much wider debate about second jobs and whether Westminster should make MPs a full-time profession with no outside interests. Particular attention was paid to Geoffrey Cox, the former attorney general, who registered £970,000 for 705 hours of legal work during 2020. A week after Paterson announced he was quitting politics, the House of Commons endorsed a new code of conduct that banned MPs from acting as paid lobbyists.

The Spencer–Rees-Mogg–Lyons trio slowly grasped how much damage they had wrought. 'They bungled the handling of it obviously. It led to a by-election and damaged the prime minister hugely,' one senior Tory said. So why did Johnson make such an obvious mistake? Some MPs put it down to loyalty to his old *Telegraph* chums. One Cabinet minister told *The Sunday Times*,[31] 'The first rule of politics is that if you listen to Charles Moore and do the complete opposite of what he says, you won't go far wrong.' The same article noted that there was a spilt between different generations about whether to let Paterson off the hook. 'Younger MPs, many in red wall seats, are furious with the old guard – ageing Eurosceptics, Old Etonians and Johnson's former *Telegraph* colleagues.' In turn, the old blamed their youthful colleagues for the second jobs row that risked scuppering their retirement nests. Everyone, meanwhile, was seething at Johnson.

The Spencer–Rees-Mogg–Lyons trio were well intentioned in their efforts to save Paterson, but they failed in their duty to deliver the cold, realistic political advice Johnson desperately needed. With the hundreds of decisions across his desk each day, the Paterson plot should never have reached the prime minister. Equally, though, instead of listening to his former *Telegraph* colleagues, Johnson should have heeded the warnings from some of his aides that it would blow up and was impossible to sell to MPs and the public. Kathryn Stone's report should have been accepted but Johnson made the fatal decision to listen to a too tight group of advisors, instead of more widely consulting the Cabinet.

One senior Tory said, 'He was getting bad advice from the chief [whip] and Jacob at the time. He agreed to do it as, "This is my instinctive reaction, so it'll be fine." And then two days later it's, "Why the fuck has this happened, why did no one tell me?"' Others blamed Lyons, 'I don't think Declan had the nous to spot how big of a problem it was going to be.' A longstanding ally of Johnson piled in, 'He was surrounded by a very mediocre group because they all want to touch the orbit of the Sun King. He didn't think of the consequences of how people will react to this. There was no mechanism for a considered approach. He runs the government like an Oxford tutorial, when people float in with interesting ideas.' But one person who spoke to the prime minister said he was unhappy with his own decision-making as well as the advice he was receiving.

Ultimately, however, it was Johnson's decision to press ahead with the Paterson ruse. 'Boris's greatest fault, which ties into lots of other things, is that he's not ruthless enough,' one minister said. 'He's too kindly and you need to deal with unpleasant business that arises as a PM.' His lifelong desire to be liked meant he often tried to please everyone.

MPs were furious about being marched up the hill to vote for a scheme that cost them political capital for something that was then jettisoned within less than twenty-four hours. More so than the madness of the plot to save Paterson was the indecision. Throughout his premiership, delegation after delegation of MPs had made it clear to Johnson that the U-turns – characterised by Dominic Cummings's frequent use of a trolley emoji, which Johnson initially came up with to describe his own journey towards Brexit in 2015 – were ruining the government. One Tory aide said, 'They had made it clear that all the fucking U-turns had to stop. MPs told Number 10 they're happy to take brickbats, but not if we have to U-turn a few days later. It's one of the most corrosive, painful things you can ask MPs to do.'

The botched Paterson plot marked a turning point for Johnson. The shine of the party conference, the globetrotting premier and the Garrick Club supper was entirely worn off by the affair. Allies of Johnson said at the time that the prime minister 'admits it's a complete own goal'. The damage, however, went far deeper: it created a fissure with the parliamentary party that widened and was never addressed.

One of those tasked with smoothing over relations between Downing Street and MPs explained why the Paterson plot had such an impact: 'It opened up a lot of vulnerabilities in the parliamentary party because all Tory MPs are paranoid about being accused of sleaze. They didn't understand why there had been a sort of special pleading, in Owen's case, because they felt that nobody else would have been treated like that.'

To the party's strategists, Paterson also created a public image issue. 'It looked like Boris is not doing things in parliament that are relevant to me, they're looking after their mates, it's all about politics again.'

Having an eighty-seat majority had acted as a big cushion for Johnson and the government that could absorb its failings and U-turns. But it would not be long before the broken bonds that had begun with the Paterson affair would become an even greater problem, one that threatened to undermine his whole government at the very moment it faced two of its greatest threats to date.

1. Partygate and an Omicron Christmas

Boris Johnson was glum. It was Saturday 27 November 2021 and he was back in the Downing Street press briefing room, speaking to the nation again about the one topic he most wanted to avoid: coronavirus. A few days earlier Chris Whitty, the chief medical officer for England, and his scientific counterpart Patrick Vallance, had visited Number 10 to warn the prime minister's team that a new ominous Covid variant had emerged, one that that might evade the vaccine. 'It was one of those doom-monger moments,' one senior aide said.

Although only two Omicron cases had been detected in the UK, Johnson warned[1] in his televised address that a third wave was coming: 'It does appear that Omicron spreads very rapidly and can be spread between people who are double vaccinated.' The prime minister announced the return of restrictions to buy scientists time to understand whether the existing Covid jabs offered substantial protection. Day two tests for those arriving in the UK returned, along with enforced self-isolation for those who tested positive with Omicron. Face coverings in shops and public transport were reintroduced and Johnson announced that the booster programme for a third round of jabs would be hugely accelerated.

As the pandemic neared its two-year anniversary, daily Covid meetings still took place in Downing Street, usually at around 9 a.m. The cast was small and included Dan Rosenfield, the prime minister's chief of staff, his communications director Jack Doyle, health secretary Sajid Javid and a 'handful' of other aides who drifted in and out depending on the severity of the situation. Those who attended recalled there was often 'indecisiveness' from Johnson between the need to protect from Covid and his constant yearning for freedom. When Omicron arrived, the debate about what to do was no exception.

After three lockdowns, at least two of which Johnson was deeply sceptical about, his gut was against the return of restrictions – echoed by many advisors in his inner circle. One person involved said, 'There were some arguing, "You've been sold a pup" by the scientists, others who said, "You've got to take draconian measures, this is a Doomsday we're fucked scenario." Then there were the mainstream people who said, "Hang on, we have no idea how severe this is." . . . So we took the middle-ground approach.' When considering measures, Johnson's team gave little or no thought to Tory MPs – a repeated critical error.

But in parliament, a growing band of Conservative MPs felt much more strongly and were appalled, thinking that Johnson was making a historic mistake that would ruin the economy, destroy Christmas for the second year in a row, and curb liberties without due cause. A potent caucus emerged known as the Covid Recovery Group – led by arch-Conservative libertarians and former ministers Mark Harper and Steve Baker. The former, who was chief whip, was a longstanding Johnson sceptic who had challenged him for the leadership in 2019. But it was the role of Baker, one of the party's most feared campaigners who had played major roles in the defenestration of two Tory leaders, which concerned Downing Street the most. Johnson had offered Baker a junior ministerial role in his first government, but the MP had rejected it as *too* junior. Their relationship had always been strained, and Covid made it more so. Baker argued that the previous lockdowns were an error, and the government should be focused instead on 'living with' Covid. They were certainly not willing to give Johnson the benefit of the doubt on Omicron.

On 30 November, parliament voted on the new restrictions. Johnson failed to win over Tory MPs to the new restrictions: thirty-four of them opposed the return of self-isolation for those with Omicron and twenty-one opposed face masks in public spaces. Johnson's eighty-odd seat majority was almost eroded. In the chamber,[2] Baker attacked the scientists and data behind face masks: 'the issue is that we are taking away the public's right to choose what they do, based on flimsy and uncertain evidence.' For Baker, an evangelical Christian and messianic Brexiter, the debate was about more than Omicron. For him, it was 'how we react and the kind of nation and civilisation that we are creating in the context of this new disease. What is the relationship between the state and the individual?'

The votes on the first round of Omicron measures underscored the damage the Owen Paterson affair had done to Johnson's relationship with his party. In growing numbers, his party was no longer listening to him. 'MPs were waiting to give us a kicking at that point, and that was the point,' one government insider said. 'We'd lost the benefit of the doubt and everything we brought to parliament was going to be a row.'

Johnson was all too aware that if Omicron went wrong, either with collapsing the health service or thousands of excess deaths, it could undo all of the progress gained with the success of the UK's vaccination programme. But hours after the Covid vote on 30 November, a far greater political problem arrived on Johnson's desk. His communications chief Jack Doyle, along with the prime minister's spokespeople Rosie Bate-Williams and Max Blain, warned Dan Rosenfield that Pippa Crerar, the tenacious political editor of the *Daily Mirror*, was to publish a story that accused the prime minister and his staff of breaking Covid lockdown rules[3] the previous November. Rosenfield, who had not been in Downing Street at the time, asked all three what had happened. The sentiment of their discussion was that some things had gone on and that 'with hindsight, it's not something we should have done' but no one argued that restrictions were not observed. The aides then went to see Johnson, who needed no second invitation to get into a scrap with the left-leaning paper and take a firm line. With the pressure of deadlines, they sought to bat away what was initially seen as a one-day story.

The *Mirror*'s front page that night reported that Johnson had spoken at a 'packed leaving do' when the country was in lockdown in late 2020. It stated that another event took place closer to Christmas that year where officials 'knocked back glasses of wine' and played Secret Santa, at a time when London was under restrictions banning indoor gatherings. Crerar's report went on to state there were many more 'social gatherings' beyond these initial two. One of her sources spoke about the hypocrisy of what allegedly happened: 'While there was one message for the public, the prime minister gave the impression that it could be very relaxed in No 10.' Within Team Johnson, there was the widespread view that the story was briefed by former Number 10 officials close to Dominic Cummings, who were set on bringing down his premiership.

Crerar's story landed at a point when Johnson had just suffered a major rebellion, and while the country was facing another wave of Covid. The accusation of breaking rules was bad enough – playing into the perception that it had been one rule for the establishment, one rule for the rest of the country – but it came at a moment when the country was facing the return of restrictions, which made the story far more potent. It would take some weeks and a drip-drip of reports before the moniker 'partygate' was attached to the scandal, yet the deeply problematic response by Johnson's office was already forged. At the bottom of the *Mirror's* first story, Downing Street said, 'Covid rules have been followed at all times.'

That line was lifted from the pages of the *Mirror* and repeated the next day in the House of Commons where Crerar's story was a prime focus at prime minister's questions. The preparation team – including cabinet secretary Simon Case, chief of staff Dan Rosenfield, levelling up secretary Michael Gove and a bevy of political aides – were all aware of what he was going to say. Johnson was asked about the gatherings, and bound by the ministerial code, which states that knowingly misleading MPs means resignation, he duly said,[4] 'All guidance was followed completely.' Every aide to the prime minister realised in hindsight that a fatal mistake had been made. From that first discussion in Number 10 with Rosenfield, no one questioned whether Crerar's story was the thin end of the wedge; whether there were more illegal gatherings that breached the government's own laws. No one thought to put together a scoping exercise to find the facts. No one thought to leave any room for flexibility in the press line. 'Of course we should have got someone to do a review, but it was already too late,' one insider said.

***

The end of 2021 for Johnson was dominated by the intertwining tales of partygate and Omicron, both of which exposed flaws in his character and how his Downing Street was run. The schism with Conservative MPs that started with the botched plot to save Owen Paterson grew and the prime minister's approval ratings began to drop rapidly. Although MPs baulked at the Covid restrictions they were being asked to vote on, it was the drip-drip of allegations about historic rule breaking at the heart of his government that was to cause the biggest headache.

A week on from the Covid rebellion, *ITV News* broadcast footage[5] of Allegra Stratton, Johnson's COP spokesperson, answering a question at a mock press conference about a party that breached Covid rules. Plans for holding televised press conferences, in the style of White House briefings in the US, heralded from the Dominic Cummings era, when his (and the prime minister's) desire to circumvent political journalists gave birth to plans for daily briefings where Number 10 could pump its slogans straight to voters. Cummings and the then director of communications Lee Cain wanted Ellie Price, a BBC reporter, to take the press secretary role. Johnson instead plumped for Stratton, previously a *Guardian* and BBC journalist before working for chancellor Rishi Sunak. Reportedly, Johnson's wife Carrie had privately advocated[6] for Stratton.

Although Johnson was initially keen on the idea of communicating directly to the country – particularly after the success of the pandemic press conferences – his aides were not sold on it. 'Boris Johnson is a good communicator and knows he is,' one ally said. 'Was he really going to subcontract his words to somebody else? This is a guy who writes his own speeches and articles.' Along with many others in Number 10, they felt the idea of putting an aide on screen to represent him every day was 'really stupid'. After Cummings and Cain left their jobs, plans for the daily press conferences were unceremoniously scrapped in April 2021.

In the forty-seven seconds of leaked footage, recorded in December 2020, Stratton was asked by a staffer, 'I've just seen reports on Twitter that there was a Downing Street Christmas party on Friday night, do you recognise those reports?' With titters of nervous laughter around the room, Stratton joked that this 'fictional party' was in fact a business event featuring cheese and wine. The clip gave the strong impression that Stratton and the other aides knew that the event in question – 18 November, the one Pippa Crerar had previously revealed – broke rules, contrary to the official Downing Street line.

That night, Johnson and his aides were reeling from the Covid rebellion in the House of Commons. When senior figures in Johnson's inner circle saw the leaked video footage on Twitter, many had no idea what Stratton was talking about. One said, 'My initial response was: what the hell is this? Where the fuck did this come from?' Given the turnover of officials after Cummings and his allies had left Number 10, those running the government had no idea Stratton had been holding practice press conferences. Once again, the finger of blame among Team Johnson was pointed in the direction of the Vote Leave cabal for leaking the footage. Universally it was acknowledged to be a disaster. Tory MPs soon picked up their phones to express their anger at Johnson, realising that the jovial nature of the clip hit a nerve.

After the initial *Mirror* story, communications director Jack Doyle had assured Johnson and chief of staff Dan Rosenfield that it was his belief that all the rules were followed in the press office. As one senior member of his team said, 'The Allegra video was the first point I think we realised this was going wrong and we had a big political problem.'

Only now were the reports about the 18 November party taken seriously and a limited fact-finding exercise began to figure out what had happened. Dan Rosenfield tasked his civil servants with exploring if any rules had been broken, but the inquiry did not span beyond a small team. 'Dan was always motivated to reduce the size of cast lists in meetings and close the loop on conversations because he wanted to protect information,' one colleague said. At the time, Johnson was constantly asking his aides, 'How much more of this is there to come?' A full answer never came. Rosenfield's fact-finding exercise produced a few sides of A4 paper; many of the events that were to prove most embarrassing to Johnson were not even mentioned.

Alongside frustration at the internal process, Johnson's inner circle believed external forces were seeking to bring down the government. Cummings had begun voicing his opinion that Johnson was unfit for the role, remarking[7] he was a 'a joke prime minister' and accused Number 10 of lying[8] about the Christmas parties. Johnson's team suspected that people involved in his Vote Leave gang had access to the archived footage of Stratton via cloud storage and had a role in leaking it to ITV (her former employer) to cause maximum damage. One insider said their first reaction was to realise Stratton was 'going to go through the absolute ringer', swiftly followed by 'a sense of preservation about what else do they have?'

Within Number 10, there was much sympathy for Stratton. The following day, in a tearful video outside her home, she announced her resignation from government. 'The British people have made immense sacrifices in the ongoing battle against Covid-19.' Stratton went on: 'I now fear that my comments in the leaked video . . . have become a distraction in that fight.' She added it was never her intention to make light of Covid rules. 'I will regret those remarks for the rest of my days and offer my profound apologies to all of you at home for them.' Stratton had taken the hit, but she had not even attended the 18 November party.

The following day, 8 December, Johnson addressed the House of Commons about the Stratton video. He told MPs he was 'furious' about the clip, but did not change his official response from the *Mirror*'s first report: 'All rules had been followed.' He was asked directly by Labour MP Catherine West, about whether another party had been held in Number 10 on 13 November 2020. His response was, 'No, but I am sure that whatever happened, the guidance was followed and the rules were followed at all times.' Whether Johnson said 'no' to telling MPs or 'no' to whether there was a party is still unclear and became key for the Commons' privileges committee's investigation into whether he knowingly misled MPs.

Some in his team were becoming nervous at the handling of the crisis. 'I remember being surprised it was such a clear-cut sentence,' one Number 10 aide said of Johnson's words in the Commons. A Cabinet minister was told by Downing Street that in response to questions about the Stratton video they should say, 'The rules were followed at all times.' He declined to do so. 'I never did say it because I thought it wasn't something you could be that categoric about.' The minister added, 'The PM was badly advised to be too certain about things in which you can't be certain – bearing in mind nobody really knew what the rules meant precisely.'

What Johnson should have done at this stage was to tell MPs that his team would look into what had happened and he would report back. Instead, the prime minister and his allies became 'like rabbits in the headlights', according to one official. 'They just got caught and went further and further with the denials.' The issue was that too many in the prime minister's core team were directly implicated in partygate. Within the Cabinet, it dawned that a real scandal was brewing. One member said, 'It's the classic Watergate lesson, the cover-up is worse than the event.' The blame was rightly portioned on both Johnson personally and those around him. 'The fundamental flaw for Boris was that his team are not strong managers,' one friend says. 'The lack of political management and understanding is at the core of it. Good leaders put around them people who don't exacerbate their weakness, they offset them. The people who are most loyal to him feed his weakness.'

Yet he cannot escape culpability. When Johnson asked Jack Doyle about whether all the rules had been followed, he did not question his aide's response, or ask him to investigate further whether any more illicit parties had taken place. On the other hand, his chief media aide should have given him the right advice. One senior Tory who observed Johnson at work said he consistently failed to consider the consequences of denying rules were broken. 'What you would normally do is you have a meeting and somebody would say, "Hang on, you can't sustain that argument." Boris would say, "We will get through this, we will get through this." No one bothered to tell him, "No you won't."'

After the leaked Stratton video, calls grew[9] from opposition MPs for the Met police to investigate whether Covid rules had been broken, but, at this stage, they declined. The police said that the footage and other material 'does not provide evidence of a breach' of Covid rules and said it would not retrospectively open an investigation. But it left open the possibility of an inquiry if further evidence of wrongdoing was found.

Johnson, however, was forced to act. On 8 December, the day after the Stratton footage was published, he announced that Simon Case, the head of the civil service, would carry out an inquiry into partygate and disciplinary action would be taken against those found to have broken the rules. The decision to appoint Case was 'rapid', according to those who spoke to the prime minister about it. 'It was just muscle memory. What happens when you need something sorting out? A cab sec's investigation. It's tried and tested.' Another aide close to Johnson felt otherwise: 'It was a really stupid decision.'

The prime minister knew he needed someone credible. 'It couldn't be a politician, it needs to be a civil servant,' one aide said. He considered a retired mandarin but decided that an external inquiry would risk becoming ungainly. Case, who had been appointed as the youngest ever head of the civil service under Dominic Cummings's auspices, was 'furious' at the position he was put in by the prime minister. Case fumed at Johnson's team, 'You're asking me to judge my colleagues. I'm going to do it, it's going to be difficult, and it will find things out that you don't like.'

***

Johnson and his team were also contending with another media storm around Omicron. On the morning of 8 December, Sajid Javid was due to tour the broadcast studios ahead of a major pandemic announcement, but knowing the focus of the questioning after the Stratton footage leaked, he asked Number 10 for a 'categorical assurance' that rules had not been broken. The health secretary did not hear back from Dan Rosenfield or the prime minister directly, so he cancelled the morning media tour.

On this same day of 8 December, before his Commons statement on partygate, Johnson accepted that more restrictions were necessary. An informal ministerial Covid quad of Johnson, Javid, chancellor Rishi Sunak and Cabinet Office minister Steve Barclay had formed around the daily 9 a.m. meetings to monitor the worsening situation. Johnson then lumbered into the Downing Street press room on the evening of 8 December to inform the nation that a 'Plan B' of measures would be introduced, including mandatory indoor face coverings in public places. Guidance to work from home would return. And, for the first time, nightclubs and large events would require vaccine certification or proof of a negative lateral flow test. It was the last measure that would prove particularly controversial with Tory MPs, who decided vaccine passports were a red line they were unwilling to cross.

Compared to the lockdowns of 2020, the measures were limited. 'Boris was never minded to do more than the minimum that could be negotiated,' one close colleague said. But he brought in the measures knowing fully that Tory MPs would not be happy. As one minister summed up: 'The path he ended up taking was not only very courageous and the right call, he did it knowing that the parliamentary party wouldn't be happy. He went in knowing that, but he thought it was the right thing to do to keep the economy open while slowing the spread of the virus.' When his position as prime minister was under threat in the months ahead, Johnson's allies often claimed he 'got the big calls right' and this was one instance when it was true.

It was not only MPs who were divided on vaccine passports, but the Cabinet too. One minister said, 'I was never convinced that certification makes any difference. In practical terms, it would be very hard to actually implement and to be meaningful.' Those in the discussions said Johnson was 'absolutely gang-busters' about introducing them. 'He thought it was a massive incentive to get vaccinated.' The eventual compromise was to allow individuals to show their testing status in lieu of their jabs history. Sajid Javid, who had to present the measures to parliament, focused on the compromise nature of the proposals in his (unsuccessful) efforts to tame the Tory rebellion.

The next day, 9 December, Rosenfield and Number 10 communications director Jack Doyle pleaded with Javid to tour the broadcast studios to sell the new package of Covid restrictions, aware that a major rebellion was brewing. Javid was told by Downing Street, 'You have to do it, otherwise we're up shit creek and it looks very bad.' But the health secretary was still concerned about partygate questions and how he would respond. Eventually Javid was assured there were no parties and no rules were broken – a line he trotted out on TV. But as one friend of Javid put it, 'It turned out to be total bullshit.'

If November's Omicron restrictions vote had damaged the government, the vote on the second round was much more severe – leading to the biggest rebellion of Johnson's premiership. Steve Baker, the ringleader of the Covid rebels, ominously warned[10] the government was 'creating a miserable dystopia'. Many of his colleagues agreed and followed his lead. On the night of the vote, Johnson was distraught, aware it would not pass with Tory votes. A total of ninety-eight of his own MPs rebelled against the measures. He was saved by the opposition parties, who supported the measures, but Johnson had lost his tribe.

Inside Number 10, a large rebellion was expected but not as high as it turned out to be. One Johnson ally said, 'The chief [whip] told us very clearly that it was going to be maximum eighty.' Declan Lyons and Ben Gascoigne, two of Johnson's closest political aides, cautioned against pushing ahead with the vote, telling the prime minister, 'We are going to get completely hammered.' One senior minister realised Number 10 was drifting away from the parliamentary party. 'It became overall Tory political correctness to be anti-lockdown. The vibe was simply against it.' Johnson's problem was that within the Conservative party and outside the government ranks, there was no organised support network for lockdown measures.

One government figure particularly disgruntled about 'Plan B' was David Frost. Known to all in Westminster as 'Frosty', he had taken the Brexit journey with Johnson from the Foreign Office as his special advisor, to the heart of Downing Street as the prime minister's chief negotiator for the revised withdrawal agreement and later negotiating the UK–EU free trade agreement. He was briefly considered to be the prime minister's national security advisor and nominated for a Conservative peerage. After a backlash, Johnson opted to make him a Cabinet Office minister overseeing the domestic and overseas consequences of Brexit. An unashamed right-winger, he became the prime minister's Thatcherite conscience.

In the summer of 2021, Frost had expressed[11] concerns that the Northern Ireland Protocol, which governs trade between the province and the rest of the UK, was broken. 'The EU needs a new playbook for dealing with neighbours, one that involves pragmatic solutions between friends, not the imposition of one side's rules on the other and legal purism,' he wrote of the very deal he negotiated. In October, the EU put forward a package of changes to the protocol that were soon dismissed by Frost as failing to speak to the scale of change required. The situation was deadlocked.

Johnson's team was aware Frost was becoming disillusioned over a range of policy areas, including the Northern Ireland Protocol, the rise in National Insurance, Covid restrictions but also Brexit. One senior government figure said, 'His frustration was that we weren't going far enough on regulation and Brexit opportunities. Number 10's response was, "That's your job, you're the Cabinet minister in charge so go and fucking do it." You've got all the latitude, you've got all the authority. If anybody gets in your way, we will take the Boris Johnson baseball bat out of the cupboard and swing it very hard at them for you.'

Throughout the pandemic, Johnson had ensured the tub-thumping Frost was at the key Covid decision meetings to buttress Johnson's arguments against restrictions. At the time of Omicron, Frost felt the arguments made by Chris Whitty and Patrick Vallance were not credible and insisted that there was not enough data from South Africa, the source of the variant, to support more measures. 'He could never believe Boris would ever do it. But then it was rushed in overnight, Plan B was presented to the Cabinet as a done deal,' one minister said. After the package was agreed, Frost told Johnson he simply could not defend it.

Frost duly agreed he would leave government in January to avoid further drama, an acknowledgement of the precarious standing partygate had put the prime minister in. Yet on 18 December, the Sunday following the second Covid vote rebellion, news of his resignation leaked[12] and he was forced to quit immediately (Johnson's inner circle believe he leaked it, but Frost firmly denies this). In a hasty resignation letter, written in a tone more sorry than angry, Frost cited 'concerns about the current direction of travel' – in other words, concerns about Johnson's policy agenda.

Frost praised the prime minister's delivery of Brexit but urged, 'I hope we will move as fast as possible to where we need to get to: a lightly regulated, low-tax, entrepreneurial economy, at the cutting edge of modern science and economic change.' Frost echoed the language of Steve Baker in stating 'we need to learn to live with Covid' and said he was hopeful the country would be 'back on track soon'. His tone later hardened as he urged in a tweet to those in Downing Street[13] and to Johnson to sack 'the neo-socialists, green fanatics and pro-woke crowd', widely interpreted to be friends of Johnson's wife Carrie.

Frost's departure spoke to the wider mood of the party of Johnson's government, according to one of his ministerial colleagues. 'Covid fitted into a broader narrative: bureaucrats in the blob are thwarting Brexit, bureaucrats and the blob thwarting living with Covid. Frosty's critique of the government brought all those things together in one thread.' Although he had been on resignation watch for some weeks, Johnson was 'very very hurt' by his decision to quit. 'He felt it was a personal betrayal because he felt he had made Frost's career.'

***

The sole blessing for Johnson at this time was the vaccine booster programme. After the second vote, Johnson spoke to the country on 12 December where he unveiled the 'Get boosted now' slogan and announced a target of offering third jabs to every adult by 31 December. With the threat of the NHS being overwhelmed once again, his tone was sombre. 'I am afraid we are now facing an emergency in our battle with the new variant, Omicron, and we must urgently reinforce our wall of vaccine protection to keep our friends and loved ones safe,' he said. 'The evidence [is] that Omicron is doubling here in the UK every two to three days.' The military teams behind the first vaccination drives returned: clinics opened seven days a week, over forty planning units were deployed across Britain to deliver jabs into arms.

Johnson's scientific advisors were already warning him that the 'Plan B' measures did not go far enough. On 15 December, chief medical officer Chris Whitty said that Omicron was becoming a 'serious' threat and told people to limit their social interactions ahead of the festive season. One of the most important Cabinet meetings of Johnson's premiership took place on 20 December, a meeting to decide whether the UK would have a second Christmas disrupted by the pandemic – or whether it could go ahead at a risk to the health service.

Rishi Sunak, who was in California at the time, spoke to the prime minister by phone[14] to 'urge restraint' before flying back to London. The chancellor met with Johnson and Number 10's chief of staff Dan Rosenfield on his return to dissuade them on further measures. An official who was present said, 'Rishi privately argued strongly against any further lockdown. He said there was not enough evidence.' Johnson was nervous. If he publicly hinted at more restrictions, Tory MPs might move against him. If he came out strongly against restrictions, he risked losing the fragile support of Whitty and Vallance, both of whom had proved instrumental in maintaining confidence in the government's Covid strategy. 'Public confidence mattered far more than parliamentary confidence, and we came very close to losing Chris [Whitty] in that December,' one insider said.

Five days before Christmas, a much-anticipated two-hour-long Cabinet meeting that would decide whether a second festive season would be ruined by Covid took place virtually on Microsoft Teams. SAGE, the government's official body of scientific advisors, warned ministers that hospital admissions could reach 3,000 a day. Stephen Reicher, one of its associate members, said,[15] 'A circuit breaker is the way to save the NHS and the way to save Christmas.' Johnson was being squeezed both ways. 'In Number 10, the PM was under enormous pressure. He had people saying at this point "You must lock down now,"' one aide said. 'The rest were pretty against, arguing the data could not support what was on the extreme end of being discussed.'

The debate commenced with the customary frequent confusion over who was muted, then Chris Whitty told ministers 'just how bad' the infection rates of Omicron were. But there was a scrap of positive news: the existing Covid vaccines offered a decent degree of protection against the new variant, but not as great as the previous Delta strain. One Cabinet minister recalled Whitty stating, 'If the jabs were 95 per cent against effective Delta, even if they're 90 per cent effective against Omicron, that five percentage point difference in terms of hospitalisations, given its high infection rate will make a huge difference.'

The pro-measures camp was led by health secretary Sajid Javid and levelling up secretary Michael Gove. Javid was the most cautious, highlighting the SAGE modelling and threat of 3,000 admissions a day. But the health secretary did not ultimately back new measures. Pointing to the balance of risks, few of those arguing for restrictions were pushing for another lockdown, unlike some members of the SAGE committee. 'The less risky route in terms of the pandemic would have been more restrictions, but there was no discussion whatsoever by anyone, even from the officials, about lockdown-type restrictions,' a minister present said. Javid told ministers he was happy with whatever decision was made but 'the Cabinet must accept that it is a risk and we're going in with our eyes open'.

The anti-measures camp was led by Jacob Rees-Mogg, leader of the House of Commons. Johnson phoned him the evening before the virtual Cabinet meeting, aware of his longstanding lockdown-sceptic views and urged him to speak out – clearly in need of a comforting voice. Johnson came to Rees-Mogg early in the meeting, before more senior colleagues, and he duly stated that behaviour had already changed as a result of Omicron messaging. One minister present said his argument was essentially, 'We should let people decide for themselves.'

Sunak did not intervene significantly in the meeting, stating Johnson was aware of his views. But one Cabinet minister said the chancellor was 'very upset' with Simon Clarke, his number two at the Treasury, for taking the opposing view and favouring restrictions. Other ministers who spoke out included the business secretary Kwasi Kwarteng and transport secretary Grant Shapps. Oliver Dowden, chair of the Conservative party and an ally of Sunak, had privately told colleagues he was 'pro-freedom' but sat on the fence in the meeting.

The anti-measures ministers focused on the same point: many

of the Covid models had been wrong before and there was not enough data to ruin the nation's Christmas. Instead, they argued that vaccines and an abundance of lateral flow tests would protect Britons. Bizarrely, the decisive voice proved to be David Frost, who was present at the meeting despite having resigned two days before. Like Rees-Mogg, Johnson had asked him before the meeting to make the case against restrictions.

To the surprise of no one in Downing Street, Johnson sided with those who wanted more data before more restrictions. At the end, Johnson summed up 'okay, we're all agreed that we're not going to lock down' but he made it clear it was a risk and his ultimate decision. The prime minister was aware of an argument made by Rees-Mogg that you aren't rewarded politically for locking down. It was such thinking that had convinced Johnson that the previous restrictions had been too onerous and should not be repeated.

After the Cabinet meeting, Johnson delivered another press conference that came as a sigh of relief to the nation overall, but was of great concern to the doctors and staff of the NHS. Christmas would go ahead with no further restrictions. 'Naturally we can't rule out any further measures after Christmas. We're going to keep a constant eye on the data and we'll do whatever it takes to protect public health,' Johnson said, urging, 'but in view of the continuing uncertainty about several things ... we don't think today that there is enough evidence to justify any tougher measures before Christmas.'

Had partygate not dominated the coming weeks, Johnson would have been able to claim a victory lap with the booster programme, which was 'pure Boris' according to his aides. Johnson was facing the potential collapse of the NHS 'without hyperbole and exaggeration' and the only thing that could save it would be the booster programme and more jabs. The Cabinet Office's marketing department disseminated the 'Get boosted now' slogan relentlessly across the country. Unlike some of the convoluted Covid messaging of the past, this wave came with a straightforward one: get jabbed or Christmas will be ruined.

The practical triumph of the booster programme, however, was almost entirely down to one individual, Emily Lawson, a senior civil servant who had won much favour with Johnson[16] overseeing the rollout of the first and second jabs in 2020. During the first waves of the pandemic, the highest number of jabs delivered by the NHS in one day was 800,000. During December 2021, a million boosters a day was hit consistently. 'We had never as a country done anything like that before,' one senior minister said. Vaccinations were even delivered on Christmas Day and Boxing Day.

Johnson's decision to put Lawson in charge of the booster rollout was inspired, a rare occasion where his grasp of management structures was correct. As with the government's vaccine taskforce, when Johnson hired Kate Bingham to oversee the procurement of Covid vaccines, a small swift team with confident leadership delivered results. Her team was not burdened with Whitehall bureaucracy or the Number 10 squabbling that dominated the rest of his inner circle. 'The brilliance of Boris's leadership came in,' an ally said. 'There is the positive side of never taking "no" for an answer. Boris was personally the one who said, "Nope, I want to go hell for leather, I want us to get everybody boosted by Christmas."'

January 2022 was a bumpy time for the NHS, with hospitalisations rising high just as Chris Whitty had predicted. But it did not tip over. One senior health service official said, 'There was a point in January when we were concerned about it, but thankfully it did level off.' The focus on Covid exacerbated the backlog of non-urgent work facing the health service, which continued to trouble Johnson for the rest of his time as prime minister. 'We knew there was going to be a price to pay to speak in terms of an even bigger backlog.' But out of those tortuous debates, another major Johnson gamble paid off. 'With the benefit of hindsight, Boris got it right when he decided against more measures or lockdown,' one minister said. 'By hook or by crook, in the end, he made that call on Omicron.'

***

Two other developments took place away from public eyes in December that were to have greater ramifications for Johnson's final months in office. During the debate on Covid restrictions, Johnson's allies became concerned that Rishi Sunak was increasingly unhappy – particularly during back and forth over Covid restrictions and the impact they would have on the economy. Throughout 2020, Sunak was briefly the most popular politician in recent British history due to his billions of pounds of economic support during the pandemic. Now he was chiefly worried about stalling the country's recovery.

While some close to Sunak say that he was never serious about his intentions, one figure close to Johnson claimed Sunak 'genuinely thought about going' and that a draft resignation letter had been written over Number 10's handling of the partygate allegations, plus the threat of more Covid restrictions. 'It was well known within Whitehall at a very senior level that he was thinking of going,' one government insider said. 'The PM called him multiple times and they had several long discussions, which stood him down from going. But it was definitely in the ether.' Sunak had taken soundings from his friends in the media at this time, while his campaign handily purchased ready4rishi.com.

The other significant change was in the media. The *Daily Mail*, one of the most influential newspaper in Conservative circles, saw a sudden change of editor. Out went Geordie Greig, the smooth Old Etonian socialite who was close to Johnson's nemesis David Cameron and had run a series of stories about the controversial redecoration of Johnson's Downing Street flat, known as 'wallpapergate', and in came Ted Verity, a protégé of legendary *Mail* chief Paul Dacre and a far more sympathetic editor to his premiership.

A senior Johnson ally said Verity's arrival marked a 'key turning point' in the government's fortunes. 'Geordie was totally hostile with Boris. For some reason, they clearly had a bad personal relationship . . . there was an animus between the editor of the *Daily Mail* and the prime minister, which is never a good mix,' the person said. Under Verity's editorship, the paper became one of Johnson's staunchest defenders until the very end. One government insider remarked, 'If the editor of the *Daily Mail* had changed six months earlier, before all the campaign about wallpapergate, that would have been helpful to us.'

In the background of Omicron, the trickle of partygate stories continued in the run-up to Christmas as political journalists delved into every possible avenue of rule breaking. On 9 December, the BBC reported that Jack Doyle, director of communications, doled out awards at a Christmas party the previous year. On 12 December, Downing Street confirmed that Johnson was part of a semi-virtual Christmas quiz at a time when indoor gatherings were banned. As each story was revealed, the picture painted for the public was that Downing Street seemed to be party central while the rest of the country was locked at home.

On 15 December, a photo emerged of a party at Conservative party headquarters featuring Shaun Bailey, the party's London mayoral candidate, and billionaire property developer Nick Candy. The picture showed that catering had been laid on, including a deeply unappetising selection of snacks. The partygate saga took another turn for the worse on 16 December, when reports emerged that Johnson had attended a do in May 2020, during the first lockdown. Downing Street explained it away as a work meeting. Three days after, a photograph emerged of the event that showed nineteen people drinking wine and sharing cheese in the garden. Dominic Cummings was present, along with Johnson's wife Carrie and their newborn son Wilfred. It patently did not appear to be a meeting.

Then, on 17 December, the final partygate bombshell of the year landed. Simon Case, who had been appointed by Johnson to investigate all the claims, was forced out of the inquiry after it emerged a party had been held in his own office the previous year. Once again, Johnson was furious with his aides, even though he had failed to ask Case if he was aware of any such parties. It was another example of the incurable combination of his aides failing to do due diligence, while Johnson failed to ask the right questions and think through the consequences of what he was doing.

There still seemed to be no strategy for dealing with party-gate, which his inner circle increasingly saw as a concerted campaign prosecuted by his former aides with an axe to grind. Johnson continued to tell his friends, 'This is inconsequential, it's ridiculous rubbish.' That dismissive instinct had served him well in the past, ignoring scandals that all eventually went away. It wholly failed with partygate because he failed to understand its scope and potency for a country facing a second ruined Christmas. Johnson, in the words of a close Cabinet colleague, 'broke every rule of how to deal with a scandal in politics – to first of all establish the facts to satisfy yourself absolutely and fully'.

At its heart, it was also a failure of communications. One strat-egist advised Johnson to make a public statement when the Case inquiry began, with full accounts of the other events and an apology along these lines: 'People who worked eighteen hours a day, seven days a week, did some things that they shouldn't have done, they had some drinks after work while no one else in the country was going into offices. We made mistakes, put our hands up.' The Tory official added, 'It would have been a bumpy couple of weeks, but we could have toughened it out.' Instead, Johnson continued to dismiss the problem until it was way too late.

Any sense that Number 10 could be able to control the direction of the official partygate inquiry disappeared with their choice of replacement. In Johnson's political team, the decision to ask Case to conduct the review meant they felt they had some ability to 'manage' the outcome. 'I don't think we would have been able to shape the views, but we would have had an understanding of where it was heading,' one official said. In his place, however, came one of Whitehall's most senior officials and adjudicators who would certainly take no notice of what Downing Street or the prime minister wanted. Her name, which was soon to be on lips across the country, was Sue Gray.

2. Sue Gray

On her way into the office, a petite, middle-aged civil servant made a regular stop at the Pret near St James's Park station to pick up breakfast. In normal times, no one would have taken any notice of her and the order, but Westminster was experiencing one of its fevered emotional breakdowns. Tony Diver, a political correspondent at the *Telegraph*, recognised Sue Gray in the coffee queue and tweeted out:[1] 'Black Americano. No sugar, no messing around. Ruthless.' The tweet was liked over 13,000 times.

Writing in *The Times* Polly Vernon mused:[2] 'Sue Gray ordering a black Americano in Pret A Manger weeks before finishing and releasing a report that might bring down the prime minister of the United Kingdom is the civil servant equivalent of a mobster doing a line of cocaine before shooting up the headquarters of a rival gang.' During the long gestation of her partygate report, Westminster and the media lost its marbles.

After Simon Case was forced to step aside from the partygate inquiry in December 2021, Johnson had few realistic choices about who could replace him. One close colleague said, 'When Simon stepped down, we thought immediately, "Fuck, we've got to get somebody to do this and do it quickly."' One option considered by Downing Street was a panel of experts, another was bringing in an external lawyer. But the prime minister wanted to keep the inquiry within Whitehall. It could not be the permanent secretary of another ministry – someone junior to the Cabinet secretary – nor could it be a partisan political figure. Gray was recommended for the task by Simone Finn and Henry Newman, both deputy chiefs of staff at the time.

Little is known about Gray and even her age is still a matter of dispute. She was born in 1957 or 1958 in north London, the daughter of Irish immigrants. After her father died of a sudden heart attack in her late teens, she abandoned plans to go to university and headed straight into the civil service. Little again is known about her early mandarin career, except that she took a highly unusual career break in the 1980s to run a bar in Newry in Northern Ireland's 'bandit country' with her husband Bill, a country singer. Some in Whitehall have speculated she worked in an intelligence role at the time, given that the career break took place during The Troubles, though Gray has denied it.

Back in London from 1987, after roles in the transport, work and pensions and health ministries, she joined the Cabinet Office in the late 1990s. Her most influential role came in 2012 as director-general of the propriety and ethics team – known as PET. Gray adjudicated on everything from pay and conditions for political special advisors, to all behaviour covered by the civil service code. Whitehall was littered with political bodies from her past findings: Andrew Mitchell, the former chief whip, was forced out following alleged comments to police officers at the gates of Downing Street. Damian Green, deputy prime minister, was also forced to quit following a Gray inquiry that concluded he misled colleagues over pornography on his work computer.

Gray's power flowed from her close working relationship with the then head of the civil service, Jeremy Heywood. Her influence was private but immense. In his memoirs, Oliver Letwin, a former Cabinet Office minister, wrote, 'Our great United Kingdom is actually entirely run by a lady called Sue Gray . . . unless she agrees, things just don't happen.' The BBC described her as 'the most powerful person you've never heard of'. Heywood praised her as 'user friendly' as she would typically give advice that ministers liked to hear. She is said to have a warm sense of humour, enjoys karaoke and has a passion for cats.

Those who have worked with Gray over the last decade praised her work ethic. Above all else, she existed to protect the civil service from political interference. One aide close to Johnson said, 'I'm fucking terrified of her but not for any real reason.' A Tory minister who worked closely with Gray said they assumed her private views were 'to the left of centre' but added it did not matter. 'She is absolutely dedicated to serving the government of the day.'

Her numerous critics, mostly external to Whitehall, argued that she was too secretive, too devoted to shoring up power for the administrative state. Gray had a reputation for not leaving any paper trails: when the Labour party wanted to nominate someone for a peerage, for example, they would call up Gray for a 'yes or no' on whether the person would pass vetting. No one questioned her advice, there were no records or explanations of her guidance. 'It's fairly obvious that very senior people are scared of her,' one Cabinet Office insider said. 'Everyone knows she can be utterly steely.'

In 2018, Gray abruptly left Whitehall to become permanent secretary of Northern Ireland's finance department, a surprising move for a civil service high-flyer. She then applied to be head of the Northern Ireland civil service but was unsuccessful – she later remarked,[3] 'People may have thought that I perhaps was too much of a challenger, or a disrupter. I am both.' Others reckoned it was political, suggesting her appointment was blocked by the Democratic Unionist party, who felt she was too close to the nationalist Sinn Fein ministers.

In May 2021, she returned to Whitehall to be the second permanent secretary at the Cabinet Office with special responsibilities for the union of the United Kingdom – working closely with the levelling up secretary Michael Gove. The appointment, at the age of sixty-five, suggested that her era as one of Whitehall's most senior figures appeared to be coming to an end. That was until she received the call from the prime minister's office in December 2021.

Gray's arrival into partygate came with Simon Case's blessing – the head of the civil service told colleagues he was relieved to no longer be involved. Her colleagues said she was 'acutely aware' of the balancing act she now had to oversee: go too easy on Johnson and she would be accused of a whitewash, go too hard and a civil servant would be accused of removing a democratically elected prime minister. Gray was nervous and later told colleagues she felt she had been misled by Case. 'She absolutely had no concept of what she was getting herself into. If she had, she would have said no to the inquiry. She was sold a pup by the Cabinet secretary,' one official said. Another added, 'Simon was very much figuratively rubbing his hands.'

The partygate investigation came with wide-ranging terms of reference: Gray was instructed to establish 'a general understanding of the nature of the gatherings', and it could include disciplinary action. There were certain prescribed events she would look at, including all the parties in the run-up to Christmas 2020. But there was a deep contradiction about what she was being asked to do. Catherine Haddon of the Institute for Government think tank summed it up: 'No matter how thorough her investigation, she has effectively been asked to investigate her own political boss.' Or as one senior Tory figure said, 'Cabinet Office inquiries never find the PM guilty.'

Gray's inquiries started before Christmas, while Downing Street was preoccupied with the pandemic. The focus, however, was starting to shift onto partygate. After the Owen Paterson scandal and the Covid vote revolts, Conservative MPs were unwilling to give Johnson the benefit of the doubt any longer. One Downing Street insider said, 'My conversations with MPs about partygate all became negative. I can remember thinking that unless we grip this situation very quickly in January, change the line and clarify our position, it will become a major problem with the parliamentary party.' And so it proved to be.

During the festive break, Johnson's two youthful Conservative strategists – the bearded Australian Isaac Levido and former journalist Ross Kempsell – sought a reset of the strategy for dealing with partygate. They were aware that the media was now chasing the story and would not leave it alone. Levido and Kempsell wanted a 'big war room', with outside legal advice, that would sift through all the evidence from throughout the pandemic to finally figure out what happened, how to repair public perceptions and protect the prime minister's standing. But their hopes were dashed when outside forces struck again and the partygate leaks resumed early in the new year.

***

Dominic Cummings was the first true digital native person to work at the top of a British government. After he left Downing Street, he returned to Twitter and created a Substack account, writing dense but enticing posts about his time in government, particularly now about the partygate scandal. With thousands of subscribers paying £10 each, it was a lucrative enterprise for an apparatchik who might have struggled to find work elsewhere. It became increasingly clear that Johnson's former chief advisor was hellbent on removing him from office and saw partygate as his weapon to do so.

On 7 January, Cummings posted an entry[4] that suggested Gray should focus her inquiries on an event that happened on 20 May 2020 that he said was heralded as 'socially distanced drinks'. His post dismissed *The Guardian*'s photo of the 15 May 2020 garden gathering, stating it was taken after a series of outdoor meetings. The long entry – full of dense language and repetition, a hallmark of his writing – reiterated many of Cummings's critiques of Johnson's decision-making during the pandemic and his long-standing criticisms of how the government was operating. But much of it was devoted to this hitherto unknown event.

Cummings wrote, 'I and at least one other spad (in writing so Sue Gray can dig up the original email and the warning) said that this seemed to be against the rules and should not happen. We were ignored. I was ill and went home to bed early that afternoon but am told this event definitely happened.' The post also marked the first time that he described Johnson as 'the trolley', in a reference to his habit of veering from side to side on policy decisions, akin to a wonky object in a supermarket. Cummings was explicit too that he wanted to remove the prime minister: 'The only way to avert this existential threat to many seats, including much of the "Red Wall", is to replace the trolley with a team that can actually deliver meaningful workforce changes.'

On 17 January, Cummings wrote a lengthy appendix to his blog about the 20 May party where he accused Johnson of lying when he said there were no parties and no rules were broken. 'No10 is throwing out as much confusing chaff as possible, such as nonsense about a "drinking culture" intended to shift blame,' he wrote. 'The events of 20 May alone, never mind the string of other events, mean the PM lied to Parliament about parties.' Cummings argued that Johnson's principal private secretary Martin Reynolds invited people to the drinks party, that he had checked with Johnson, and that both agreed it should go ahead and both attended the party.

Four days later, the invitation that Cummings had discussed handily turned up in public in another leak[5] to *ITV News*. Reynolds, who ran his private office, provided undisputable evidence that a party took place on 20 May 2020:

> *Hi all,*
>
> *After what has been an incredibly busy period we thought it would be nice to make the most of the lovely weather and have some socially distanced drinks in the No10 garden this evening.*
>
> *Please join us from 6pm and bring your own booze!*
>
> *Martin*

ITV reported that around forty staff gathered in the garden with drinks and picnic food. When the revelations had been leaked about the previous events, Number 10 had insisted they were purely work events, impromptu 'gatherings'. This one was impossible to pass off with a formal invitation where individuals were invited to 'bring your own booze'. The timing of the BYOB party was particularly embarrassing as hours before the bash began, the then culture secretary Oliver Dowden had delivered a press conference where he told viewers, 'You can meet one person outside of your household in an outdoor, public place provided that you stay two metres apart.' Gatherings in greater numbers were not allowed until a month later. Yet seemingly Number 10 had taken no notice of their own rules. When the invitation was leaked, there was no comment from Downing Street.

Inside Number 10, however, the atmosphere instantly became like a circular firing squad. The event had not appeared in the slender report into the parties ordered by Dan Rosenfield a few weeks prior, and he had no idea it even existed. Diaries were checked, though, and the ITV report was accurate: Johnson and his wife Carrie had attended. The prime minister was, again, utterly furious with his team, but apparently not at himself for attending the event. He felt his aides had let him down. In a crisis meeting, Johnson shouted: 'How has all this been allowed to happen? How has it come to this? How haven't you sorted this out?'

Much abuse that evening was naturally thrown in the direction of Reynolds from his colleagues. 'People went apeshit with Martin over that email, absolutely apeshit,' one senior civil servant said. 'Not that he had sent it, but at the fact he hadn't bothered to tell people when we asked around about what parties had taken place.' Some officials put the blame on decision-making structures in Number 10 'essentially collapsing' after Johnson suffered Covid, while others put the blame on Dominic Cummings, who had 'disengaged' after the Barnard Castle scandal according to colleagues. Reynolds told colleagues that some of the partying in Number 10 had even been self-medicating: 'When people drank excessively, they weren't doing it for fun.'

Civil servants within Number 10 were anxious they were going to be dobbed in during the Gray inquiry, which was now widened to include the BYOB party. 'People were all running scared, they didn't know who to trust and they had nowhere to go. It was a horrific, toxic atmosphere,' one said. Faced with potentially misleading parliament and lying to the public, Johnson's political team were unforgiving. 'The civil service chronically let the boss down,' an ally said. 'Nobody stepped up, Martin [Reynolds] or others. Nobody stepped up and said "We know things are happening that probably shouldn't have happened. Let's get it all out, let's pull it all together." Officials were giving the PM an incremental impression that it was going to be okay.'

Some vague attempts were made to figure out who had leaked the email. Johnson's closest allies blamed Cummings again, pointing out that the timing of his blog and the leaking of the email were 'too close to be a coincidence'. One ally said, 'It really was a concerted campaign of an extraordinary nature against a sitting prime minister by his previous closest advisor.' Others felt it was the civil service seeking revenge for Johnson dismissing their concerns. One close ally said, 'A lot of the partygate stuff was leaked by junior civil servants, particularly in the press office. There's about thirty of them, all quite young and junior. One person leaking had quit on bad terms the previous summer. Another was selling pictures to the *Mirror*.' Whoever was responsible, trust began to break down between the prime minister and those who were supposed to be running the country.

The following day, 12 January, Johnson appeared in the House of Commons to apologise for the second time. To a deathly silent chamber, the prime minister spoke without his usual rhetoric flourishes or ebullience. He told MPs about the BYOB event that he 'believed implicitly ... was a work event' but admitted 'with hindsight I should have sent everyone back inside'. The prime minister acknowledged the anger and anguish people will have felt 'when they think in Downing Street itself the rules are not being properly followed by the people who make the rules'.

Yet Johnson sought to justify the gathering, stating that Number 10 is a 'big department' with the garden used 'as an extension of the office'. Despite these excuses, the prime minister said he would take responsibility and there was little more he could say until the Gray inquiry was complete. Remarkably, Johnson's words were his own. While journalists took the 'believed implicitly' line to be the result of careful legal advice, to avoid misleading MPs, it was Johnson's effort. 'It wasn't a heavily legalised statement, that was the whole problem!' an aide said. 'The PM was writing a lot of these lines himself.'

After a bruising time at the Despatch Box, Johnson visited the members' tearoom – he typically turned up when things were going badly. Some MPs he chatted to recall he repeated his line that he had given to parliament, that he had personally done nothing wrong. Others said he looked 'almost ill' and showed contrition. The mood among the Cabinet was no better. Rumours began to surface that a major shake-up in his Downing Street staff would follow the full Gray report, whenever it was concluded, described by one MP at the time as 'the Night of the Long Scapegoats'.

The scandal took one of its routine turns for the worse the following day when *The Daily Telegraph* reported[6] on 13 January that yet another illegal gathering took place, this time on the evening of Prince Philip's funeral in April 2021. The imagery of this third party was the starkest yet: the evening before the Queen sat alone in the chapel of Windsor Castle when nationwide Covid rules forbade people from gathering in large numbers to attend funerals, not one but two boozed-up parties took place in Downing Street. A government official had been dispatched to a nearby Co-op supermarket to fill up a suitcase with wine. Once again, the parties had not appeared in Dan Rosenfield's previous fact-finding dossier of parties.

One party was for James Slack, Johnson's former director of communications, while the other took place for a personal photographer. The *Telegraph* reported that 'excessive' levels of alcohol were consumed and guests danced late into the night. The Covid guidance at the time stated that indoor gatherings beyond household bubbles were forbidden and it was impossible to justify this as a work meeting. Johnson was not present in Number 10 as he had travelled to Chequers, his countryside residence. For Slack's party, drinks were consumed in the press office before transferring to the garden. Staffers at the other do partied in the basement, with a raucous atmosphere. When the two events merged, music began blaring out of a laptop on top of a photocopier while someone played on a swing belonging to Wilf, Johnson's baby son. The seat was snapped off.

When the revelations became public, senior officials were incredulous. All of those in Downing Street were aware that the revelations about the Prince Philip party, where guests were reportedly 'lathered', made the partygate crisis far worse. 'It was the idea of the Queen sitting alone while everyone was getting drunk,' one insider said. At such a sensitive moment for the nation, Number 10 staffers had been reminded by the building's custodians that it was a time of national mourning and they should not exit the black door of Number 10 with grins on their faces. 'I didn't think anybody would need reminding not to have a massive piss-up in the garden,' one senior official said.

At this point, the partygate furore expanded beyond specific events with further revelations about the general culture in Downing Street. Reports emerged that 'wine time Fridays' had been commonplace for a decade, with the suitcase being used to smuggle booze into Number 10 since David Cameron was prime minister. The suitcase began as a carry-on bag, before gradually expanding into something sturdier with wheels. Under Johnson's premiership, a wine fridge was installed that could hold dozens of bottles.

Gray's report had been set up to explore failures by various individuals, but Tory MPs began turning on the prime minister – blaming him personally for allowing such lax standards. One long-serving ministerial aide said, 'There is no doubt the culture is set from the top. It would be impossible to imagine some of the pandemic parties happening under Theresa May or even David Cameron. It's hard to dispute that the atmosphere relaxed under Boris.' While there was still no sign of the Gray report, anticipation for her findings was building each day. Social media was full of memes around 'waiting for Sue Gray',[7] likening her to Mr Bean standing in a field, US Democrat Nancy Pelosi ripping up paper behind Donald Trump, and Gromit the dog, building a train track as he was gliding along.

Throughout January, as the leaks continued, Gray was in regular contact with Johnson's inner circle. While some close to Gray said she 'loathed' the attention and that it was 'the very worst' job she did in government, others in Number 10 thought she was lapping it all up. 'Sue loved being the centre of the story,' one said. 'She became obsessed about her status, her reputation, her position.'

When Gray picked up the partygate inquiry from Case, a fair chunk of work had been done by the Cabinet Office's propriety and ethics team, which Gray used to lead. Her successor Darren Tierney led the investigation day to day and although she conducted some of the interviews personally, for more senior individuals, Tierney and his team did the grunt work. One official on the Gray inquiry described it as a 'very pressured intense environment'. The officials were only too aware they were not just investigating their colleagues, but the most powerful people in the country. 'Sue was concerned, but her aim was not to bring down the government. It might sound old-fashioned but she just wanted to get to the truth,' one official involved said.

While waiting for Sue Gray to complete her work, Johnson desperately formed two new support networks of his closest confidants (his official political team was barely functioning). 'Operation Big Dog' was the first, consisting of minister without portfolio Nigel Adams, chief whip Chris Heaton-Harris, transport secretary Grant Shapps, his political strategist Ross Kempsell and Charlotte Owen, a special advisor who oversaw administration of the team. *The Independent* reported the existence of the gang but missed one key fact: the 'big dog' was not in fact Johnson but Nigel Adams – a humorous nickname for one of the prime minister's most loyal soldiers who is far from big in stature.

Operation Big Dog was a parliamentary operation to counter waning support for Johnson among Tory MPs. Their efforts were directed through a complex spreadsheet, masterminded by Shapps. It ranked Conservative MPs on their loyalty, voting record, constituency needs and how they could be expected to vote in a potential confidence vote to remove the prime minister. From early January onwards, the Big Dog team concluded it was 'inevitable' that the prime minister would be challenged. Unlike partygate, they wanted to be prepared. Dan Rosenfield and the formal Number 10 team welcomed the support. 'He didn't feel undermined or anything, he was happy for the help,' one aide said.

The second support organisation formed at this point was the 'Brains Trust', consisting of Tory strategists Isaac Levido, Lynton Crosby and Ross Kempsell, plus Will Lewis, Johnson's former editor at the *Telegraph*. The latter was brought in as a close friend of Johnson and communications expert. 'He was a very sensible guy and at that stage, the PM had very low trust in any of the actual team,' one person involved said. From the Brains Trust came a slew of policy announcements intended to regain his footing after Sue Gray: the end of all Covid restrictions, a major policy paper on the levelling up agenda to tackle regional inequality, freezing the BBC licence fee for two years. One minister said its efforts were broadly successful: 'The critique most MPs had was, "This Conservative government isn't doing anything that's conservative right now." They sought to change that.'

Two events during January gave Johnson a respite from party-gate. On 18 January, the first plot to unseat Johnson burst into the open thanks to the work of the 'Big Dog' team. Dubbed the 'pork pie plot', it was named after the ringleader Alicia Kearns, MP for the Rutland and Melton constituency, home to famous pies. It was formed of fifteen to twenty MPs from the 2019 intake who were plotting to force a no-confidence vote in Johnson. The membership of the plot was much disputed, but Gary Sambrook, MP for Birmingham Northfield and Chris Loder of West Dorset were both involved. One Cabinet minister said[8] of the plotters, 'They were only elected because of him [Johnson]. Most of them are a load of fucking nobodies.' Within Number 10, the plot brought some relief and comedy.' That was a good moment in party management because things began to swing back to us a bit,' one insider recalled. 'We also just laughed at how achingly bad they were.'

The second event came on 19 January, when the *Financial Times* broke the news that Christian Wakeford, Tory MP for Bury South, would be crossing the floor to the Labour party at prime minister's questions. Wakeford, one of the pork pie plotters who had sworn directly at Owen Paterson several months prior, cited partygate and the cost of living crisis for his reasons for defecting. Johnson received the Wakeford news (he was privately named 'Christian Wokeford' among Tory MPs) just as he arrived at the Palace of Westminster. The prime minister cheered. 'He immediately knew it was a win because it would allow us to claim that the pork pie plotters had committed the cardinal sin of going to Labour,' one senior aide said. Instead of further dividing the party, as Wakeford had hoped, his defection had a unifying effect.

Gray's investigations rumbled on with no hint of when she might be finished and what the final report would look like. And still the partygate leaks continued. On 24 January, *ITV News* reported that Johnson had attended a birthday party in June 2020 at a time when indoor gatherings were banned. The cast list at this particular party was said to have included the chancellor Rishi Sunak, Johnson's wife Carrie and Lulu Lytle, who was redecorating Johnson's Downing Street flat with furnishings financially out of reach for most of the population. The mood inside the government soured dramatically. 'It's death by a thousand cuts,' one Cabinet minister remarked. Other senior Tories came to the same conclusion as the Big Dog Operation: it was 'inevitable' that Johnson would face a no-confidence vote.

The efforts to defend all these parties became farcical. Conor Burns, the Northern Ireland minister and a devoted Johnson loyalist who was occasionally involved with the Big Dog team, was questioned on Channel 4 that evening about the birthday party. Burns argued that the prime minister 'was in a sense, ambushed with a cake' when staffers produced the dessert to celebrate his birthday. The ridiculous phrase entered the partygate lexicon, leading celebrity chef Nigella Lawson to announce[9] 'Ambushed By Cake' would be the title of her next book. When Johnson saw the clip of Burns's interview, he was 'massively pissed off' according to colleagues. There was cake at the birthday do, but it was never taken out of a Tupperware box. Still there was little contrition. Nadine Dorries, the culture secretary and easily the most ardent Johnson loyalist, mused, 'When people in an office buy a cake in the middle of the afternoon for somcone else they are working in the office with and stop for ten minutes to sing happy birthday and then go back to their desks, this is now called a party?' The Brains Trust team was 'tearing its hair out at these shit lines', according to one official involved.

Had Gray's full inquiry been published at this point, a no-confidence vote in Johnson could have finished off his career.

With partygate, the prime minister had waded into quicksand and he was gradually being subsumed by each new revelation. Back in December, he could have grabbed a rope to safety by ordering a fact-finding exercise and perhaps sitting down for a comprehensive interview to sincerely apologise and take responsibility for what had gone wrong. Yet no internal fact-finding exercise had ever taken place and the press office never properly softened their response that no Covid rules had been broken and that there had been no parties.

And then, partygate went from a political problem to a criminal one. After weeks of vacillation, the Met police picked the last week of January to formally open an investigation. Gray's team had been passing information to the Met since December and were baffled as to why the police had so far opted not to investigate. One person close to her inquiry said, 'They could have feasibly started an investigation before Christmas, based on the photos and witness statements they received.' The civil servants put the Met's stalling down to incompetence or perhaps concern that it would look politically motivated.

On 25 January, the head of the Met, Cressida Dick, told[10] the London Assembly that her force would look into 'a number' of the parties. Johnson's inner circle was given warning a few hours before the announcement but in a Cabinet meeting that morning, Johnson did not tell his colleagues that he was now under police investigation as it was 'too sensitive' to be shared in advance – again a sign of the low regard he held of those purported to be loyal to him. Johnson's inner circle accepted they would have to cooperate '100 per cent' with the inquiry but most realised they had lost all control of the partygate strategy.

The decision came as a complete shock to the Cabinet Office, throwing Gray's inquiry into chaos just as it was about to conclude. 'From our perspective, they massively dropped the ball and then tried to do a huge overcorrection by kicking off when they did,' one official close to Gray said of the police inquiry. To her colleagues she expressed huge anger and frustration that the report was going to be delayed just as it reached the final drafting. Had the Met not launched their probe, the full Gray report was due to be out by the end of January. A codename was given to the Met inquiry: Operation Hillman.

One ally of the prime minister said they had no visibility of how the police work was going to pan out. 'We didn't know when it was going to end, when it was going to report, there was zero communication between the Met and Number 10. There was no sense of how long the process would take, how many people would be questioned. At this stage, we were massively out of control and the police were fully in the lead.' Some in Johnson's inner circle saw an opportunity to reset the narrative around partygate: with the police investigation underway, they could no longer answer questions from the media or from their own MPs. Everything was paused and stopped, or 'thrown into a bucket called "the Metropolitan Police investigation",' as one insider said.

Sue Gray, however, had other ideas. She told Number 10 that day she still intended to publish an interim report that would skirt around the Met's inquiries. That came as a huge frustration to Johnson's team, who dispatched Simon Case to try and persuade her to wait until the police inquiry was finished. She roundly told Case that was not going to happen.

On 31 January, Gray's dozen tersely worded pages came out. She concluded that many of the gatherings were 'difficult to justify', stating there had been 'failures of leadership and judgment by different parts of Number 10 and the Cabinet Office'. The interim report lambasted the culture of 10 Downing Street and the 'excessive consumption of alcohol' which she said was 'not appropriate in a professional workplace at any time'. Some government staffers had wanted to raise concerns about behaviour but felt 'unable to do so' due to the drinking culture at the time. Although more detailed findings would have to wait, she concluded 'there is significant learning to be drawn from these events which must be addressed immediately across government. This does not need to wait for the police investigations to be concluded.'

When copies landed in his Number 10 private office, the prime minister's reaction was relatively positive according to those in the room and it 'wasn't as hostile as it might have been'. 'He was mostly pleased it was not too personal,' one person present said. Another aide said, 'The interim Sue Gray report was the first time he had a comprehensive understanding of a lot of things that happened.' When setting out a plan to respond, the inner circle knew the only option was another apology – but one that came with a plan to reset the government.

Johnson returned to the House of Commons for his third partygate mea culpa. The prime minister told MPs he was 'sorry for the things we simply didn't get right and also sorry for the way that this matter has been handled' and said he would act immediately to fix some of the structural problems highlighted by Gray.

Despite his relative optimism at the interim report, the ensuing debate revealed that backbench support was draining away from his leadership. Theresa May, his grudge-holding predecessor, said that Gray's report had shown 'Number 10 Downing Street was not observing the regulations they had imposed on members of the public' and posed a question to Johnson: 'Either my right honourable friend had not read the rules or didn't understand what they meant, or others around him, or they didn't think the rules applied to Number 10. Which was it?'

The criticism in parliament went on for hours and Johnson had to take it. Andrew Mitchell, the former chief whip who had supported Johnson's leadership bid, said he had lost confidence in him. Aaron Bell, a 2019 red wall Tory MP, told the prime minister he had not attended his grandmother's funeral due to Covid restrictions. 'Does the prime minister think I'm a fool?' he asked. The testiest exchange, however, came with Keir Starmer, the opposition leader, who called Johnson 'a man without shame', saying, 'Just as he's done throughout his life he's damaged everything and everyone around him.'

In his response, Johnson made one of the most remarkable comments of his time in public life. He suggested that Starmer had failed to prosecute the notorious paedophile Jimmy Savile during his time as director of public prosecutions and that as such he would not be taking any lectures from him. It was untrue and not rehearsed beforehand but seemed to be picked up from Jacob Rees-Mogg, the leader of the House of Commons, who was beside him on the front bench and had yelled it across the chamber. 'People say stuff on the front bench and in the atmosphere of the Commons, you need ideas the whole time,' one Johnson ally said. 'He had a bad habit of repeating what others had said. He has no filter sometimes.' Back at Downing Street, his aides were stunned. Priti Patel, the home secretary, made it known she was 'livid'.

Gray's interim findings, though, allowed Johnson to launch a major reset of Downing Street, planned out by the Brains Trust team. First was structural: her report said 'as a matter of priority' there should be a major effort to address the fact Number 10 had 'not evolved sufficiently' to deal with the 'size, scale and range of responsibilities' that it now had. In response, Johnson announced that a new 'Office of the Prime Minister' would be created, hiving off half of the Cabinet Office's domestic functions to better support his position. 'The PM was genuinely seized of the need to reform how Number 10 was working,' one colleague said. 'He felt he'd been massively locked out of the system by those around him.' One example were the press lines on partygate. 'All of those lines being issued weren't repeatedly signed off by the PM, it wasn't reaching the PM. That was a big structural problem.'

The second part of the reset came on 3 February with the departure of three of Johnson's most senior aides. The first resignation was not planned: Johnson's policy chief Munira Mirza who had worked with him since his City Hall days, was a huge shock for Johnson and his team. In her resignation letter, she cited her reason for leaving as the Jimmy Savile slur against Keir Starmer in the House of Commons. 'This was not the normal cut-and-thrust of politics; it was an inappropriate and partisan reference to a horrendous case of child sex abuse,' she wrote in an excoriating letter that concluded, 'It is not too late for you but, I'm sorry to say, it is too late for me.' Mirza's departure was bitterly felt among Team Johnson, as a minister reportedly[11] said: 'If he's lost her, he really is screwed, there really isn't anyone left.'

Many officials in Johnson's inner circle remained puzzled as to why she quit. 'It certainly wasn't about Jimmy Savile,' one official said. 'When Munira didn't like something, you knew about it immediately. She didn't raise the Savile remark once.' One Johnson ally said, 'There is not a chance on God's earth that a remark about Jimmy Savile would have made a blind bit of difference to Munira. She is as hardcore as it comes.' One minister who worked with her said that the Savile remark was 'the straw that broke the camel's back in Munira's mind', adding that she privately shared Dominic Cummings's views of Boris. 'She loved him, still loves him, but was infuriated by his trolley-like leadership.'

Her departure, though, precipitated the Number 10 shake-up that had been planned for weeks. Martin Reynolds, who acquired the nickname in Whitehall 'Party Marty', after his infamous email about the BYOB email, quit. Dan Rosenfield was out as chief of staff and Jack Doyle was out as director of communications. Doyle had found himself at the harsh end of dealing with the partygate scandal and had fundamentally failed with the unyielding comments to the media he had overseen, and that left no room for manoeuvre. According to one colleague, 'Jack was hollowed out by then, he wasn't functioning in his job.'

Rosenfield realised his position had become untenable. Well before the Gray report, he had attempted to persuade Johnson of the need for some significant personnel changes in Number 10. After months of fruitless discussions, where he warned the prime minister if the calibre of advisors didn't improve it would cost him his job, he concluded it was not going to happen. The day of Mirza's resignation, he travelled in the car with the prime minister to Stansted Airport where the pair came to a mutual agreement he should go. 'Dan was humble enough to accept it was over,' one Johnson ally said. Johnson held no animosity towards Rosenfield and Doyle. The following day, Johnson gathered all Downing Street staff to discuss the shake-up and supposedly herald a new era of calm competence after the Gray report. He quoted[12] Rafiki from *The Lion King* that change was 'good and necessary'. There was no mention of Operation Hillman. The mood was unsettled, however, and it was unclear who or what was coming next.

Despite the reset, relations between Johnson and Sunak began to fray further. Following Mirza's resignation, the chancellor was asked publicly about the Jimmy Savile remark. 'Being honest I wouldn't have said it,' he said in a press conference. Johnson loyalists fumed that it was another sign of betrayal, that Sunak was drifting away from the prime minister's camp. The prime minister's inner circle became convinced that Sunak had again begun planning an exit from government in an attempt to seize the crown for himself. 'December had been an emotional wobble for Sunak, but in January he was strategising and organising a bid,' one ally said. The unhappiness went further when Sajid Javid was also publicly asked about the Savile remark and said he had 'absolute respect' for Starmer's work.

On 4 February, the Brains Trust met to map out what a new Downing Street would look like after the departure of Mirza, Rosenfield and Doyle. The meeting began with bacon sandwiches at 7 a.m. and ended with some 'godawful' takeaway food late that evening. To replace Jack Doyle as director of communications several seasoned political journalists were approached, including George Pascoe-Watson, the former political editor of the *Sun*, Neil Darbyshire (organiser of the Garrick dinner back in October), Andrew Porter, a former political editor of the *Telegraph*, and Sarah Sands, the ex-editor of Radio 4's *Today* programme. Johnson asked Will Lewis to take up the role, but he politely declined and opted to remain an informal advisor.

On Monday 5 February, the new Downing Street team was announced. Steve Barclay, who was appointed as Cabinet Office minister in September's reshuffle, was made Number 10 chief of staff, to run alongside his ministerial duties (something that had never been done before). He was not Johnson's first choice for the job: the Brains Trust tapped up a range of people who all rejected the role. One person involved said, 'We went through all the political advisors and they were all rejected for political or personal reasons.' Another senior official said, 'it was hard to find an advisor who was, by that stage, senior enough or respected enough, to take the job or who wouldn't piss off everybody else.' Grant Shapps was asked to take on the role and declined. 'We needed an outsider. Boris liked the idea of having a minister and he thought that Steve was a competent administrator.'

The other appointment was a familiar name in Team Johnson: Guto Harri, a former BBC political correspondent who worked with Johnson during his time as mayor of London, would be his new director of communications. The always cheerful Harri rapidly made his mark when he told Golwg360,[13] a Welsh-language news site, that he had enjoyed a brief rendition of Gloria Gaynor's 'I Will Survive' and 'a lot of laughing' during his job interview with Johnson. For good measure, Harri went on to insist that his new boss was 'not a complete clown' and a 'very likeable character'. Hari was sharply reprimanded by the prime minister, which did not portend well for their relationship.

The next piece of Johnson's government reset came later that week on 8 February with a mini Cabinet reshuffle that was to have severe consequences. The first aim was to deal with the ministers implicated in the Owen Paterson farrago: Mark Spencer was shifted from chief whip to leader of the House of Commons, while Jacob Rees-Mogg was moved to the Cabinet Office in a new role as minister for government efficiency and Brexit opportunities. Two core members of the Big Dog team were brought into formal roles: Chris Heaton-Harris was made chief whip and his friend and ally Chris Pincher was appointed his deputy.

Two final appointments capped off what would be Johnson's final Number 10 team. Andrew Griffith, a former Johnson aide, was made head of the Number 10 policy unit. Again he could not find a political appointee to fulfil the role but turned to the smooth, well-dressed MP for Arundel and South Downs, who had loaned his Westminster house for Johnson's leadership bid in 2019. Coming from the right of centre of the party, the Big Dog team tried to turn the fact he was an MP into an advantage.

'Andrew and the PM go back a long way with their personal relationship, they do speak and trust each other,' one official said. But those involved in the discussions were aware he was not universally popular. 'He rubs a lot of people up the wrong way,' a colleague said.

The last new figure to arrive in Johnson's orbit was David Canzini, a slight, goateed Tory party official who worked at Lynton Crosby's political consultancy firm, who was tasked to improve relations with Tory MPs. But unlike many of the appointees, he was not close to Johnson – the prime minister told colleagues, 'This guy Canzini, I don't know him.' One longstanding aide to the prime minister said Canzini was a 'very weird addition' to the team and 'it was not clear what he was there to do.' He was often to be spotted skulking around the glass atrium of Portcullis House, which MPs walk through to their offices.

The new team were soon faced with another crisis, this time not at home. With Omicron receding and the pandemic finally over, Johnson's attention turned to the worsening situation in mainland Europe. The first full-scale invasion of a European country since the Second World War would provide Johnson with what some would say were some of his greatest achievements as prime minister. As far as the daily news was concerned, Sue Gray and the Met drifted into the background as President Vladimir Putin drew up plans to invade Ukraine. Johnson would soon find himself playing a leading role on the world stage, as he had always dreamed.

3. Putin's Move

Boris Johnson was nudged awake at 4 a.m. on 24 February 2022 to hear the news he had been dreading but feared was coming. Jamie Norman, the prime minister's military assistant, informed him that Russian troops had crossed several borders into Ukraine from the north, east and south. Missile attacks from Russia had been launched on Ukraine's major cities including the capital Kyiv. What President Vladimir Putin termed a 'special military operation' was given its genuine name in Downing Street: an invasion. The prime minister pulled himself out of bed and Downing Street kicked into what officials termed 'crisis gear'.

For months, the military and intelligence apparatus of the British state had warned publicly and privately that the colossal build-up of thousands of Russian troops along Ukraine's border was not another bluff. Johnson had shared these concerns more widely and some had accused the prime minister of stoking the crisis; of seeking to focus on international matters in order to detract attention away from his growing domestic woes. Both of those accusations were proven false as the horror of Russia's disastrous invasion decision unfurled. The depth of planning that had taken place in Moscow to seek to collapse Ukraine as an independent, democratic state was now obvious to all.

In the early hours of that February morning, Johnson spoke to Ukraine's president Volodymyr Zelenskyy to reaffirm the UK's support for its vital eastern European ally – a partnership that would be central to the final months of his premiership and his legacy. The pair had established a relationship through a series of in-person and virtual meetings, and it was to evolve into one of the deepest geopolitical bonds of recent times. Johnson's critics argued that any British leader would have been forced to develop such bonds by the reality of the UK's foreign policy need to curb Russian aggression. Yet those who have been in the room with Johnson and Zelenskyy attest that their affinity is deep and personal.

Unlike the other crises that hit the UK during Johnson's time in office, such as the pandemic and partygate, the Ukraine war was one that the prime minister and his Downing Street team were well-prepared for. In the weeks leading up to the invasion, detailed plans were made for the prime minister to address the country, hold a debate in parliament, and slap waves of sanctions on Russia to penalise Putin. Johnson had even road-tested a snappy soundbite among senior Number 10 colleagues that he hoped would define the West's response to the invasion: Putin Must Fail. The plans were duly activated that morning.

In the televised address that lunchtime from Number 10, Johnson announced:[1] 'President Putin of Russia has unleashed war in our European continent. He has attacked a friendly country without any provocation and without any credible excuse.' The prime minister sought to differentiate Ukraine from other conflicts the UK had entangled itself with. 'This is not in the infamous phrase, "Some faraway country of which we know little." We have Ukrainian friends in this country; neighbours, co-workers.' He said that the UK and its allies could not allow the values of democracy and freedom to be snuffed out. Johnson summed up the UK's approach: 'Our mission is clear: Diplomatically, politically, economically – and eventually, militarily – this hideous and barbaric venture of Vladimir Putin must end in failure.' Those final words spoke to a lofty aim, but one that Number 10 believed, or hoped, was achievable. He did not, however, warn that the Russian invasion and the West's economic response risked a disastrous impact for consumers at home through the impact on the supply of goods and energy – something Tom Tugendhat, chair of the foreign affairs select committee had suggested. All Johnson said in reply was, 'We will of course do everything to keep our country safe.'

During the first day of the invasion, Johnson spoke to Jonas Gahr Støre, the Norwegian prime minister, and German chancellor Olaf Scholz, urging both countries to join forces with the UK for a coordinated approach with strong sanctions. Downing Street's robust approach was shared by the Foreign Office – typically far more cautious on diplomatic matters. Across the road from Downing Street, a testy meeting between foreign secretary Liz Truss and Andrey Kelin, Russia's ambassador to the UK, broke down[2] after a few minutes. She chastised the ambassador for the invasion, stating 'he should be ashamed of himself' after he 'spouted the usual propaganda'. Truss kicked him out of her office after warning Russia would become 'an international pariah'.

As Johnson prepared to set out the UK's sanctions that evening, he continued to seek a tougher response. The *Financial Times* reported Johnson pushed 'very hard' during a virtual call of G7 leaders that Thursday for Russia to be ejected from the international SWIFT payments system, making it almost impossible to move money in and out of Russia. But German chancellor Scholz did not support such a dramatic move at this stage. Number 10 warned after the call, 'The prime minister underscored that Western inaction or underreaction would have unthinkable consequences.'

The 'Putin Must Fail' sentiment was restated when Johnson addressed the House of Commons with trenchant rhetoric. 'I'm driven to conclude that Putin was always determined to attack his neighbour, no matter what we did. Now we see him for what he is – a bloodstained aggressor, who believes in imperial conquest,' he told MPs. Johnson went on to set out the 'largest ever' set of sanctions, including a ban on Aeroflot, the Russian airline, a full asset freeze on its second largest bank VBT, and export controls on equipment that could be put to military use. Over a hundred individuals would be sanctioned later, with a full range of measures applying to Belarus too, which had been the launchpad for the invasion.

Over the following weeks, Johnson would garner some of the greatest praise of his premiership thanks to the confident response to the situation in Ukraine. At the close of 2021 and the start of 2022, Downing Street was still struggling with the chaos of partygate and the Sue Gray inquiry, as well as the instability within the prime minister's inner circle. But with the warning lights flashing on the government's diplomatic dashboard with increasing alarm in the lead-up to the invasion, Johnson's nimble foreign policy team guided him into the rare position of being fully briefed and prepared and, as a result, in the vanguard of global opinion. Unlike the unwieldy structures elsewhere at the top of his government, Johnson's approach to Ukraine was effective thanks to a small team dominated by expert special advisors and civil servants.

Led by his chief foreign policy advisor Professor John Bew, historian, academic and one of the world's foremost experts on realpolitik, the prime minister relied on a handful of advisors to navigate the UK's response to the most serious land war in Europe in a generation. Johnson's core Ukraine team included Jamie Norman, his civil service military aide, national security advisor Stephen Lovegrove and Simon Gass, chair of the joint intelligence committee. From the off, the core team wanted to go hard on Russia. 'Our job was to go around and push the envelope as far as possible,' one senior official said. Number 10's political and press team had minimal involvement – they were only drafted in for major media interventions, although Johnson continued to write most of his own speeches.

At cabinet level, Johnson was supported by two close ministers who shared his hardline approach: defence secretary, Ben Wallace, and foreign secretary, Liz Truss. Wallace was a long-time supporter of Johnson's political ambitions and had served in the Scots Guards for seven years; Truss had been promoted to the Foreign Office the previous year, importing her enthusiastic yet disruptive approach from the Department for International Trade. Both ministers were trusted by Number 10 during the crisis. 'We had an activist foreign secretary, who was very good, and an activist defence secretary with huge credibility on the issue,' a government insider side. 'It worked well because there weren't that many people involved.'

Since his tenure as foreign secretary, Johnson had taken a keen interest in Ukraine and was deeply engaged with its complex history. Unlike the often tedious management of Conservative MPs, or the exasperation he felt about Covid rules, his persona was fully engaged with the war. One senior Foreign Office insider said, 'Every time we got these giant maps out, Boris knew where everything was – the villages, historical moments, it fitted into a particular part of his brain.' An ally of Johnson said the conflict reflected on his admiration and aspirations of being a latter-day Winston Churchill; 'I genuinely suspect his worldview clicked with the subject. He has this great appreciation for the history of conflict and battles. It was all completely genuine.' None of his team sensed he was leaping into the subject to distract from his troubles closer to home. 'The suggestions that he was doing a cynical ploy to distract are rubbish,' one Number 10 insider said.

As with his views on almost any topic, Johnson's foreign policy stances had shifted and morphed over the years. During his years editing *The Spectator*, he set out its editorial line[3] as 'always be roughly speaking in favour of getting rid of Saddam, sticking up for Israel'. He had supported the invasion of Iraq and Afghanistan, but sharply criticised Tony Blair's handling of the conflicts. Officials who sat through crisis meetings on Ukraine stated, 'He's not an instinctive hawk, he's not a Russophobe. His basic theory of international relations is cultural and civilisational respect. He is not a kind of shrill neo-con.'

Since Russia's invasion of Crimea in 2014, the UK was at the forefront of the Western military response. Following the annexation, David Cameron's then government offered[4] nonlethal equipment at the request of the Ukrainian government. The following year, the UK launched Operation Orbital, a programme to train nonlethal Ukrainian armed forces with a focus on logistics, medical and intelligence support. In March 2015, the Ministry of Defence ramped up its supply of equipment. Michael Fallon, then defence secretary, said, 'Ukraine is our friend, it is in need and we should respond to requests.' Any requests for help were fulfilled by the UK in coordination with its NATO allies, but an early divide opened up: America supplied lethal equipment early on, France and Germany openly opposed arming Ukraine. Britain fell somewhere in the middle.

In March 2016, the UK and Ukraine signed a fifteen-year agreement on closer defence cooperation, intelligence sharing on potential threats and further cooperation in the training of armed forces. The UK government gifted Ukraine £2 million of military equipment between 2015 and 2017. By the time Boris Johnson became prime minister in July 2019, the defence ties between the two nations were already strong and he sought to make them even firmer, urged on by his advisor John Bew. As well as humanitarian and moral concerns, taking a leading role in the Western defence in Eastern Europe was part of his 'Global Britain' foreign policy.

In October 2020, Zelenskyy visited Johnson at Downing Street to sign[5] a deeper strategic defence partnership that the Atlantic Council think tank described[6] as 'the most consequential foreign relations act of his presidency to date'. It was a full state visit: after meeting Prince William at Buckingham Palace, the Ukrainian president visited one of the UK's gigantic aircraft carriers in Portsmouth and nodded approvingly at the Operation Orbital training of Ukrainian troops. Both countries' defence ministers signed a dense agreement promising £1.25 billion to help rebuild the Ukrainian Navy following early signs that Russia may have been looking to attack from the south. Johnson welcomed Ukraine's move towards NATO membership with 'enhanced opportunities partner' status and pledged whatever further support he could offer.

Johnson and Zelenskyy had grown closer as the threat from Russia increased. In June 2021, the partnership between the two nations had been further deepened with supplies of lethal military aid, the UK following in the steps of the US. Britain agreed to supply two refurbished Royal Navy minehunter vessels, along with the sale of missiles. NATO's largest member matched Johnson's commitment: that summer, US president Joe Biden pledged $150 million of security assistance, which was followed by another package of lethal and nonlethal equipment that autumn.

Come September, Johnson addressed the UN General Assembly (UNGA) and warned 'the adolescence of humanity is coming to an end'. While his message was driven by the impact of climate change as head of the COP26 climate summit in Glasgow, Ukraine was on his mind too. The prime minister met

Zelenskyy for a meeting on the sidelines of the summit, where British diplomats began to stress that the threat from Russia was real and urged Ukraine to supercharge its preparations for an invasion. Zelenskyy's public reticence to acknowledge or discuss how he would cope with an invasion alarmed many in Downing Street, but it later turned out to be a mask for comprehensive private preparations.

One of Johnson's closest aides who witnessed their UNGA meeting said, 'He had a real rapport. We joked that a politician who's famous for playing the piano with their penis is naturally going to get on with Boris,' a reference to a comedy sketch[7] from the Ukrainian president's days as an actor and comedian.

Washington and London were increasingly fearful that war was coming. Biden and Johnson made it clear that additional support for Ukraine could be available well beyond what was already being offered, but the prime minister's affinity with Ukraine was not entirely shared by the Whitehall foreign policy establishment. When intelligence reports suggested in late 2021 that a Russian invasion was a serious prospect, Ben Wallace and Johnson pushed for a further significant increase in the UK's assistance. Although the Foreign Office was seen by some as 'hawkish' on Russia – a topic that crossed the Remain and Leave divide – officials remained concerned at prodding the Russian bear, particularly about the decision to supply 'lethal' weaponry to Ukraine. Events were to prove Johnson correct. 'He and Ben Wallace got it right quite early on against a lot of resistance,' one senior Downing Street insider said.

***

Russia had built up troops along the Ukrainian border previously in March and April 2021 that had not resulted in an invasion. But when the second build-up followed in the autumn, British intelligence believed that an invasion was no longer a bluff. Over 100,000 Russian personnel were deployed – including forces in neighbouring Belarus and navy assets in the Black Sea. London's concerns were shared in America: Joe Biden was visited by his military and diplomatic chiefs in October[8] to inform him that their assessment had changed from uncertainty to alarm that military action was imminent. The US president was told, as was Johnson, that Putin had almost everything in place for an invasion. According to *The Washington Post*, Biden was informed of a plan with 'staggering audacity' that threatened to destabilise NATO and rip up Europe's post-war security model.

Bedecked in white tie, on 15 November, the prime minister used the annual Lord Mayor's Banquet to warn[9] that Western nations would face the unenviable choice between safeguarding their principles and energy supplies. 'A choice is shortly coming between mainlining ever more Russian hydrocarbons in giant new pipelines and sticking up for Ukraine and championing the cause of peace and stability,' he told the City of London's great and good. Downing Street had said earlier that day that the situation on Ukraine's border was 'concerning' and reiterated 'unwavering support' for its territory. Johnson criticised Belarus for being an enabler of Russia's aggression and accused it of engineering an 'abhorrent' migrant crisis. Russia still denied any plans to attack.

All Western military nations sought to strike the delicate balance between the classified nature of their intelligence, while continuing to plan for an invasion. Intelligence sharing by NATO members suggested that Russia would initially focus on an invasion from the north, heading for Kyiv with plans to seize the city within several days. Putin hoped to remove Zelenskyy and install a more Kremlin-friendly regime. Further attacks would follow in the east and the south. One US national security official said,[10] 'It did not seem like the kind of thing that a rational country would undertake.' Biden and Johnson were both receiving analogous intelligence and were left in no doubt that Putin was hugely determined. This time, the UK and US felt that an invasion was going to happen.

Johnson and Biden urged Ukraine to take the threat seriously and to prepare for war. 'The British and Americans were alarmed they were not taking the intelligence seriously enough,' one government insider said. 'It turns out they weren't telling us much about their plans. They were actually better prepared than we presumed at that point.' Another senior official involved in the response said that Ukraine was eager not to give any sense that the invasion was 'imminent or inevitable'.

On 7 December, Putin and Biden held a virtual summit, where the Russian president suggested[11] that NATO's expansion in the east was the reason behind his plans to send troops to the border – essentially that he was guarding his own territory. The US president countered that Ukraine was not on course to join the Western defence alliance. Biden advised there would be severe economic costs if Putin duplicitously proceeded. Johnson spoke to Putin on 13 December. Putin told him Russia wanted clear agreement that NATO's border would not expand at all. Johnson later told the House of Commons how he had responded during the call,[12] 'If Russia were so rash and mad as to engage in an invasion of sovereign territory of Ukraine, then there would be an extremely tough package of economic sanctions, mounted by our allies, mounted by the UK and our friends around the world.'

A few days later on 12 December, a communique[13] was issued by the G7 foreign leaders of France, Germany, Italy, Japan, the EU, US and the UK calling on Russia to 'de-escalate, pursue diplomatic channels, and abide by its international commitments on transparency of military activities'. The statement echoed Biden's message that any military aggression would be countered with 'massive consequences and severe costs in response'. But throughout December Russia continued to build up its presence on Ukraine's border and the US significantly ramped up its supplies of arms, along with the deployment of more of its troops to Europe.

Early in 2022, Ben Wallace, the defence secretary, pushed hard against opposition at the Ministry of Defence to send 2,000 'next generation light anti-tank weapons', known as NLAWs, to Ukraine. Wallace succeeded in his aims and British personnel were sent with the weapons to instruct soldiers how to use the equipment. Wallace said[14] he would not shy away from sending more NLAWs if required: 'I will keep the question of sending more defensive weapons to Ukraine under close review. I do not rule anything out within helping Ukraine deliver self-defence.'

In Downing Street, the rising crisis in Ukraine became the primary focus, yet all the while Johnson was distracted with his growing domestic woes around the partygate inquiry as a potential no-confidence vote loomed. Given his warning at Mansion House, specifically referring to forthcoming problems with energy supplies, it is a surprise that perhaps more was not done early in 2022 to prepare for such difficulties. Downing Street was aware of what was likely to come, yet there seemed little preparation for a short-term solution to energy security and rising prices. An energy security white paper[15] was prepared, which was chiefly focused on nuclear power and other projects that would take years to come to fruition.

On 24 January, Johnson warned[16] that any invasion would be 'painful, violent and bloody'. Based on the joint US and UK intelligence, the prime minister outlined how the conflict could be very rapid: 'The intelligence is very clear that there are sixty Russian battle groups on the border of Ukraine. The plan for a lightning war that could take out Kyiv is one that everybody can see.' Despite the darkening storm, the prime minister still hoped sense and peace could prevail. And if it did not, the UK was preparing to punish Russia.

The following day, 25 January, when the Met police announced their criminal investigation into Covid rule breaking at the heart of his government, Johnson insisted in[17] the House of Commons he was not distracted from Ukraine. 'I and the whole government are focused 100 per cent on dealing with the people's priorities, including the UK's leading role in protecting freedom around the world.' He reminded MPs that the UK had trained 21,000 Ukrainian troops under Operation Orbital since 2015, along with supplying anti-armour missiles and training personnel. But a sign of Whitehall's concern was evident in its decision to 'temporarily' evacuate some diplomats from the embassy in Kyiv.

At this moment, ministers were clear that the UK would not provide 'active military support', nor would it countenance a no-fly zone – which would considerably raise the possibility of direct conflict with Russia. Within Johnson's foreign policy team, a significant debate took place about whether the UK should mirror the US in supplying military equipment that went beyond defensive needs. One senior government insider said, 'The internal debate was whether we announce another tranche of nonlethal aid, or do we move it beyond what we've done already?' Again, the domestic and international collided. Johnson was scheduled to speak to Putin on 30 January, but the call was cancelled as the prime minister was forced to make a statement to MPs on partygate. The Kremlin enjoyed the distraction and declined to immediately rearrange.

On 1 February, Johnson visited Zelenskyy in Ukraine to buttress the UK's 'unwavering commitment to Ukraine's sovereignty, independence, and territorial integrity within its internationally recognised borders'. As he flew across Europe, 135,000 Russian troops had now amassed on the border with Ukraine – increasing by thousands every week. Officials who accompanied the prime minister recall the visit as bittersweet. 'I'll never forget that trip,' one senior aide said. 'It was very sad because Kyiv is the most beautiful city – it's very Western and not what I expected.' A senior diplomat said that pro-British sentiments were strong during that visit. 'Everyone in Kyiv was obsessed with Brits. If we went to a bar, we were definitely getting drinks because we were British. They thanked us for training their troops and being really supportive.'

As Johnson landed in Kyiv, Poland announced it would supply Ukraine with lethal weaponry – including surface-to-air missiles and artillery shells. While Putin met with Hungary's Viktor Orbán at a ludicrously long, socially distanced table, Johnson's headline announcement was £88 million to fight corruption within Ukraine. In a joint press conference with Zelenskyy, he dismissed the notion that a war was being talked up. 'Someone said we were exaggerating the threat, that the US and UK are trying to big this up. It's not the intelligence we are seeing. It's a clear and present danger.'

After their press conference, the leaders enjoyed an upbeat but focused dinner with their closest aides. One person present said, 'We went to a restaurant, I remember jousting with Zelenskyy, we talked about NATO membership. Our overall impression that night was the Ukrainians weren't fully prepared for what was coming. Our intelligence picture suggested it was really bad.' But the Ukrainian president might have had good cause for dampening the prospects of war. 'What Zelenskyy kept saying was if they spoke out in a way that caused a flight of capital, Putin might be able to get what he wanted, which is regime collapse and a massive crisis without even having to step a foot in Ukraine,' one government insider said.

On 10 February, the Ministry of Defence announced supplies of more defensive equipment – including body armour and helmets. But in another sign that the Brits expected an imminent invasion, all military trainers were withdrawn. The British state threw all of its diplomatic might at the crisis to ensure every option was exhausted. Having missed the Kyiv visit after catching Covid, Liz Truss made a futile trip to Moscow on 10 February, touted as a last major UK peace effort. The trip was a disaster: the foreign secretary was on the receiving end of a belligerent attack from Russian foreign minister, Sergey Lavrov. 'The conversation turns out to be between the dumb and the deaf,' he said, standing right beside her. 'We seem to listen, but we do not hear.' The press conference ended when Lavrov simply walked off and left Truss alone. From her perspective, the only positive was a photo in Red Square, wearing a faux-fur hat that seemingly channelled a visit by Margaret Thatcher thirty-five years earlier.

The same day, Johnson visited NATO headquarters in Brussels and warned the crisis had reached 'the most dangerous moment' as Russia's military build-up reached its climax. The delegation was well received, as Johnson's warnings proved prescient. 'Boris was quite strong,' one civil servant said. 'We'd spoken to the Dutch delegation, we felt like the leaders of this diplomatic campaign – members of the Ukrainian parliamentarians were coming over to hug Boris and get photos.' The last-ditch diplomacy with Russia was rounded off on 11 February when defence secretary Ben Wallace visited Moscow. He warned his Russian counterpart Sergei Shoigu that an invasion would be a 'lose–lose' situation and the UK had 1,000 troops on standby. Cooperation had reached 'close to zero'.

The UK's role as an interlocuter came to the fore. Johnson was 'locked in' on a tough no-compromise stance by this point, according to his aides, and there was 'much scurrying around' to ensure all Western nations were on the same page. 'Boris's role to bang heads together at this stage was quite important, he did his best to ensure everyone moved in lockstep in case the worst happened,' a diplomat said. Several groupings were at play. The core 'quad' of NATO defence powers spoke regularly: France, Germany, America and the UK. It was occasionally expanded to a 'quint' to bring Italy into the discussions. France and Germany may have operated around Johnson at certain times, but his close relations with the Baltic countries proved important.

All of the diplomatic efforts ultimately failed, as they were perhaps always going to. A sham vote took place in the Russian Duma on 15 February to recognise the Donetsk People's Republic and Luhansk People's Republic as separatist regions from Ukraine. Putin continued to insist 'of course' he did not want a war, and Russia muddied the waters by withdrawing some troops from the border. Johnson signalled there may be a 'diplomatic opening' but warned their foes were sending 'mixed signals'.

That following weekend, Johnson attended the Munich Security Conference – the annual gathering for Western political and military leaders. Johnson had a conversation on the sidelines with US Republican senator Lindsey Graham, who assured the prime minister, 'During a crisis, when shit hits the fan, the Brits and Americans are in one place.' John Bew and the Number 10 team were eager for smooth relations with Washington. One official explained, 'It was our job to get the Americans in the best possible position. We had to stay close because we know their heft does far more than anything we can achieve.'

Johnson's keynote speech proclaimed that Britain would always defend freedom and security around the world, reiterating his core message from the start of the conflict: 'If dialogue fails and if Russia chooses to use violence against an innocent and peaceful population in Ukraine . . . then we at this conference should be in no doubt that it is in our collective interest that Russia should ultimately fail and be seen to fail.' Zelenskyy received a standing ovation during his call for peace in his twenty-minute address and lambasted Western leaders for failing to fulfil their security pledges.

Johnson held bilateral meetings with Zelenskyy and delegations from Estonia and Poland. With Brexit still dominating the UK's foreign policy approach to Europe, he had struggled to find a new role until this crisis. 'Until that point, we didn't have a massively activist Europe policy,' one insider said. What alarmed Johnson's team the most was complacency among some other leaders. 'We thought everyone was being very complacent in Munich, we're like, "What the fuck is going on here?"'

The trigger for the invasion came gradually, then suddenly. On 17 February, Johnson said that the shelling of a nursery in Ukraine's Donbas region could be part of a 'false-flag' operation to destabilise the Zelenskyy government and offer Russia a pretext for an invasion. 'We fear very much that that is the kind of thing we will see more of over the next few days,'[18] he warned. A Kremlin disinformation campaign ramped up to purportedly show Ukrainian forces killing Russian troops. On 21 February came the official 'recognition' of the Donetsk and Luhansk republics, followed by tanks moving into the Donbas on 23 February. Russia evacuated its embassy in Ukraine and at 4 a.m. the following morning, the war began.

The UK immediately significantly increased its aid to Ukraine. On 9 March, Ben Wallace told MPs over 3,600 NLAWs had been delivered to Ukraine – along with anti-tank Javelin missiles. He insisted[19] all of the weapons were defensive and the supplies were 'calibrated not to escalate to a strategic level'. Wallace, who had not had the smoothest of relations with Downing Street under the Dominic Cummings regime, was lauded by Johnson's inner circle for ensuring the weapons were delivered. 'Ben broke the mould and Boris explicitly pushed the state further with each step,' one senior official said. 'We didn't realise at the time but he was being advised, "If you want to do this, we should be cautious." That happened on a number of issues during the escalation.' Another senior government insider said they felt Johnson's response on weapons and sanctions showed his gut political instincts at their best: 'It was guts, a willingness to take risks, commit resources and be difficult. He showed genuine leadership.'

***

After the invasion, Johnson pushed on with diplomacy. On 29 February, he visited Estonia and pledged[20] the 'biggest possible' offer of doubling the number of British troops to help protect Eastern Europe. He later went on to Estonia and met British troops stationed in Tallinn. Along with Jens Stoltenberg, NATO general secretary, and Estonian prime minister Kaja Kallas, he praised their efforts as 'fundamental for the safety and security of all of our nations, but also of our values – freedom, democracy, independent sovereign nations'. The prime minister privately picked up an NLAW for the first time during that trip, but photographs were forbidden.

On 1 March, he arrived in Poland and faced Ukrainian anger and frustration directly for the first time since the invasion had begun. Daria Kaleniuk, an activist who had fled her country when the war broke out, told Johnson in a highly emotional appearance, 'You're coming to Poland, you're not coming to Kyiv because you are afraid, because NATO is not willing to defend, because NATO is afraid of World War III, but it has already started.' Kaleniuk urged the prime minister to introduce a no-fly zone to stop 'the bombs and missiles which are coming from the sky' that would kill women and children. A pained-looking Johnson responded, 'I'm acutely conscious that there is not enough that we can do, as the UK government, to help in the way that you want,' explaining why a no-fly zone would result in the Royal Air Force shooting down Russian planes. He was deeply moved by the encounter according to colleagues. 'He was so emotional,' one official said. 'On the flight back to the UK, we were being told to avoid further escalation and be calm. That really pissed him off too.'

On 7 March, Johnson published[21] a six-point plan in *The New York Times* to try and rally an international response – including a humanitarian coalition; supplying more defensive equipment; going further on sanctions (including expelling Russia from the SWIFT banking system); preventing any 'creeping' normalisation of what Russia has done; remaining open to diplomacy and de-escalation; and looking to strengthen NATO. The Biden administration informed Number 10 through backchannels that it did not appreciate the intervention, but it spoke to the pugilistic approach Johnson was taking. He also felt vindicated by the US response; 'It was a conscious decision, we're willing to disrupt and make ourselves unpopular,' one ally said.

All of Johnson's worlds came together on 8 March when Zelenskyy addressed the House of Commons. Quoting the prime minister's political hero Winston Churchill, he told MPs, 'Just in the same way you didn't want to lose your country when Nazis started to fight your country, you had to fight.' Channelling the famous pledge to fight 'on the beaches', the Ukrainian president pledged, 'We'll fight in the forests, on the shores, in the streets.'

More than almost any other topic during his premiership, Johnson was emotionally invested in the conflict. He would often call his foreign policy aides late in the evening, after the 10 p.m. news bulletin, and ask them: 'Why aren't we doing more on x when there's atrocities happening?'

During the frequent rounds of the G7 leaders' calls in the first weeks of the invasion, Johnson did not seek to be a harmoniser. One diplomat said, 'Boris was always willing to piss people off in a way that does slightly go against the conceived wisdom that he always wants to be liked. Quite a few people in the diplomatic establishment were uncomfortable with it and would report back that [Olaf] Schultz or [Emmanuel] Macron were unhappy. But the PM would just come back and say "We're not doing enough."'

As the UK's financial sanctions gradually tightened in further rounds targeting oligarchs and key figures linked to Putin, Johnson's foreign policy team felt they had won the argument – especially when Germany announced it would freeze the Nord Stream 2 gas pipeline. 'We dealt in primary colours, we were explicit,' a British diplomat said. 'We didn't move an inch, whereas Macron or Schultz thought in terms of settlements and realpolitik.' Johnson's constant slogan of 'Putin Must Fail' was eventually adopted by other leaders (Number 10 officials were amused when Canada's liberal prime minister Justin Trudeau emphatically endorsed the slogan in one meeting). 'There was no backsliding by our senior partners. We felt we'd had a huge policy success because everyone landed on our position,' one insider said.

Johnson's central role in the West's response to Ukraine was confirmed on 9 April, when he made a surprise visit to Kyiv as 'a show of solidarity' soon after Russian troops had pulled back. British security officials opposed the visit, arguing it was too dangerous. Johnson overruled them. During a remarkable walk around the city, surrounded seemingly by half the army, Number 10 undertook meticulous planning to ensure no one knew he'd gone. 'It was the most satisfying trip to pull off, it never leaked,' one of his inner circle said. Johnson was cut off from Downing Street for twenty-four hours – except for a burner phone for emergencies – so the last his team heard of him was from a train in Poland. He was videoed greeting ordinary Ukrainians, many of whom embraced and thanked him. Later, at a press conference, Johnson praised Zelenskyy for his 'resolute leadership and the invincible heroism and courage of the Ukrainian people'. He added, 'Ukraine has defied the odds and pushed back Russian forces from the gates of Kyiv.' During the trip the UK increased its loan guarantee to £770 million and pledged yet more military support. One senior official in Zelenskyy's office said, 'The UK is the leader in defence support for Ukraine, the leader in the anti-war coalition, the leader in sanctions against the Russian aggressor.'

The personal rapport between Johnson and Zelenskyy as witnessed in that visit baffled some in Downing Street. One official who saw the pair closely said, 'I find it difficult to say why they get on so well because often his [Zelenskyy's] English isn't perfect and a lot of the time they speak through a translator. It's quite difficult to really understand their relationship. But I don't think it was a romance of convenience.' Another senior official added, 'Zelenskyy admired Boris as a politician and Boris has a sense of Zelenskyy as a significant figure. Boris has a whiff of the zeitgeist and Zelenskyy captured it.' It was arguably Johnson's finest hour as prime minister.

He would remain closely engaged with the Ukraine war throughout the rest of his time in Downing Street, although Johnson was unable to see through to victory his slogan that 'Putin Must Fail'. Officials in his foreign policy team admit now that 'there's no easy way out' of the conflict and that in late 2022 things on the ground are moving towards stalemate. One senior government insider said, 'No one thinks that is acceptable. With the initial Russian invasion against Kyiv repelled, the Donbas has been slightly stabilised and much of the war is now about access to the Black Sea and the land strip. That's really where the question is. If you froze it, Ukraine would not have the ability to function as a state.'

Another person said that it was 'completely possible' that the war could result in some form of disputed territory stalemate with Ukraine. 'There's so much political build-up, you can't go from full-scale war into a sort of neat solution,' the official said. 'Can you have a peace that theoretically may stop short of Ukraine's headline war aims, which is where life was before February 23? Yes.'

***

The Ukraine war had two consequential impacts on Johnson's premiership. The first was to heighten his personal interest in defence matters beyond his previous instincts on foreign policy. During a visit to an NLAW factory in Belfast in May 2022, the prime minister impressed the manufacturers with his 'quite detailed knowledge about the whole weapons systems'. One of his inner team said, 'He got far more into defence.'

The conflict also further developed his foreign policy views. 'Many of Boris's views are instinctive and quite emotional and I think that's probably also the way the British people see it,' one ally said. 'The way the invasion happened is such an egregious insult, all the things we're taught that were bad about the Second World War we thought had gone away. It was a shocking moment.' Although he faced much scepticism from the Whitehall establishment over his support for Brexit, the Ukraine conflict improved his mastery of foreign relations – leading some in the UK's diplomatic establishment to conclude he could turn to an international role after exiting Downing Street. 'He's quite well orientated, he's got a solid sense of it. After three years as foreign secretary, he's got a smell for it and knows the leaders,' one diplomat said. His foreign policy advisors think 'quantum leaps' were made with relations with Japan, South Korea, Australia – as well as the Baltics, Nordics and Poland – during his time as prime minister.

His relationship with Joe Biden was publicly somewhat distant, not least due to the US president's Irish heritage tying into the dispute over the Northern Ireland Protocol. Yet Whitehall officials who listened in on the pair's calls said that the two leaders would often find 'they're completely of the same mind', especially when they spoke one to one outside a formal setting. The protocol did not feature as heavily in their relationship as some reports suggested. 'The whole time Biden never ever mentioned Northern Ireland to Boris once, not once,' a senior diplomat claimed. One of Johnson's closest allies said that the war delivered him one fundamental insight: 'This crisis exposed and reaffirmed the massiveness of the United States and it's vital importance for all our security.'

One foreign policy area that was not resolved was Europe. Relations over the UK–EU trade deal came close to collapsing over the opposing approaches of Brussels and Westminster to the Northern Ireland Protocol. Johnson's team were acutely aware that their hopes of reconstructing Anglo-French relations were unfulfilled. As Johnson entered his final months in office, his foreign policy aides had hoped things may shift. 'I thought we turned the corner,' a senior official involved said. 'We had agreed to reset. That's one of the tragedies, we threw the boomerang really hard and fast and it didn't have time to come home.' Despite the difficulties of Brexit, Johnson's inner circle believed his right calls on Ukraine had left him with a respectable foreign policy legacy. 'His reputation in the world is strengthening, although some may still regard him as a bit untrustworthy. The UK is now more of a player, we are seen to act strategically instead of going along with the pack.' With Liz Truss's pledge to raise defence spending to 3 per cent of GDP by 2030, her approach is likely to follow much of what Johnson pursued. 'That gives us real heft and leverage.'

At the start of the Ukraine war, Johnson warned that the conflict would have a huge impact at home – but few realised the extent to which it would trigger inflation and expose the decades of policy mismanagement of the UK's energy security. When the first rounds of sanctions were discussed, Johnson's team were disgruntled by warnings from Rishi Sunak. One minister recalled the chancellor told the Cabinet, 'Of course we can do sanctions but we should be careful because this will have economic consequences.'

In the subsequent Cabinet debates, Johnson found an ally in Liz Truss as the most hawkish on action. One Number 10 insider said, 'It would always come back to us "Liz wants to push harder" and Boris would always go for the hardest position.' Ministers present said Sunak would not actively argue against action, but saw it as his job to flag the political and economic side effects. 'He didn't push hard, he never undercut what we decided,' one said. Johnson's foreign policy team also dismissed the notion that the UK could opt out of sanctions. 'If we'd sat the whole thing out, first it was politically implausible. Second, we'd all still be suffering from the economic crisis anyway. There's no specific UK sanction that's been self-harming, it's the Western sanctions collectively.'

Sunak was later to state[22] that he never opposed any sanctions but noted they came with consequences: 'I remember saying at the beginning of this thing: "Defending freedom is important, but you've got to tell people that it is likely the energy bills go up to £4,000 or £5,000 in the worst-case scenario . . ." I was like: "You need to go into it knowing that is what might happen. You've got to prepare the country for it, make sure that everyone is on board with that.'" He was right that not enough ground-work was done to explain to Britons the potential cost at home, of inflation, of rising energy bills, of correcting the failures in energy security.

The immediate political effect of the Ukraine crisis revived Johnson's standing. By the end of March, most of the decline in his popularity by partygate over Christmas and into the new year had been restored. Pollsters Redfield & Wilton reported[23] in early March that Johnson's popularity had increased by eleven points at home. His approval ratings were even higher abroad: in Ukraine it was 50 per cent. The Number 10 political team were not intimately involved with the war, but his fixers appreciated a different topic to talk about. 'Everything got better politically – there was a period where the media focused on Ukraine and the heat was off on partygate. At that time, we thought, "We are going to get through this,"' one Tory strategist mused. Another senior Tory party figure said, 'It did significantly move the news agenda on. He did demonstrate incredibly good instincts.'

A Cabinet minister close to Johnson argued Ukraine was his 'Falklands moment' akin to Margaret Thatcher's decision to send the navy halfway across the globe in 1982. 'Nobody other than Boris would have set off on this course. The PM was truly world leading in this. It all goes back to the agreement to send arms to Ukraine which started some months before despite enormous official opposition. He took on the blob and won, it was a shame he could not do it on other matters too.' Another minister who observed him closely in the Ukraine response said, 'It showed him at his genuine best. Boris's strengths and weaknesses are the same thing, it just depends on which way the wind is blowing. He's crashing through with "I'm going to lead on this, I don't care about the norms and sort of hesitations about moving too fast on things and not considering them."'

Throughout his premiership, Johnson sometimes failed to demonstrate the knowhow on bending the civil service to his way. Ukraine was the notable exception. 'When the PM pushed something, we'd discover there had been a big internal fight within Whitehall,' one senior Number 10 figure said. 'I remember a top civil servant saying all the time, "Oh, well it's on you then." On a couple of occasions with Ukraine in general, on sanctions, there was a bit of stress transference. We felt in the Number 10 team, we were absolutely at the sharpest point. But we'd also fight, fight and fight for the toughest measures.'

Those who worked with him on the Ukraine conflict could still see the flaws that would bedevil other parts of his government, but felt he was more temperamentally suited to the crisis. 'He was nice to work with,' a Western diplomat said. 'He's obviously flawed in organisational ways. But he can listen to reason, listen to challenge. I sometimes worried he wasn't challenged enough by some seniors around him, but he certainly was on Ukraine.' Whereas Johnson's legacy on Covid and Brexit will be disputed, Ukraine is harder to quibble with. 'We did change the course of international opinion on Ukraine,' one government insider said.

Unfortunately for Johnson, his new-found popularity over Ukraine was short-lived. Partygate had not disappeared, the Met police's inquiries had continued throughout February and March while he was often abroad. His political standing in the UK would rapidly crash back down to earth when an email dropped in his personal inbox one April morning from the Met police, inform-ing him of a penalty notice, bringing all of his troubles back into the limelight.

4. Operation Hillman

Boris Johnson's fifty-sixth birthday party was probably the most miserable of his life. Around 2.40 p.m. on 19 June 2020, the prime minister wandered into Downing Street's grand Cabinet room to discover a select, surprise gaggle of colleagues and those close to him – including his wife Carrie, the Cabinet secretary Simon Case and chancellor Rishi Sunak. Laid out on the coffin-shaped table was a tray of pre-packaged Marks & Spencer sandwiches, with big jugs of orange and apple juice, and cans of beer.

The gathering had not appeared in Johnson's official diary and he was not aware of it before it took place. The morning of 19 June was like many others for the prime minister: work commenced at 7 a.m. with eight meetings in Number 10 – including the daily Covid update. Johnson went off to visit a primary school in Hemel Hempstead, which had reopened earlier that month for the first time since the pandemic. Johnson chatted to the pupils,[1] joined a socially distanced class and was photographed on the playground demonstrating the two-metre rule, his arms raised up on either side. Before returning home, he posed for a photo with a luscious strawberry birthday cake, with dark chocolate oozing down the sides. The image would haunt him again and again during every subsequent partygate story.

According to Sue Gray, the gathering that would see Johnson becoming the first ever British prime minister to have broken the law while in office lasted no more than twenty minutes. Those attending consumed food and drink and 'some drank alcohol'[2] she would conclude. The leaked photos of the gathering present a rather lame sight: aside from Johnson holding aloft a small beer, birthday merriment was thin on the ground. One Tory aide present in the room said it was 'ridiculous' to describe it as a party. 'People were too fucking busy, it was the height of the pandemic.'

A few months shy of the two-year anniversary of this birthday do, Johnson, Carrie and Sunak were issued fixed penalty notices (FPNs) by London's Metropolitan Police for their attendance. The fines, issued on 12 April 2022, could have been challenged but all three instantly accepted and paid the £50 required of them. That evening, Johnson offered a 'full apology'[3] in a pained televised clip from Chequers. 'I have to say in all frankness, at the time, it did not occur to me that this might have been a breach of the rules,' he said. Johnson did not hint at any thought of resignation. 'Now I feel an even greater sense of obligation to deliver on the priorities of the British people.'

His remorseful sentiments were echoed by Carrie who also offered 'unreserved' apologies for breaking Covid rules. Sunak said the same in his public apology':[4] 'I understand that for figures in public office the rules must be applied stringently in order to maintain public confidence. I respect the decision that has been made and I have paid the fine. I know people sacrificed a great deal during Covid, and they will find this situation upsetting.' Surprisingly, the Cabinet secretary Simon Case was not fined, despite being photographed opposite Johnson. There was no pattern as to who the police fined or not: other Number 10 employees in the room also avoided a fixed penalty notice.

The penalties issued to Johnson and Sunak were easily the most significant result of Operation Hillman. The Met commenced its criminal partygate investigation back in January 2022, just as Sue Gray was preparing to release her full report. The Met had often seemed disinterested in investigating historic Covid law violations but with a stipulation that significant evidence would change that. As the leaks and reports of rule breaking stacked up, pressure from the opposition parties undoubtedly played a significant role in their decision to investigate. The police warned that if regulations were violated without a 'reasonable' excuse, then penalty notices would be issued – with fines increasing significantly with each breach.

Within Downing Street there was dismay at the criminal investigation. 'We were all assured for a long time by senior people that this wasn't going to happen,' one civil servant said. When the Met's inquiry began, the then chief of staff Dan Rosenfield gathered the thirty-odd political special advisors in the Cabinet room to reassure them about the inquiry, likening the prospect of any fixed penalty notice to a speeding fine. Despite the reassurances, 'It became a very anxious time for everyone who walked into the building because you were waiting to see if you or the person next to you was going to be fined,' one insider said.

When Operation Hillman began, Johnson's allies were strikingly upbeat that he could avoid a fine. Those close to the prime minister told[5] the *Financial Times* there was a 'good chance' that his reasonable excuses for the events he attended would hold because he considered them to be work gatherings. 'Legally the situation is not as black and white as it might seem. Some of the gatherings may have become full-blown parties later on but not while the PM was in attendance,' one ally said. Unlike some of his previous statements, Johnson took legal advice to oversee his response.

Despite these optimistic briefings to the media, the reality inside Johnson's political team was different. 'Nobody had a fucking clue what was going to happen with the Met,' one figure close to the prime minister said. 'There was no specialised knowledge on what was happening with the investigation, there was no back channel to the Met. People were theorising about what would or wouldn't happen out of thin air.' Throughout March and April, Johnson was constantly asking his aides – often on a daily basis – 'What's going to happen? What's going to happen?' His team simply did not know. The Met communicated only through Sue Gray and the Cabinet Office. Operation Hillman was so secretive that most of it was carried out on paper in a sealed room at New Scotland Yard.

The process took the Met's legendary opaqueness to new highs. At the end of January, the force helpfully said it would not name those issued with the fixed penalty notices, which only succeeded in creating a media witch-hunt to track down the rulebreakers. A few weeks into the inquiry, it was announced that ninety people would be sent questionnaires. Number 10 confirmed on 11 February that Johnson had received one, with the requirement for it to be returned 'truthfully' within a week. These forms held the same status as being interviewed under caution, meaning Johnson became the first prime minister to acquire this dubious accolade (one of his predecessors, Tony Blair, said he would quit if questioned under caution during the 'cash for peerages' scandal).

The forms, with some dozen questions,[6] asked individuals to provide a 'lawful exception' or 'reasonable excuse' for attending the event under investigation. The questions, which included the timings of the person's attendance at the gathering, included the following:

- Did you participate in a gathering on a specific date?
- What was the purpose of your participation in that gathering?
- Did you interact with, or undertake any activity with other persons present at the gathering? If yes, please provide details.

The Met said individuals could remain silent and answer 'no comment' to the questions, provide written responses, or attach a statement in their own words. Downing Street declined to say how Johnson had answered. But junior civil servants were petrified, fearing that the responses they had given to Sue Gray would be used against them in a criminal investigation – in turn, she allowed those who had spoken to her inquiry to review her notes before filling in the questionnaires.

Johnson's inner circle felt that the most problematic event would be the event that took place in May 2020, the 'Bring Your Own Booze' party, although their argument that the prime minister did not see Martin Reynolds's email invite ultimately held. The birthday party in June 2020 was far from the top of their radar: his allies insisted there would be no fine because it involved work colleagues and was not pre-planned. As the Ukraine war dominated the news, Downing Street had some breathing space from the restive Conservative MPs. 'The rage was gone so it didn't feel that bad,' one insider recalled.

But the fines kept coming and the scale of law breaking at the heart of the British state became apparent. By 29 March, twenty fines had been issued – and again the Met did not clarify who had received the £50 notices. The *Telegraph* reported that the first batch of fines covered the infamous 'Prince Philip' leaving party for James Slack, previously Johnson's director of communications. Another notable figure fined was Helen MacNamara, Sue Gray's successor as the Cabinet Office's director of propriety and ethics who procured a karaoke machine at one party that ended with a physical altercation between guests. She apologised[7] for 'the error of judgement I have shown'.

By 12 April, a batch of thirty FPNs were issued – including the ones issued for Johnson, his wife and chancellor. When the Met tipped off Downing Street that the fine was coming, the response was summarised by one press office aide to another as 'Fuck fuck fuck.' There was 'complete bafflement' as to why the Met had gone for that particular event. 'It was mad,' one insider said. 'Any objective person looks at that event and would say "What the hell is this?"' Johnson's closest colleagues concluded the fine was due to the presence of non-government staff.

Many in Downing Street felt sorrow that Johnson was taking responsibility for the rule breaking of others. 'I did feel a bit sorry for the PM because he was carrying the can,' one close colleague said, 'but Covid was something which literally every single person in the country related to because it affected their lives in a very bad way.' The sympathy for the prime minister extended into the Cabinet. 'Boris was as much a victim as anyone,' one minister said. 'The fine was ridiculous. His legal defence, which I think is right, was that he was demonstrating leadership. Boris doesn't even particularly like parties, when he went to all these events, he was doing it genuinely because he thought "These guys have been working hard and I've got to say thank you."'

The bewilderment was shared at the Department for Levelling Up. Sue Gray, who had returned to her day job until the police work was complete, privately expected Johnson to be fined but not necessarily for the birthday party. 'Sue had not put the birthday party at the top of her list,' one colleague said. 'There wasn't a surprise [among the team] that he was issued a fixed penalty notice, but there was surprise it was that event – particularly those who had seen the photos and all of the witness statements.'

Gray's team was privately quizzical that Simon Case, who was photographed laughing at Johnson raising a can of beer, had not received an FPN. 'Nobody understands that,' a senior official recalled. 'The only credible assumption is that they filled out the forms differently.' Johnson and Case did not coordinate their responses and took separate legal advice. Another person close to the process said, 'It can only be that there was sufficient doubt or excusable factors about Simon's actions, which is remarkable because they were all in the same room, for the same thing, for the same amount of time.'

The following week, Johnson was questioned in the House of Commons about the fine. Keir Starmer accused him of using the Ukraine war as a 'shield' to stave off resignation. Johnson admitted[8] he had been mistaken about the Covid rules: 'It did not occur to me then, or subsequently, that a gathering in the cabinet room just before a vital meeting on Covid strategy could amount to a breach of the rules.' Starmer, irate, retorted that his response was a joke and accused him of being dishonest (he was forced to withdraw the remark by the Commons speaker). On the Tory benches, Mark Harper, the former chief whip and one of the successful organising forces behind the Omicron rules rebellion the previous December, called on Johnson to resign.

Later that day, Johnson addressed a meeting of the 1922 Committee of Conservative MPs to stabilise his position – telling them, 'We're going to get on with our one-nation Conservative agenda.' Plenty of Johnson critics within the party piled into him. One advisor said that the fine became 'another excuse for people who wanted him to go' but they did not believe that a confidence vote was imminent. Tory strategists were increasingly aware that voters were becoming fed up with the story. 'The thing that people were most pissed off about partygate was the distraction from the things they actually cared about,' one said.

Among Johnson's closest allies, a visceral anger towards the police festered. Some of his supporters put the decision to investigate the parties down to internal leadership issues within the Met. One Johnson ally, who called the partygate investigation 'an abuse of power' and a 'waste of taxpayers' funds', mused, 'The Metropolitan Police was going through a bad time.

It was used as a distraction to give the commissioner some political strength by saying, "You can't get rid of me as commissioner now I'm investigating you.'"

But what was done was done. Johnson had broken the law and accepted the punishment. It may have been a minor infraction, yet his standing was undoubtedly harmed. Throughout partygate, the prime minister and his core team failed to understand why there was so much anger about parties that in normal times would never have been considered parties at all. In essence, they did not experience the same pandemic as the rest of the country with many of the 400-odd staffers in Downing Street continuing to work in the office, due to security issues and practical reasons, and as such they never suffered as much of the isolation and loneliness as the rest of the nation.

Johnson's failure to emotionally grasp the exceptional situation led to an over-optimistic sense that the fine would not be lethal to his career. Once again, his core political team miscalculated the mood. 'There was a consensus in Number 10 that it would be impossible for the police to fine the PM because it would be a massively political thing. Most people in Number 10 thought it wasn't going to happen. Turned out that was total bullshit.'

***

As well as worsening relations with his MPs, the strained relations between Johnson and Sunak sunk even further. The day after the fines were issued, *The Times* reported[9] that the chancellor devoted seven hours to debating his own future, having also told parliament that no Covid rules were broken. The paper reported that Sunak thought both he and Johnson should go, but 'friends warned him that his resignation could be considered an act of regicide against Johnson and damage any chances that Sunak might have of succeeding him'. One Sunak ally said he 'feels very badly let down by being dragged into this' and it was only natural for him to consider his position.

Relations between Number 10 and Number 11 Downing Street also faced policy pressure during the spring statement on 23 March when the cost of living crisis came to the fore. Due chiefly to the Ukraine war and the pandemic, inflation was soaring – reaching a four-decade high of 8.7 per cent. The Office for Budget Responsibility, which produces the UK's economic forecasts, warned that the country would suffer its biggest fall in living standards in sixty-six years.

To burnish his tax-slashing credentials within Tory circles, Sunak announced a 5p cut in fuel duty – in a publicity stunt he was later photographed filling up a Kia Rio in a Sainsbury's car park, only for it to later emerge the car was borrowed. It backfired when another photo suggested he could not use a contactless card machine. He also preannounced a 1p cut in the basic rate of income tax for 2024, something that Johnson's team thought was 'mad' when informed of it hours before the spring statement was delivered. 'That stupid income tax cut in two years was entirely on the Treasury's shoulders,' one Johnson ally said. 'They wouldn't even share with us what was in it until the morning.'

Rising inflation meant rising tax receipts, handing Sunak an extra £30 billion of 'headroom' that could be saved for a rainy day. Yet instead of spending it immediately, as some in Team Johnson wanted, he banked it to weather the turbulence ahead. Number 10 was 'attracted' to cutting VAT on energy bills in the spring statement, but was blocked by the chancellor according to those involved in the conversations (curiously Sunak went on to make this very pledge during his leadership bid). The package was widely judged as underwhelming, particularly the fuel duty cut. The shine was rapidly wearing off Sunak, who had briefly been wildly popular during the pandemic.

A far bigger problem, however, was emerging: Johnson and Sunak had fundamentally opposed economic views and approaches to governing. These differences were masked during the pandemic but had now come to the fore. Number 10 felt that the Treasury had to be dragged 'kicking and screaming' into taking action to tackle the cost of living crisis. One senior Johnson aide said, 'You can really tell when the Treasury are forced to do stuff they don't believe in. We didn't get the data, it was a very poor process.' After the spring statement, both sides openly criticised each other. Sunak's supporters said[10] the prime minister was 'unreliable and unpredictable'; Johnson's allies retorted Sunak was a 'privileged billionaire' and his energy offering was 'absolutely rubbish'.

Sunak's political woes were to rapidly worsen a fortnight later. *The Independent* broke the news[11] on 6 April that Akshata Murthy, Sunak's billionaire tech heiress wife, had held non-dom tax status while he was chancellor, living in the UK while stating that her home residence was in India. This revelation, which suggested she paid £30,000 to avoid an estimated[12] £20 million in taxes (according to the Labour party) could scarcely have been more toxic. A leak inquiry was duly launched, as Sunak's tax affairs were held tightly in Whitehall. Aides close to the chancellor believed that a civil servant leaked it to the Labour party, who in turn passed it to the media in order to discredit the chancellor.

After the revelations, some Number 10 officials admitted 'slight schadenfreude' after being on the receiving end of negative briefings from Team Sunak. The chancellor spoke to Johnson when the story was first published to reassure him that 'his wife was not going to be a political problem'. Yet Johnson's team were alarmed at both how badly Sunak's team had handled the story and the fact they had not anticipated what was to come next. 'It was very naive,' a Johnson ally said, adding that the timing ultimately benefited Sunak's future leadership hopes. 'In hindsight, they must be very glad that came out when it did, not in the summer' when Sunak was running for leader.

The following day, 8 April, Number 10 had reason to become even more exasperated when it emerged that Sunak had held a US Green Card, a route to permanent residency in the United States, for a significant period of time while he had been chancellor. Sunak had deep connections to America: he studied at Stanford University from 2004 to 2006, where he met his wife. Sunak's response was pugnacious: he gave a testy interview to *The Sun*[13] claiming the stories were a smear on him and his wife. 'She loves her country. Like I love mine, I would never dream of giving up my British citizenship. And I imagine most people wouldn't,' he said.

The chancellor called several newspaper editors to try and smooth the situation but decided that transparency was the best solution. Sunak referred himself for an investigation by Christopher Geidt, the government's independent advisor on ministerial interests, who later cleared him[14] of any wrongdoing and praised him for being 'assiduous in meeting his obligations and in engaging with this investigation'.

Johnson publicly defended Sunak, stating he was doing 'an absolutely outstanding job' and echoed his long-held personal views that families should be kept well out of politics. But behind the scenes, trust was thin. One senior Downing Street figure admitted the Sunak–Johnson relationship was 'always a bit tricky', adding, 'The PM did really value his relationship with Rishi and put a lot of time into it, even though he knew they were very different characters.' One of Johnson's closest aides argued that the difficult relations between Number 10 and Number 11 'dominated everything'.

That ally added that Sunak's unscheduled arrival in the Treasury, replacing health secretary Sajid Javid in February 2020 after he refused to sack all of his aides at the behest of Dominic Cummings, was a critical juncture in Johnson's premiership: 'If I was going to pick one moment that set the fate of the entire government, I would pick out the arrival of Sunak because it meant the PM lost control of the Treasury. He didn't have a close ally in the Treasury from day one.' The person added that Sunak's appointment was advocated by Cummings, and Johnson did not know him well. 'They met him a few times on the campaign and knew him as a talented young minister. But he didn't have a close personal relationship with him like he did with Saj.'

When relations deteriorated further in the months ahead, Johnson's team became convinced that Sunak had forged 'an alternate powerbase in Whitehall' from next door. Those close to the prime minister denied they had anything to do with the tax leaks. 'It was not planned. They dealt with it as if it was a crisis,' a colleague said. Another added there was no capacity to work at destabilising the chancellor: 'There was barely an operation in Number 10 to try and protect the PM, let alone doing in the chancellor.'

As the spring of 2022 drifted towards summer, the combination of the Operation Hillman fines, the policy differences over the spring statement and Sunak's struggles with revelations about his personal finances, meant the relationship that defines all British governments between the prime minister and the chancellor became 'very, very strained'. One figure close to Johnson concluded, 'The fines destroyed it. Rishi blamed the PM for creating this environment.'

***

Beyond the Conservative party, the Hillman fine brought another problem to a head. After Johnson accepted the fine, his MPs were braced for the opposition parties to refer the prime minister to the Commons' privileges committee for an inquiry on whether he had misled parliament. The investigation would be serious: if the bipartisan group found Johnson had knowingly misled MPs, he could face a suspension. And if that suspension was over ten days, that could in turn lead to a recall petition and a by-election. So if the inquiry investigation was successful, Johnson would plausibly face the end of his career.

With a direct echo to the Paterson saga, Johnson's political team hatched a plan to buy time before an inquiry could begin. On Tuesday 19 April, the day the fines for Johnson and Sunak landed, the Commons' speaker Lindsay Hoyle granted a request from all the opposition parties – including Labour and the Liberal Democrats – to refer the question of misleading the house to an investigation into whether Johnson was in contempt of parliament. The vote would take place two days later.

Much like the Paterson scandal, when Johnson was in Rome and Glasgow, Johnson was due to be out of the country and away from a moment of political danger. A thrice-rescheduled trade junket to India had been planned for the same day as the vote – a trip the prime minister was eager not to miss after the pandemic. The third iteration of Johnson's political team, with a new chief whip, the thinning-haired and efficient Chris Heaton-Harris, would need to stay behind and help Johnson wriggle out of his latest hole.

The motion,[15] proposed by Keir Starmer on Wednesday 20 April, noted that Johnson had told MPs the following: 'All guidance was followed in No. 10', 'I have been repeatedly assured since these allegations emerged that there was no party and that no Covid rules were broken', 'I have been repeatedly assured that the rules were not broken' and 'guidance was followed and the rules were followed at all times'. It said the words 'appear to amount to misleading the Commons' and called for a privileges committee to investigate whether his conduct 'amounted to a contempt of the House'. Finally, it said that the inquiry would not begin until Operation Hillman was concluded.

It was over to Heaton-Harris to produce an amendment that would allow Johnson to manoeuvre his way out of another inquiry. The chief whip devoted the afternoon speaking to concerned backbenchers[16] who might be minded to back the opposition motion, including former chief whip Mark Harper and Tom Tugendhat, chair of the foreign affairs select committee. Both influential MPs had called on Johnson to go and were not minded to give the government the benefit of the doubt. More junior whips spoke to a wider selection of MPs and it became clear the government did not have a majority. One Tory whip said, 'Our eighty-seat majority was gone, we couldn't vote down the investigation.'

On the Wednesday evening, Heaton-Harris produced a solution: the privileges committee investigation would go ahead, but not until the full Sue Gray report was published. The amendment would buy Johnson a little more time, but he would still ultimately face an investigation that could end his parliamentary career. One government insider said that they were eager to avoid the mistake of the Paterson saga: 'A neutral motion designed to kick the can down the road suited most Conservative MPs at that point.' Another Johnson ally said, 'The chief's view was that we didn't have the numbers to completely knock it back. But he thought an amendment was more doable. That was not gerrymandering, it was just saying, "Wait till the police report."'

But mistrust was so deep between Downing Street and the parliamentary party by this point that it became rapidly clear that Heaton-Harris's amendment would not work. One senior MP said, 'Overnight our inboxes filled up accusing us of providing a cover-up and minds begin to turn.' By Thursday 21 April, the government's majority had shrivelled and Heaton-Harris had to announce another U-turn – the single thing Downing Street had been seeking to avoid after realising how much MPs loathed such situations. 'I remember thinking "that's insane" because we have done it again,' one Downing Street insider said. "We've marched the parliamentary party up the hill to do something, we'd been briefing them for two days that they were going to have to back this. And then we abandoned them.'

Speaking from Ahmedabad on day two of his trade trip to India that morning, Johnson said, 'I'm very keen for every possible form of scrutiny . . . I don't think that should happen until the investigation is completed.' Heaton-Harris struggled to get in touch with the prime minister that day but the pair eventually spoke at 4 p.m. The chief whip said he could not guarantee the government would win the motion – and even if they did, it would lead to another huge rebellion that would further damage his government's standing. The pair agreed that he would climb down in a televised clip from India. Johnson stated: 'The House of Commons can do whatever it wants.' Watching the clip from Downing Street, one of his aides remarked, 'Another disastrous decision because he was away.'

Inside Downing Street, the mood was 'utter chaos' as they waited to hear confirmation from Johnson and Heaton-Harris that the climbdown had happened. One official remarked to another, 'This makes no sense, why are we such morons?' The climbdown on the privileges committee investigation was not made public until minutes before the Commons debate on the privileges investigation was due to begin. Having spoken to

Johnson, Heaton-Harris shuffled onto the frontbench and passed a note to Mark Spencer, his predecessor who had botched the Owen Paterson scandal and was now leader of the Commons. The green benches were sparsely attended and the vote meekly passed.

The vote itself came on the Friday morning, but recriminations had already begun in Downing Street. One senior official said to another that morning, 'Why the fuck are we causing ourselves absolute pain again? We've spent the whole of yesterday saying we're doing this because we should wait for the Sue Gray. Everyone had coalesced around the fact that that was an okay place to be. Then the chief told us actually no, we can't do that.' The answer was that the Tory whipping operation had failed, and relations had further soured between Downing Street and Tory MPs, just as more no-confidence letters in Johnson began flowing to the 1922 Committee.

***

Throughout the partygate scandal, the prime minister's allies insisted the saga was primarily a concern of the Westminster bubble and that 'real' voters were anxious about other priorities. The opinion polls told a different story. The last time the Conservatives had led in the polls was reported[17] on 8 December 2021 by Redfield & Wilton, before a run of leads for the Labour party that remained unbroken until Johnson left office in September 2022. Even when Ukraine temporarily boosted Johnson's ratings in March, the Tories never regained their lead. By mid-April, as the campaign for the local elections began, the party fell as far as eleven points behind.

Conservative party HQ was aware they were facing a shellacking at the elections. Although they set expectations high, journalists were frequently briefed that, given the last local elections came three years since the last general election, losing 800 council seats would be a good outcome for the Tories. There was particular concern among strategists that the party would lose its remaining council footholds in London and bleed votes to the Liberal Democrats in prosperous southern England, where partygate was proving particularly unpopular.

As the results filtered through overnight on 5 May, many of their fears were confirmed: Wandsworth in south-west London, praised as Margaret Thatcher's favourite council, went red for the first time. Westminster council also flipped to Labour, as did Worthing and Southampton on the south coast. The Tories lost control of scores of councils across their traditional home counties heartlands including West Oxfordshire and Tunbridge Wells. The party lost 485 councillors and control of 11 councils, yet the results were not spectacular for Labour who only gained 108 councillors. The real winners were the Lib Dems, returning as a significant political force with 224 gains.

Johnson was fortunate that the order of the results meant the worst did not arrive until the next morning. 'We were helped because the overnights were okay,' one Johnson ally said. 'Then, as we went through Friday, they got steadily worse. We actually lost a lot of seats but the narrative was we were doing okay.' The prime minister spoke constantly to Ross Kempsell, one of his strategists, to calibrate a response. He also spoke to party chairman Oliver Dowden after the results for Sunderland council in the north east of England landed, where Labour fell back by one seat. Overall the Tories did not capitalise on their previous gains in pro-Brexit England but Johnson voiced the opinion to Dowden, 'It was not such a bad night.'

One senior Conservative party official said partygate was to blame for the losses. 'It was broadly where we expected it to be, which was shown by the expectations management ... But obviously, it was not a good night.' Johnson's position remained precarious, but his inner circle felt assured a challenge was not forthcoming. 'We knew it wasn't going to be the locals that killed him, the results were all in the ballpark of what [David] Cameron suffered,' one insider said. The losses did frighten Conservative MPs facing off a Lib Dem challenge in their seats. 'It continued to scare the shit out of Lib Dem-facing MPs,' one Tory strategist said. 'On the doorstep, they were hearing "I'm sending a message to Boris Johnson."'

Any possibility of an uprising at this point, however, was thwarted by an announcement on Friday afternoon from Durham Constabulary: Keir Starmer would be investigated for potentially breaking Covid rules. A new scandal was born: 'beergate'. Its origins lay in events that had taken place in April 2021, when the opposition leader was reported to have quaffed a beer and enjoyed a curry after a day of campaigning in Durham when indoor socialising was banned under Covid rules. Soon after, a grainy video of Starmer, beer in hand, was published. The Starmer clip was eventually sent to anti-lockdown activists who posted it on social media. It was largely ignored, with the media focused on Johnson's Covid troubles.

In January 2022, the *Daily Mail* ran on its front page a still from the video footage and called Starmer 'the Covid Party Hypocrite' but in February Durham police cleared Starmer over allegations of rule breaking. Deep within Conservative party HQ, the footage was put in a metaphorical filing cabinet until the party decided to unleash it to try and score political points. The Conservative Research Department revisited the story in April to help Johnson's ailing position. 'We were desperate at that stage for something that the PM could actually use at PMQs as a tactical distraction,' one person involved said. A dozen people were set to dig into the matter to find evidence to refresh the story. They hit upon a Facebook post on the Durham constituency Labour party showing a quiz had taken place that night.

After Johnson's fine in April for attending the birthday party, the Conservative MP for North West Durham, Richard Holden, wrote to Durham police arguing there was 'a strong public interest' in reopening the investigation and that the Covid rules should apply equally. Via Conservative HQ, Holden provided the police with the Facebook post promoting a quiz night; the Labour party said Starmer had not been involved but the Tories' efforts to turn beergate into a scandal analogous to partygate seemed to have come to pass when Labour had to issue a statement admitting that its deputy leader Angela Rayner had attended the event, having previously stated that she hadn't been present.

Durham Constabulary said it had 'significant new information' and an investigation would commence. Much like the Met's inquiries into partygate, Durham did not state how long it would go on for and whether its thresholds would equal what happened in Downing Street.

Starmer could not bat away the scandal as a smear because he had called on Johnson to resign as soon as he was investigated by the Met police. The pressure from Tories for him to quit began. One senior MP said, 'Keir Starmer had called for Boris to resign, so by his own standards, he'd should have resigned on the day the police announced they were investigating. I thought he was a complete hypocrite, the stuff that he was doing was almost identical to the stuff the PM was doing.'

With willing help from the *Daily Mail*, the story was splashed in the paper for over ten consecutive days. Even senior Tories acknowledged that the prominence of beergate became 'ridiculous'.

What the scandal did, however, was to provide the government with some respite from partygate. The opposition party's attacks on Johnson were blunted and the message to voters became 'they're all the same'. Further beergate allegations came in May, when a leaked schedule[18] showed that the takeaway was planned in advance. It was also reported[19] by several outlets that Starmer did not return to work after the curry and some junior Labour staffers were drunk. After days of stories and pressure, Starmer announced on 9 May he would resign as leader of the opposition if he received an FPN to show 'different principles to the prime minister'. Rayner also said she would resign as deputy leader.

While the police investigated, Conservative party HQ continued to pour resources into keeping the beergate story alive to distract from partygate. One person involved said a lengthy 'war book' on beergate existed that included much information that was never published. The scandal was aided by sources inside the Labour party – one known in Tory HQ as 'red throat' – who 'wanted to do Starmer in' and provided the media with details and reports on what happened in Durham. Conservative officials believed 'there was quite a high chance' Starmer would be fined and had legal opinions to back it up.

For some weeks, it appeared Starmer might have made a major miscalculation. He and Rayner received police questionnaires on 31 May. Conservative MPs piled pressure on Durham police not to be lenient given the Met's treatment towards Johnson. The prime minister enjoyed the focus on his rival, dubbing Starmer 'Sir Beer Korma' during the investigation. But on Friday 8 July, the police announced the investigation was finished and no fixed penalty notices would be issued. Durham police said:[20] 'A substantial amount of documentary and witness evidence was obtained which identified the 17 participants and their activities during that gathering ... it has been concluded that there is no case to answer for a contravention of the regulations, due to the application of an exception, namely reasonably necessary work.'

The Tories pushing beergate discussed seeking a judicial review of the outcome. 'There was an inconsistency in approach between Durham and the Met. If Starmer was looked into by the Met I think he would have been fined,' one person involved mused. But events soon overtook any such plans. Starmer pivoted back to partygate and drew a clear moral line with Johnson. 'For me, this was always a matter of principle. Honesty and integrity matter. You will always get that from me,' he tweeted.[21] Rayner said, 'The contrast with the behaviour of this disgraced prime minister couldn't be clearer.'

***

Throughout this time, the number of fines for partygate kept rising. On 12 May, the number of FPNs reached one hundred. There was much speculation Johnson would be fined again, and with it would come more pressure from MPs. Operation Hillman concluded on 19 May with 126 fines issued[22] to 83 individuals. The Met's conclusions were opaque and confusing: it is unknown who the other eighty-odd persons fined were, or which of the dozen events they attended.

The investigation had been significant in terms of time and resources. A total of twelve police detectives worked on Operation Hillman, sifting through 345 documents passed in their direction from Gray's team – including internal emails, diary entries, security door logs and witness statements. A whopping 510 photographs and pieces of CCTV footage were submitted. None of the fines were contested, but the Met said, 'We took great care to ensure that for each referral we had the necessary evidence to prosecute the FPN at court, were it not paid.'

Crucially for the prime minister, he received no further penalty notices, leading his internal critics to herald that the 'greased piglet' – former prime minister David Cameron's nickname for Johnson – had wriggled free once again. Charles Walker, a veteran Tory MP, predicted in February it was 'inevitable' he would be forced out. By May, Walker said,[23] 'He's a bit like that cricket all-rounder who's been written off time and time again, and then grabs the bowling ball and takes five for 15, or smashes a hundred, or does both things in the same match.'

Johnson had some political breathing room, but it did not last long. With the police work complete, the country reverted to waiting for Sue Gray; there were no further obstacles for her full investigation into partygate to be published. Throughout Operation Hillman, Gray had returned to the Department for Levelling Up and the inquiry was 'put into storage' until the all clear was given from the police.

The Met did not inform Gray of who had been issued with penalties, posing a challenge for the redrafting of her report. On Monday 16 May, though, three days before the public announcement, the Met privately told Gray that Operation Hillman was soon to be wrapped up. She called colleagues to inform them 'the Met think they might be done on Thursday' and rapidly reassembled her team and began the redrafting of the initial 'full fat' report that was meant to be published in January. But it was not until Wednesday 18 May that her team was certain that the police were done. The reaction by officials on her inquiry was, 'Oh shit it's actually coming.' According to those involved, around 10 to 20 per cent of the report was reworked following Hillman fines, with 'a lot of toing and froing over bits of the wording'. A critical sticking point was whether photos should be included: some officials were pressuring Gray against, others felt it was necessary to

Boris Johnson and Charles Moore, former editor of *The Daily Telegraph*, leaving the Garrick Club.

Owen Paterson looks on in the Commons as MPs debate an amendment calling for a review of his parliamentary punishment.

The press conference where Boris Johnson announced the first Omicron cases had been found in the UK.

Allegra Stratton announcing her resignation.

Sue Gray – the shadowy civil servant who led the partygate inquiry.

The three senior aides who departed Downing Street
after Sue Gray's interim report was published.

Dan Rosenfield, chief of staff.

Jack Doyle,
communications director.

Munira Mirza, director of the
Number 10 policy unit.

Boris at the Munich Security Conference, which took place as Russian troops massed on the Ukrainian border.

Johnson and Volodymyr Zelenskyy walking through the street of Kyiv.

Rishi and Boris at the latter's infamous birthday party during Covid restrictions.

Cressida Dick arriving at Scotland Yard the day the investigation into rule-breaking parties in Downing Street was announced.

Key members of Johnson's support network.

Grant Shapps,
transport secretary.

Chris Heaton-Harris, chief whip.

Nigel Adams, minister
of state without portfolio
and chief fixer.

Ross Kempsell, key strategist.

Will Lewis, key fixer.

Graham Brady of the 1922 Committee announces
the vote of no confidence result.

Chris Pincher, whose alleged
behaviour was the final scandal
that led to Johnson's fall.

Sajid Javid's resignation
letter as health secretary.

New ministers that were appointed to prop up Johnson's government.

Nadhim Zahawi had one of the shortest tenures as chancellor in history.

Michelle Donelan became
education secretary for
forty-eight hours.

Steve Barclay escaped Number 10
to become health secretary.

Boris announces his resignation.

Liz Truss and Rishi Sunak at a debate as they vie to be Conservative leader.

Boris Johnson gives his farewell address outside Number 10.

show that the inquiry was not a whitewash. A decision on this was not immediately reached.

The publication of her report, however, did not go smoothly. A month before its release, Gray had an 'informal catch-up' with Samantha Jones, a civil servant who was appointed chief operating officer of Number 10 in February's shake-up. At the end of their meeting, Jones suggested to Gray it would be a 'good idea' if she caught up with Johnson at some point. Gray responded that she was more than happy to do so and Jones (perhaps oddly) suggested she should 'stick it in the diary'. In a brief moment that would later become significant, Gray forgot to revert to Jones and was soon chased for a date. One colleague said, 'The fact Sam then chased Sue to say "Can you please sort this invite out?", you could either interpret as Sam being efficient or having a reason for Sue to arrange a meeting.'

Given that Johnson has the largest diary team in Whitehall (and probably the country), it was natural to assume his office would have arranged it. The crunch meeting eventually took place in Johnson's private office, with Gray and Jones in attendance with Steve Barclay, his chief of staff and Cabinet Office minister. Much of the meeting was a 'general discussion' about the Met's inquiries, what Gray knew about their progress, and how ready she would be to publish when Operation Hillman concluded. The question of whether photographs should be included was not raised.

But there was a 'throwaway comment', according to officials, about whether the report needed to be published at all. 'By that point everything had been leaked,' one Downing Street insider said. 'It was almost a question asked to the air.' Gray's team did not take it seriously but thought the Number 10 officials were being 'very careful not to be seen to be suggesting that directly, but they were looking for Sue's reaction.' Gray did not take the suggestion seriously, until a senior official approached her after the meeting and said, 'I understand you had a meeting with the PM where the idea that you wouldn't publish a report came out?'

Gray was furious and insisted it was not seriously discussed. Johnson's political team suggested Steve Barclay had raised the prospect of binning the report in the meeting. 'Steve had this big idea that he was going to be able to prevent the publication of the second part of the report. I don't think anybody seriously thought that that was possible,' one ally said. 'No one serious thought that we could get away with not publishing the report.' One person who worked with her said, 'Sue was massively angered with this suggestion, but it was quickly quashed. The idea that the report would be binned was stamped out immediately.' Another colleague said, 'she was cross because there were only four people in that room.'

On Saturday 21 May, two days after the Met concluded their inquiries, Sky News reported[24] that the Johnson–Gray meeting had taken place. That weekend, a furious internal row broke out between Gray's team and Number 10. Guto Harri, Johnson's director of communications, insisted Steve Barclay was not present when he in fact was. Harri also stated that Gray had instigated the meeting, which she had not. Harri finally also suggested photographs had been discussed, which they had not. Gray became deeply concerned that Downing Street was attempting to discredit her and the report. One colleague said, 'Sue was enormously upset. From her point of view this was a hit job, this was Number 10 coming out trying to discredit Sue and all of her work.'

Gray's team took the highly unusual step of issuing an on-the-record statement saying that she had not instigated the meeting, which conflicted with Downing Street's account. Harri called Gray's spokesperson, a civil servant, and gave him 'the hair-dryer treatment' and accused him and the inquiry team of causing damage to the government. The battle ended in stalemate: Gray's spokesperson was forced to step back from the inquiry and Number 10 capitulated in agreeing that Gray had not organised the meeting. Whether Barclay's remark was a deliberate plot to discredit Gray that was botched, or just a silly offhand comment, their efforts at neutering the report failed.

On Monday 23 May, as anticipation for the full report hit fever point, leaked photos were published. Johnson was merrily seen in one raising a cup of wine[25] at the November 2020 leaving party, surrounded by the blurred-out faces of civil servants. With the photos in the public domain, Gray had no choice but to include them. And finally on Wednesday 25 May, six months since the inquiry began, the full Sue Gray report was published. Across sixty pages, her findings covered sixteen events between May 2020 and April 2021 in meticulous detail.

Gray wrote that many of the parties were rowdy and continued into the early hours of the morning. She was excoriating on the culture in Downing Street, particularly the political and civil service leadership. She accused officials of knowing what they were up to, renaming 'parties' as 'events' in email chains to make sure they were not caught out. She described how some tried to warn that the parties were a bad idea – the 20 May 2020 BYOB gathering was labelled a 'comms risk' by one staffer. Out of the 300 photographs submitted to the inquiry, only eight were published. Much of the detail in the full Gray report had been public for months, thanks to all the leaks. The most striking new finding was 'unacceptable' behaviour towards Number 10's cleaning and security staff from senior aides. Gray said they have been routinely rude. Johnson soon apologised to the staff. One ally said, 'Boris was totally horrified to hear that. He got up especially early the next morning to apologise in person to the cleaners and custodians.'

The report was problematic for Johnson and his team, but for the mandarins too. 'It's just as bad if not worse from the civil service point of view,' a senior figure said. One Downing Street figure said, 'It was a pretty grim read in all of its gory detail.' Gray only named the most senior officials who had attended events, including the Cabinet secretary Simon Case and Martin Reynolds. Civil servants were criticised as much as the politicians about who was to blame. One Johnson ally said: 'I don't subscribe to the idea Boris Johnson led a frat house. The report made it clear Martin was responsible for what happened in the house [Number 10] because he fundamentally led the civil service side.' Others said the report highlighted Johnson's consistently flawed judgement in who to trust. 'Fundamentally, there was a sort of person Boris wanted beside him. Appointing Party Marty, someone who was lax about such things, is much of a reflection on him.'

For Gray, the end of the report prompted relief. Although many in Number 10 believed 'she enjoyed the limelight a little too much', her colleagues insisted it was not a happy time. 'I think she regrets ever having taken it on.' Gray returned to her role as the second permanent secretary at the Department for Levelling Up and for a quieter life. She has never spoken publicly about the ordeal or the findings of her report. Her colleagues say she never intends to. But for Johnson, the moment of reckoning with his MPs had finally arrived. Throughout 2022, the prime minister's tedious and tenuous line that everyone should 'wait for Sue Gray' no longer held. It was time to see whether his colleagues had forgiven him over partygate, or whether they no longer had confidence in his position.

5. The 41 per cent

The House of Commons had scarcely heard Boris Johnson so humble. Addressing the chamber soon after the publication of the full Sue Gray report, his contrition put Uriah Heep to shame. He was 'humbled', had 'learnt a lesson' about his behaviour, and took 'full responsibility for everything that took place on my watch'. The prime minister set out the 'context' of partygate that he had been so eager to explain for months: Number 10 was full of hard-working staffers, who had made mistakes, but put in long hours in the office during the pandemic. 'I appreciate this is no mitigation,' he said to a torrent of heckling from MPs.

From the government Despatch Box on Wednesday 25 May 2022, Johnson corrected the record on partygate:[1] 'When I came to this house and said in all sincerity that the rules and guidance had been followed at all times, it was what I believed to be true. But clearly this was not the case for some of those gatherings after I had left, and at other gatherings when I was not even in the building.' His statement was followed by more jeers from MPs who believed he was once again avoiding responsibility and trying to create a narrative that took himself out of the picture.

The prime minister went on to emphasise the structural changes that had taken place in Number 10 since Gray's interim report earlier that year. Downing Street had a new chief of staff in Steve Barclay, a fresh director of communications in Guto Harri, a new principal private secretary to replace Martin Reynolds as well as a bevy of newly hired efficient officials.

Johnson concluded he would work 'day and night' to deliver his mission of tackling the cost of living crisis, the war in Ukraine and create 'high wage, high skilled, high employment' that would improve the UK's economic standing. He would not be resigning.

After the statement, there was no immediate rebellion from Conservative MPs, and Johnson had seemingly wriggled out of yet another hole, the accepted wisdom went. The only notable Tory critic was Tobias Ellwood, chair of the Commons defence committee and a longstanding Johnson opponent. He asked his fellow MPs: 'Are you willing day in and day out to defend this behaviour publicly? Can we continue to govern without distraction given the erosion of the trust with the British people? And can we win the general election on this current trajectory?' For his exhortations, Ellwood was heckled by Johnson's supporters.

In some parts of Downing Street, there was relief. They concluded that the trickle of leaked partygate stories and the elongation of Sue Gray's work meant that the moments of pressure had all been relieved. One Number 10 insider said, 'We thought he had basically survived Sue Gray albeit massively damaged – a 7 to 10 percentage hit to his polls that was probably permanent.' The fact he had not received another penalty notice added to the sense that Johnson had survived the storm. MPs had repeatedly said they wanted partygate and Sue Gray to just 'go away' and now perhaps they both had.

Those who thought Johnson had got away with it also did so because of the vast range of other scandals he had survived over the months. According to one senior Tory figure, '70 to 80 per cent of the parliamentary party came to the conclusion that if he'd made it through January – as bad as that was with morale so low – what's left to bring him down?'

Others in Johnson's inner circle believed severe trouble lay ahead. One close ally said that sceptics told Johnson that the terminal 'underlying problem' was him having lost his grip on the parliamentary party. 'It was day after day after day of bad headlines. MPs had very little for them to tell their constituents that they were doing positively,' one aide said. 'It was like sand running through our hands the whole time.'

Immediately after the prime minister's statement, his allies and aides devoted hours in parliament to seeing streams of Tory MPs and seeking to calm their nerves. The whips had told them in advance to prepare for resentment. The aim of that immediate post-Gray operation was to stabilise the situation and see Johnson through the following six weeks until summer recess, when the political temperature could cool. One Johnson ally said, 'There was a bit of complacency in Number 10. It was still a view among many that if we got into conference [in the autumn], we were probably safe.'

Yet Johnson's core political team, led by aides Declan Lyons and Ben Gascoigne, with assistance from the Brains Trust outriders, were convinced a vote of no confidence in Johnson by Tory MPs was approaching and urged him to be ready. 'There was so much parliamentary stuff going on, we were whirling for a vote coming,' one Tory official said. 'I'd always thought the greased piglet thing never aligned with the full situation among MPs. Sue Gray simply brought everything to a head again.' After Johnson's Commons statement, Downing Street kicked into survival mode in case enough MPs moved against their man.

To oust a leader of the Conservative party, 15 per cent of the parliamentary party must submit no-confidence letters to the chair of the 1922 Committee – the informal trade union of Tory MPs. In June 2022, that was 54 MPs required to write to Graham Brady, the portly genial grandee who had chaired the committee for over a decade. Brady entered parliament in 1997 and made the seamless journey from bright young spark to veteran back-bencher without skimming ministerial high office. Out of sorts with David Cameron's modernisation efforts, he devoted himself to being the house master of the parliamentary party. His first no-confidence vote was in Theresa May four years prior and MPs widely thought he handled the tricky process with aplomb and tact.

The letter-writing process is even more opaque than the Met's partygate investigations. There is no public record of who has submitted letters; they are locked in the safe of Brady's expansive office on the top floor of Portcullis House on the parliamentary estate. Whenever the Westminster village becomes bored with the topic of the day, speculation typically rises that letters are being submitted and another Tory confidence vote is approaching. Such reports are nearly always off the mark, as Brady has a long-held principle of never commenting to MPs or journalists about how many letters are in his possession.

One reason the media often overestimates how many no-confidence letters are submitted is due to the transient whims of MPs. Many Tories made a hoo-hah about submitting them – the left-leaning Roger Gale and Brexiter headbanger Andrew Bridgen being two of the most notable culprits. Others visit Brady at a moment of angst to submit a letter, encouraging a few more colleagues. Then events rapidly change and the letters are withdrawn out of a fear that the timing is unhelpful for the government or party. There was one Tory MP who publicly announced they had submitted a letter, publicly stated it was withdrawn and then publicly resubmitted it, without ever actually writing one.

One senior Tory who served on the 1922 six-strong executive committee said the process is a 'fascinating' insight into how colleagues think, describing it as, 'A swirling current where the tide ebbs and flows.' Another party grandee said, 'People don't always feel the need to publicise the fact they have withdrawn their letter. That's why you get a lot of the media miscalculation on numbers – from counting them when they go in but not knowing when they've been withdrawn.'

Back in January 2022, when partygate hit its first peak, Conservative MPs were convinced that a confidence vote was imminent. One longstanding backbencher, who has experienced several such votes, said, 'The velocity was such that it might have happened. It did not necessarily go right up to the edge in terms of numbers in January.' Another member of the 1922 executive described that moment as, 'The mood of the herd. You got a series of people writing letters in very short order. And then just at the point where you thought it's going to happen, it petered out.' As usual, Brady made no public comment.

Johnson was fortunate that there was no coordinated effort in January to oust him. With 358 fellow Tory MPs, convincing 54 of them to remove their leader was not straightforward. Such an endeavour requires several wings of the party to have unified goals and strategies. When Theresa May faced her confidence vote in 2018, it was a coalition of hardline Brexiters and disgruntled centrists that tipped the letters over the threshold. Johnson did not face such a coordinated coalition against him. In the early months of 2022, a drinks party for Tory MPs took place in parliament where the prime minister's future was the topic du jour. One MP present recalled, 'I stumbled into a conversation with a leading light of the One Nation group [left-leaning Tory MPs] and the other of the 1992 group [right-leaning Tory MPs]. They both said nothing was being coordinated at all.'

As partygate wore on, a trickle of MPs publicly called on Johnson to go. In February, it was the former education minister Nick Gibb[2] who said voters were 'furious about the double standards' Johnson had demonstrated during the pandemic. Come April, backbench MP Nigel Mills joined him[3] after Johnson had been fined, stating voters 'had a right to accept higher standards'. The most notable by far was then Steve Baker, the formidable former chair of the European Research Group who had played a key role in bringing down the last two Tory leaders. On 21 April, Baker told[4] the Commons, 'the gig is up' and Johnson should be 'long gone by now'. Following the full Sue Gray report, nineteen Tories had publicly said he should go – including former health minister Stephen Hammond.[5] By 30 May, it was up to twenty-seven.[6]

Downing Street had hoped that the week of the Queen's Platinum Jubilee would offer respite from the threats, with MPs and the nation focused on celebrating the monarch's seventy years on the throne. Two significant figures, however, announced they had lost confidence in the run-up to the Jubilee bank holiday weekend: Jeremy Wright, the former attorney general who said[7] Johnson had done 'lasting damage' to the party, and Andrea Leadsom, the former business secretary who had worked closely with him during the Vote Leave campaign. She did not explicitly state Johnson should go, but wrote that leadership failings 'are the responsibility of the prime minister' and said Tory MPs 'must now decide on what is the right course of action that will restore confidence in our government'.

It seemed inevitable that the confidence vote predicted by Johnson's core allies was getting closer. As the Jubilee weekend dawned, forty-one Tory MPs had questioned[8] Johnson's position before glumly decamping to their constituencies for the celebrations. One Cabinet minister said, 'There was a growing view amongst MPs that this stain won't be wiped clean.' Support for Johnson began to waver in the Cabinet too, but few felt there was an alternative. Another minister said, 'I knew all his flaws but thought he's still capable of winning the next election, he's still got the energy, the animal spirits. and I'm not convinced that there's any obvious alternative.' Rishi Sunak, who was widely seen as the most viable replacement for Johnson, was struggling due to his partygate fine, the lacklustre spring statement and the row over his Green Card and his wife's tax affairs. 'He had been tarnished in the public mind and lost his mojo, so I just thought we're better off with Boris,' the minister said.

Even if Johnson survived this moment, a difficult pair of by-elections lay ahead at the end of the month – plus there was the spectre of the privileges committee's investigation into whether he had misled the house and which raised the prospect of further upheavals and distractions.

Instead of offering Johnson some political respite, the Jubilee celebrations ended up providing the moment that may have resulted in the threshold of fifty-four no-confidence letters being hit. On Friday 3 June, Johnson and his wife Carrie stepped out of their armoured Range Rover at St Paul's Cathedral for a thanksgiving service. A crowd of ardent loyalists lined the City of London to catch a glimpse of the Royal Family. Many other political dignitaries, including opposition leader Keir Starmer and foreign secretary Liz Truss, had arrived with little reaction from the crowd. But during the walk from their car to the entrance of St Paul's, an audible chorus of boos was picked up on TV. Johnson, seemingly unaware, smiled and nodded as he walked into the church but the moment was captured by the BBC and then shared widely on social media. It received almost eleven million[9] views.

When Johnson returned to Downing Street after the service, he was unaware of what had happened. 'When he was going in, he was quite far away from it,' one Number 10 insider said. 'Boris didn't know what it sounded like on the microphones.' His aides soon showed him the clip. Several senior MPs also saw the moment after it was widely shared on WhatsApp, which further unsettled their nerves. One senior Tory said, 'These were not *Guardian*-reading Islington dwellers, they're arch-monarchists. If we had lost those people, our core base, everything was gone.' Another MP said, 'It was that moment I realised just how unpopular Boris had become.'

One Tory strategist said, 'The clip clearly had an effect on some MPs putting their letters in – the spectre of him getting booed walking into St Paul's.' Johnson's inner circle were scathing of the BBC, which they claimed 'pushed it very hard'. Culture secretary Nadine Dorries, Johnson's most steadfast defender said,[10] 'There were far, far more cheers, but that doesn't make a good headline does it?' In response, *ITV News*'s royal editor Chris Ship tweeted, 'The facts are, and I was there, the boos were very loud indeed. No escaping that.'

Number 10 was dismissive about those who cared about the booing. 'I think it sums up a lot of the MPs, it's such a shallow analysis,' one senior aide said. Another Johnson ally said, 'A lot of these MPs pay far too much attention to this kind of stuff rather than the actual fundamentals of politics. That's why they're bad at their jobs. If you shit the bed every time something doesn't go exactly to plan, it's no wonder everything came crashing down.' The number of no-confidence letters rose over the bank holiday weekend. After the thirty-second clip went viral, the countdown to the confidence vote commenced.

***

Sunday 5 June was the pinnacle of the Jubilee celebrations, a regal pageant featuring military parades, cultural 'highlights' from the Queen's seventy years on the throne and a street carnival.

Alongside the most senior members of the Royal Family, the Queen came to the balcony of Buckingham Palace to greet the crowds belting out the national anthem, in what would be one of her final public appearances. Boris Johnson was seated in the VIP section with his wife Carrie, beside the opposition leader Keir Starmer, and behind the Duchess of Cambridge and her children. As Prince Louis bounced around, slightly bored, the prime minister was photographed smiling. There was no indication he now knew he could be out of a job the very next day.

Between the St Paul's booing and the Jubilee pageant, Conservative MPs were agitated but fearful about upsetting the celebrations. 'A large number of colleagues were very edgy about being seen to balls up the Jubilee,' one senior backbencher said. Several contacted Graham Brady to say they would be sending no-confidence letters but asked him to be cautious around the announcement. Through a backchannel of a senior Tory MP, Downing Street made it known to Brady that Johnson was 'really keen that the Queen's party was not interfered with'. Brady passed a message back that he was well aware of how to do his job.

Just before Johnson left for Buckingham Palace on Sunday lunchtime, he received the call his political advisors had long predicted – Declan Lyons, political secretary, told Johnson before the bank holiday that a no-confidence vote was 'likely' the following week. Graham Brady informed the prime minister that fifty-four letters of no confidence had now been submitted and a vote would need to take place 'as soon as reasonably practical'. One person with knowledge of the call said Johnson responded by 'spending a little while explaining why this was an extreme folly on the part of colleagues.'

Johnson did not tell a single person in Number 10 what had happened. Instead, he hopped straight into his motorcade to the party. One close advisor said he did not have the time to inform aides, but he may have had reasons to keep it private. 'When you're dealing with that kind of information your first concern is that it will leak and if it does, you've lost any ability to control the information.' Another official said, 'He was digesting it throughout the pageant.' By historical precedent, the mere fact that a confidence vote was happening suggested his time as prime minister was drawing to an end. No previous Tory leader had survived a confidence vote and gone on to win another election.

After the finale performance of Abba's 'Dancing Queen' by the cast of *Mamma Mia*, Johnson returned to Downing Street and sent a message out to the Big Dog team that the vote was coming. The team assembled in his luxuriously decorated flat that evening to plot over cups of tea – no food or alcohol – on how best to save his position. The aides present included chief whip Chris Heaton-Harris, political fixer Nigel Adams, Tory strategists Lynton Crosby and Ross Kempsell, plus director of communications Guto Harri. One person involved said, 'The plan was to give the PM the best possible chance in the confidence vote. The Big Dog group had been planning since January, it was obvious it was coming.'

But some junior aides were frustrated more had not been done in the days before the bank holiday weekend. 'On the Friday before the vote, there was a drip-drip of letters, notably from Andrea Leadsom. I really don't think anyone spotted it until Graham called the PM on Sunday. We could have bought ourselves an extra four days,' one Number 10 insider said. Johnson did not minimise the threat. One of the first questions he asked the assembled Big Dog team was how big the rebellion was going to be. Nigel Adams told him that their infamous spreadsheet, collated by transport secretary Grant Shapps, suggested it would be in the region of 150. The aides hoped to 'chip away' at those minded to vote against the prime minister, while chiefly ensuring their base did not collapse.

Brady had told Johnson he wanted to agree a timetable for the vote as soon as possible. The 1922 Committee does not have any formal guidance on when a confidence vote should take place. In 2018, Theresa May had been abroad when the threshold was reached and Brady requested a meeting with her the next day. Someone in the Number 10 team had leaked the information that Brady wanted to see Johnson, hence why he decided to make the call immediately to Johnson. One senior figure on the 1922 executive said, 'if Graham had asked to see him, it would have been tantamount to saying it's on.' After discussions with the Big Dog group, the prime minister texted Brady that evening to say, 'Let's crack on with it tomorrow.' The pair agreed an announcement should be made early on Monday 4 July and the ballot would take place between 6 and 8 p.m., with the result an hour later. No more than ten people knew.

Before an official announcement was made on that Monday, Johnson received another blow when Jesse Norman, a former Treasury minister widely respected among MPs, published a blistering letter explaining why he had lost confidence.[11] The prime minister's fellow plummy voiced Old Etonian (and long-standing ally who lost his job in a reshuffle) accused him of allowing 'a culture of casual law-breaking' in Downing Street and called his response to partygate 'grotesque'. Norman lambasted the government's policies too: the privatisation of Channel 4 was 'unnecessary and provocative' and plans to reform the controversial Northern Ireland element of his Brexit deal 'economically very damaging, politically foolhardy and almost certainly illegal'.

At 8.20 a.m. on Monday, Brady issued a press release stating: 'The threshold of 15 per cent of the parliamentary party seeking a vote of confidence in the leader of the Conservative Party has been exceeded.' He made a brief TV appearance on College Green, a patch of grass opposite the Palace of Westminster that morphs into a village of pop-up broadcast studios and shouty political protesters during moments of crisis, to explain the time-table. That morning, Sajid Javid was representing the government on the morning broadcast round. Downing Street had alerted the health secretary that Brady's announcement would likely take place while he was on air. Javid was in the tricky spot of acknow-ledging it could be imminent, without egging on the threat.

Before taking to the cameras and microphones on Monday morning, Javid consulted with his wife and aides about whether he personally still had confidence in Johnson. In these discussions, Javid was torn: on the one hand he was frustrated with the integrity of Johnson's operation and still angry at how he had been misled earlier in the year over partygate. But ultimately, with no successor or alternative ready, Javid decided to give the prime minister the benefit of the doubt and went out to defend the government. He was not prepared to run for leadership again himself.

In Downing Street, the efforts to shore up Johnson's position began early – led by the Big Dog group in conjunction with the formal advisory team. Their first task was to prepare letters for every Conservative MP pleading with them not to vote against their leader. One of Johnson's aides performed a mail merge and he spent hours topping and tailing 358 letters by hand with a fountain pen. The printer in Downing Street was slow and kept jamming. An assortment of aides folded and sealed each letter, including Johnson's wife Carrie and deputy chief of staff Simone Finn. Some aides thought it was a 'nuts' idea, a waste of time that could be better spent speaking to MPs.

When all the letters were signed, they were driven over to the lower whips' office in the House of Commons to be delivered.

Chris Pincher, deputy chief whip, was running a 'naughty and nice' operation that day in parliament with a mixture of threats and love-bombing MPs. One whip said, 'Pinch ran a tight ship: getting all those letters out, constant phone calls, in-person meetings. Boris came in and spoke to the right people, it was incredibly efficient.' A briefing note, written by Ross Kempsell, was dispatched to MPs emphasising his electoral record and warning that three months of party infighting would only benefit Labour.

Some of Johnson's most supportive ministers, including Conor Burns and Tom Pursglove, were dispatched by Pincher to speak in turn to their closest friends – a complex network of influence based on Shapps's multi-layered spreadsheet. One whip said of Shapps's work that, 'It was hugely comprehensive to ensure we had the right level of knowledge about what people wanted, what relationships they had in parliament, in terms of who could talk to whom. It was bloody good for getting that information quickly and keeping it up to date. It was the only way to keep the show on the road.'

While Johnson geared up for the battle of his political life, the work of being prime minister went on – including a call with Ukraine president Volodymyr Zelenskyy on the Monday morning where the leaders discussed the latest supplies of British military equipment and worries about grain exports. Some commentators suggested the timing seemed suspect, given Johnson's political woes, but civil servants insisted there was no chance it was impromptu. 'The Zelenskyy call was in the diary for a while, you can't change these things around. There's about fifty Foreign Office officials on the call and it takes a week to set up,' one official said.

The next unhelpful intervention for Johnson was one his team had long expected. Jeremy Hunt, who challenged him for the Tory leadership back in 2019 and came a distant second place, had made it clear he wanted another crack at the leadership. At 10.50 a.m., the former health secretary tweeted: 'Conservative MPs know in our hearts we are not giving the British people the leadership they deserve.' Hunt said the vote of no confidence was an opportunity for 'change or lose' and he would be opting for the former. Yet Number 10 was not concerned: one aide described Hunt as 'entirely insignificant' and his support in the parliamentary party was limited. His proto-leadership campaign had been running for months in the private dining rooms and bars of Westminster: Philip Dunne, the former junior health minister, was acting as his de facto manager, along with former Cabinet ministers Andrew Mitchell and David Davis, who were sounding out support.

Johnson scoffed at the suggestion Hunt was behind a major coup, if only based on knowing the profiles of those behind it. One close ally explained: 'Philip was never going to be the leader of a great political coup. Jeremy was busted flush and had no support. Andrew has no mates and David Davis has become a figure of some absurdity.' In a sign of how split the Tory party was becoming, the 'blue-on-blue' fighting went public. Nadine Dorries, the increasingly slavish culture secretary, publicly condemned Hunt[12] for being 'wrong about almost everything' including how to deal with the pandemic. 'Your duplicity right now is destabilising the party and the country to serve your personal ambition,' she added for good measure.

***

As Monday wore on, as the WhatsApp messages became more frantic, it became clear to Johnson's team there was no coordinated effort to oust him and the fifty-four threshold for confidence letters had 'tipped over by accident', as one government insider said.

'None of the rebels were actually organised. If they were actually coordinating, they should have known that they were going to tip over the Jubilee without the votes to win the actual ballot. They should have withdrawn twenty letters until they had the numbers.' The whips knew that better coordination could have 'easily' lost them the vote. One senior rebel who wanted Johnson out said their best weapon was the transactional nature of his support: 'People supported him precisely because he was popular and a winner. I might think he's a rogue and a charlatan but he also keeps us in power. When your support is that transactional, it can just fall away. That's what was happening.'

With less than twelve hours to win the vote the whips had to prioritise who to call, which naturally led to some MPs complaining they had been forgotten, further stoking their unhappiness. 'On a vote of no confidence day, you don't waste time phoning people who you know are either going be unhelpful or are probably going to vote for you,' one whip said. 'If you're a waverer who might be persuadable, you do get a call but of different seniority. It might be from a minister, it might be from the PM – he was on the phone all day. You have to persuade those who you absolutely need to come over to survive. There were hundreds of people to target.'

Four disparate groups of Tory MPs wanted Johnson out. First were the 'pork pie' plotters from the 2019 intake of MPs who instigated the failed coup of January 2022. Second was the Covid Research Group of libertarian-minded anti-lockdown MPs. Then there were the rebellious left-leaning One Nation MPs such as former immigration minister Caroline Nokes. And finally, and most importantly, were all the former ministers. After a decade in power, over a hundred ex-members of governments who had been fired or demoted were festering on the backbenches. There was also a smattering of Brexit rebels who believed Johnson had gone soft on the Northern Ireland dispute. Altogether, one Johnson ally called them 'quite a powerful cohort of disgruntled colleagues'. The situation was worsened because Johnson had wholly failed to manage these groups since becoming prime minister.

That afternoon, Johnson addressed a 1922 Committee meeting of the Conservative parliamentary party, an idea that came to fruition late in the day. The prime minister arrived to the traditional banging of tables by his keenest advocates, mostly for the benefit of the hundred-odd journalists crammed outside trying to hear what was going on. In that packed, sweaty, overly filled room, Johnson was bullish: he warned MPs that removing him would unleash 'some hellish Groundhog Day debate' about returning to the single market (prompted by a lone suggestion from the irreconcilable MP Tobias Ellwood that the UK should tear up Johnson's Brexit deal). Johnson reminded them he had won the Tory party its biggest election victory in forty years. His message in short was: I have won before and I can win again. Despite the sour mood, he told colleagues 'the best is yet to come' and made a vague pledge about cutting taxes. During the meeting, longstanding Covid rebel Mark Harper openly criticised Johnson's conduct that had led to the vote. He replied, 'I humbly submit to you that this is not the moment for a leisurely and entirely unforced domestic political drama.'

Despite the vying efforts that day of the rebels and Johnson's whipping and Big Dog teams, very little shifted. Team Johnson failed to see off the substantial rebellion; the damage was deep and had grown for months. 'We kept it to exactly where we were on the Sunday night,' one ally said. But those seeking to oust him failed to coordinate tactics and ran conflicting strategies, failing to make much headway towards the 50 per cent mark needed to oust Johnson and put in train a leadership contest. Before the vote, Grant Shapps took one last look at his spreadsheet and placed his prediction for the rebellion in a sealed envelope: 149.

The confidence vote commenced at 6 p.m. in the Palace of Westminster's opulent committee room 14 – where Theresa May, Iain Duncan Smith and Margaret Thatcher had all faced confidence ballots that precipitated the demise of their careers. Coming less than four years since May's vote, Brady followed the same procedures. MPs drifted in and out of the room, dismissing the heckles of journalists who lined the wood-panelled corridor to try (and fail) to ascertain whether Johnson was going to survive. Few of them exited with cheerful looks or any sense of confidence about where their party was heading.

Graham Brady and the 1922 Committee executive entered committee room 14 at 9 p.m. to announce the result. The room packed with journalists and MPs, he declared that out of 359 MPs, 211 had confidence in Johnson and 148 did not. The 41 per cent of rebels had delivered a hugely damaging result. It was a worse outcome than Theresa May (she was out within six months), worse than John Major in 1995 (he lost the election two years later), and worse than Margaret Thatcher in 1989 (out within the year). Johnson was braced for it: the result was just one vote off Grant Shapps's prediction. The only positive news was that the 1922's formal rules meant he could not be challenged again for another twelve months.

As the results came through, a group of Tory MPs were watching the results over drinks in Michael Gove's official residence in Carlton Gardens, just off Pall Mall. Kemi Badenoch, local government minister, was present along with chief secretary to the Treasury Simon Clarke, skills minister Alex Burghart and junior ministerial aides Laura Trott and Claire Coutinho. All present had voted for Johnson, but felt the result was a terrible outcome for the party. One said, 'We were all sad because we thought it's not going to end the pain. It's not "Oh my god Boris is going" or "Boris is safe", it was the worst possible zone: more agony.'

Johnson was unwisely muscular in his response to this slight victory. 'I think it's an extremely good, positive, conclusive, decisive result which enables us to move on, to unite and to focus on delivery and that is exactly what we are going to do,' he said in a televised statement. The prime minister later went further, arguing the result represented 'a new mandate from my party' that showed a wider level of support than the shortlisting process in the 2019 leadership race. This was not welcomed by his advisors. 'We did quite badly and then we tried to pretend it was a success,' one said. Another added, 'It wasn't the tone that some of us advised him to take.' William Hague, the former Tory leader, offered the ominous counter view: the result showed 'a greater level of rejection than any Tory leader has ever endured and survived'.

Johnson's mood throughout the vote of no confidence was defiant, but history suggested it was a question of when, not if, Johnson would be out. 'We were in a very bad situation after that result with the parliamentary party,' one Cabinet minister said. 'A lot of us thought it was a matter of time, but we also thought the PM is the kind of guy who can do impossible things. There was still the sense that maybe this is going to be the first Tory leader who gets through that and who is going to redefine that.'

The whips and the Big Dog Operation were disappointed. 'We'd love to have had it under one hundred,' one official involved said. Despite his public bravado, Johnson's political aides urged him to seize the moment and conduct a major Cabinet reshuffle, much bigger than the one that had taken place in February, as an olive branch to MPs. Had Johnson made it through to July, a new Cabinet would have been brought together before parliament's summer recess. Declan Lyons and Nigel Adams had drawn up a preliminary plan that would have seen Chris Pincher moved out of the whips' office – 'he had done his job to bring some order, he didn't want to stay' one aide said – while local government minister Kemi Badenoch would have been promoted to the top table.

Even though Johnson loathed reshuffles – he was terrible at delivering bad news to those being demoted – he accepted the need for a reset. Members of the 2019 intake of Tory MPs would have been made ministers for the first time, according to Lyons's plan, while the whips' office would be refreshed. The plan would have 'built some bridges' by bringing back sacked ministers from the more liberal wing of the party, such as former justice secretary Robert Buckland. 'It was time to show some humility and bring people into government who had not been necessarily support- ive,' one whip said. There was another reason for a reshuffle too: based on the scale of the rebellion, the whips office concluded that not everyone in government had voted to save the prime minister.

In the days after his near miss, Johnson's team became paranoid that chancellor Rishi Sunak was masterminding an operation to oust him – despite the fact there was clearly no coordinated putsch in the confidence vote. One close colleague of Johnson said, 'The agitation against Boris back in January, when it was pork pie plotters, was from amateurs. By the time we got to the confidence vote, it was far more sophisticated. The Sunak lot knew what they were doing, they were running an alternative whipping operation by that stage.' Instead of Jeremy Hunt, the only senior Tory to state Johnson should go, the prime minister's loyalists were focused on the chancellor. 'The main problem was Sunak and his people,' one said.

Another minister close to Johnson said Number 10 believed Sunak had drawn up 'a detailed strategy' on how to replace him – suggesting Sunak himself may have had a role in leaking the details about his wife's tax affairs and his Green Card to pave the way for a future leadership challenge. 'I think he decided to get the issue about his wife out of the way because that was very confidential information and very tightly held,' one minister claimed. Those close to Sunak strongly deny he was plotting against Johnson and said it was 'totally ludicrous' to suggest he would have leaked a damaging story about himself.

Instead of focusing on his neighbour, Johnson might have been better off improving relations with MPs who had become despondent following the vote. 'It wasn't like the white-hot rage we had over partygate,' one government insider said. 'MPs were realising that we were onto our third team running Number 10 and it still wasn't working. If the aides kept on changing and the problems kept on happening, there's one fundamental problem. They came to a reluctant conclusion that he's got to go.'

After the vote, Graham Brady's tally of no-confidence letters was reset to zero but it did not remain so for long. Immediately after the 41 per cent result, the most hardline Johnson rebels resubmitted their no-confidence letters – even though another vote could not take place until June 2023 under the 1922 Committee's rules. But Brady began to receive delegations calling on him to change the leadership contest guidelines to allow another vote as soon as possible. For now, Brady declined and told them it would be unfair to move the goalposts halfway through a match.

During that week's Cabinet meeting on Wednesday, ministers told Johnson in private he had reached the last chance saloon. Sajid Javid had a one-to-one discussion with the prime minister after the Cabinet meeting. The health secretary told him 'this is a really shit result' and reminded him that four out of ten colleagues wanted him gone. Javid summed it up: 'It's huge. PM, this is your last chance. If things don't change now, it's over. You've got to put all this chaos behind you and show people things can change.' Ben Gascoigne, one of his longest-serving political aides, told Johnson, 'Now we can change or die.'

A strategy for an organised reset was the last thing on Johnson's mind. Downing Street was in total crisis. The best he could do was survive each day and hope that the Cabinet would remain firm and there would be no resignations from his government. Instead, another pair of catastrophes were soon to strike.

***

Christopher Geidt was one of the most curious appointments of Johnson's administration. Previously a private secretary to the Queen, he became the independent advisor on ministerial interests in April 2021 – the official Whitehall arbiter of the ministerial code that governs the conduct of those in government. Geidt was the ultimate steady pick: a lifetime devoted to public service through the military and the Royal Family before taking a seat in the House of Lords. 'A man very much of the establishment in the nicest possible way,' one senior civil servant said.

He took up the role in inauspicious circumstances. Alex Allan, his predecessor, resigned from the role after Johnson disagreed with his conclusion that the home secretary Priti Patel had bullied officials. Throughout his career, Johnson had shown little regard for the rules and established norms, and as the most powerful person in the country, there was little chance he was going to do so now. After several senior Whitehall figures were approached and firmly rejected the job, the Cabinet secretary Simon Case beseeched Geidt to take it. The pair had worked closely in the Royal household and Case argued he would be able to protect him from Johnson's capricious nature and that Geidt was the best placed person to restore trust in the ministerial code. His time with the Royal Family had prepared him for working in sensitive circumstances full of rampant egos. Their discussions took 'weeks and weeks', according to those involved, until Case eventually pushed him over the line.

Immediately after he took up the role, Geidt told colleagues he had made a mistake. He was forced to carry out a series of investigations into Johnson's personal financial affairs, notably into whether the ministerial code had been broken over the refurbishment of his Downing Street flat. Stoked by a series of leaks to the *Daily Mail*, the wallpapergate scandal suggested Johnson had not been straightforward in declaring a loan from David Brownlow, a Tory donor, to pay for over £100,000 of decorating work. Geidt initially cleared Johnson of breaking the ministerial code, but considered resigning eight months later when it emerged Johnson had not been wholly forthcoming as to how the Brownlow donation had been solicited.

Geidt then became embroiled in the partygate scandal and was increasingly exercised that Johnson had broken the ministerial code – namely the sections on honesty and truth – over his statements to parliament that there had been no parties and all rules had been followed. Following the Met police fine, Geidt stated there were 'legitimate' concerns about whether the code had been breached. In a meeting with Johnson, he demanded an explanation of how Johnson had been truthful; the prime minister replied[13] that his breach of Covid rules had been 'unwitting'. Across Whitehall, the advisor was on 'constant' resignation watch as he had belatedly realised Johnson had little care for his role and had no desire to face the consequences for his actions.

However, it was not the parties that ultimately pushed Geidt to quit but a peculiar row about steel tariffs. He was asked by

Johnson to consult on whether deliberately breaking World Trade Organisation commitments over a dispute with China on steel trade would count as a breach of the ministerial code. In his resignation letter, Geidt said the request put him in 'an impossible and odious position' given the prime minister was suggesting 'a deliberate and purposeful breach of the ministerial code'. He warned it would make a 'mockery' of his role.

Johnson's allies thought it was 'eccentric' that Geidt decided to go over this issue. The following day, Geidt clarified that his departure may have also been linked to the dispute over the Northern Ireland Protocol. The steel tariff request was 'simply one example of what might yet constitute deliberate breaches by the United Kingdom of its obligations under international law, given the government's widely publicised openness to this,' he said. Civil service colleagues said Geidt was 'genuinely torn' between two principles: 'Genuine concern for public service duty and to be a person in there upholding the office, and the total shitshow that was going on in Downing Street.'

After his departure, Geidt told colleagues he tried his utmost but ultimately concluded Johnson would never follow the codified structures of the ministerial code. The prime minister had lost two ministerial ethics advisors – adding to a sense among Tory MPs and the public that Johnson was leading a government that had little care for standards. Johnson could or would not find a replacement for Geidt. When he left Downing Street in September 2022, there was still no arbiter of ministerial standards in place.

The next problem struck a far stronger note with MPs. On 23 June, a pair of by-elections took place that tested both ends of the Conservative party's voting coalition. One was in Tiverton and Honiton, a traditionally safe blue seat in Devon that returned a 24,239 majority in the 2019 election; the other in Wakefield, a pro-Brexit former Labour heartland in West Yorkshire that went Tory for the first time under Johnson. Both were prompted by Tory scandals: in Tiverton, MP Neil Parish was forced to resign after admitting to watching pornography in the House of Commons (he insisted he was searching for a tractor range called the 'Dominator'). In Wakefield, Imran Ahmad Khan was forced to quit after being convicted of child sexual abuse and being jailed for eighteen months.

Given that both votes were prompted by disgraced Tories, holding them in normal circumstances would have been a challenge. With Johnson's sinking popularity – his net approval ratings had sunk[14] to -45 in June – it was impossible. Johnson's keenest supporters hoped that his popularity in pro-Brexit northern England would stifle Labour's majority, and that the sheer size of the Tory majority in Tiverton and Honiton would insulate the party from a massive swing to the Liberal Democrats, the seat's traditional challengers.

Prior to the votes, the *Financial Times* reported[15] that senior Tory strategists were braced to lose both. And so it came to pass: Tiverton and Honiton flipped to the Liberal Democrats on 23 June with a 30 percentage point swing[16] away from the Tories, while Wakefield returned to the Labour party with a 13 percentage point swing.[17] Although Labour's 3,358 majority was lower than the party might have hoped, there was particular alarm at the swing towards the Lib Dems in the south. 'I didn't realise things were going to be so bad in Tiverton and Honiton,' one Cabinet minister said. 'The South had turned against us and Boris in particular.'

Johnson's inner circle justified the results as just an example of how mid-term governments tend to lose by-elections. But the pair of results were another example of Johnson losing his electoral potency, which in turn frightened Tory MPs. 'The cost to the party was political capital,' one senior Tory party official said. 'Losing both types of seats we represent was especially painful. Bear in mind with Boris the biggest attraction is his ability to win elections. Once that's gone, there's nothing.' One of Johnson's closest officials said, 'He expected the results to be as bad as they were. He did not expect the Dowden bombshell.'

At 5.35 a.m. on 24 June, Oliver Dowden became the first Cabinet-level casualty of Johnson's final decline. The Conservative party chairman had been ill at ease for some time; it was well known within the government that he was unhappy at being moved sideways from culture secretary in the previous reshuffle. 'He didn't like the move to chairman,' one Cabinet minister said. 'He wasn't suited to that role, he quite liked to go to the opera, the premieres and all the fun stuff of being culture sec.' A briefing to the *Mail On Sunday* that reported that he was likely to be demoted in the next reshuffle had stoked his annoyance. In his letter, Dowden said[18] he must take responsibility for the losses. 'We cannot carry on with business as usual. Somebody must take responsibility and I have concluded that, in these circumstances, it would not be right for me to remain in office,' he wrote, insisting it was a personal decision.

One person close to Johnson said it came as 'a huge surprise'. On Wednesday 22 June, the day before the by-election, Dowden had assisted Johnson with his preparations for prime minister's questions. He was also lined up to do the morning broadcast round straight after the by-election results. As was often the case, Johnson was out of Westminster when the crisis hit. He received the call from Dowden while in Kigali, Rwanda for a meeting of Commonwealth leaders. Downing Street told journalists he had received the news after an early morning swim. Back at Number 10, suspicions turned on Dowden's close political friend who Team Johnson feared (again) may have stoked the resignation and could be next to quit: Rishi Sunak.

The Big Dog team believed Dowden's resignation was part of an effort to destabilise the prime minister. Grant Shapps had recorded him on the spreadsheet as an MP who could not be counted on in a confidence vote and that a move somewhere else in government, or potentially a sacking, was in the ether if the potential reshuffle had taken place later that year. One Johnson ally said, 'Those of us who were close enough to the situation knew he was disloyal. His resignation was the public awareness of the Sunak plot, which had been running for months beforehand. Sunak and Dowden were very personally close.' Sunak's allies deny this, suggesting it was paranoia on behalf of Team Johnson.

Another Cabinet minister close to the prime minister described Dowden's departure as, 'an act of great personal treachery because the chairman of the Conservative party, in that role when you're in such trouble, should be one of your closest allies.' But one minister close to Dowden said it was nothing to do with Sunak. 'Oliver's frustration was that he was offering advice in a variety of areas as party chairman. It was either not taken, countermanded or only partially implemented. He felt the people in the Number 10 operation who are not directly responsible for running the party were overriding him.'

Immediately after Dowden put the phone down, Johnson spoke to the chief whip Chris Heaton-Harris to begin finding out whether a full Cabinet coup was taking place and whether Sunak was involved (the prime minister was later furious with his communications chief Guto Harri when reports of the ring round emerged, as it looked like Number 10 were panicking). Johnson spoke to home secretary Priti Patel, who convinced him she was steadfastly loyal. He then spoke to Sunak, who professed to having no knowledge of Dowden's resignation. One official close to Johnson said the prime minister was not convinced, while another said, 'I don't think Rishi was dishonest.'

Johnson also tried to speak to Sajid Javid, but the health secretary was delivering a speech on suicide prevention with his phone on silent. It was vibrating in his pocket throughout the morning, but the calls were ignored. When he later emerged from the event, Javid saw an escalating series of missed calls from senior figures in Downing Street who feared he was about to quit. Javid rapidly rung back Heaton-Harris and assured him he was going nowhere.

Until the by-election losses, the rebellion against Johnson had remained among MPs – many of those unrequited malcontents who were never going to be won over by his leadership. But the resignation of Dowden brought the problem directly into the Cabinet. With Johnson on edge that further ministers may soon quit, the Big Dog Operation was closely watching Rishi Sunak and all the while pressure was rising for the 1922 Committee to allow another confidence vote. The government could not afford any more mistakes – the head of steam had been building for over six months and it could easily blow. It needed a period of stability and calm, and yet a week later, one of Johnson's most volatile ministers visited a Pall Mall gentlemen's club for drinks with colleagues. What happened next set in train the final fall of Boris Johnson.

6. Drinks at the Carlton Club

On Thursday evenings, after parliament has wrapped up for the day, a certain partying sort of Conservative MP heads to the Carlton Club. Situated halfway up St James's Street, one of London's most salubrious addresses, membership is open to those who pledge a vow to Conservative values, and it is considered a safe space for Tories. Around 1,500 members pay fees[1] of £1,700 a year for the privilege of membership, which allows access to its luxurious dining rooms and bars named after former prime ministers. Having long given up any formal role in the party, many of its fundraising activities are directed towards elections.

The Carlton has long had a dubious reputation. The Duke of Wellington once remarked,[2] 'Never write a letter to your mistress and never join the Carlton Club.' It lacks the social cache of, say, the nearby Boodle's gentlemen's club, or the strong ties to the governing class as the Travellers Club. For newly elected MPs, however, it is an embodiment of the party's illustrious past – as well as somewhere to relax without interlopers earwigging on any plotting. In January 2022, serial Johnson critic William Wragg (a member of the 1922 executive) was reported[3] to be 'holding court' one night with a hundred fellow MPs at the club supposedly to discuss the ongoing partygate revelations and whether Johnson should be challenged. Nadine Dorries, culture secretary and arch-Johnson loyalist, also happened to be in the club.

Underneath the grand staircase of 69 St James's Street, there is an 'inviting corner' of dark leather armchairs beneath the Tory blue carpeted staircase. One observer* described the area as 'The spot where male members could stand to stare up the skirts of female guests walking up and down the stairs.' And it was here where Chris Pincher, Boris Johnson's deputy chief whip, ended up late on Thursday 29 June as part of a typical cabal of Tory MPs and acquaintances who had gone to the Carlton for drinks after parliament had finished sitting. The club was busy that night as a party was being held in aid of the Conservative Friends of Cyprus.[4]

Born in September 1969,[5] Pincher was first elected to parliament in 2010 for the seat of Tamworth in Staffordshire, which he won from the Labour party. A compact, bearded and impeccably dressed MP, his innate love of parliament and the political game meant he was destined for the whips' office. He became a junior whip in July 2016, rising up to become assistant chief whip. But Pincher's career came to an abrupt halt when Alex Story, a former Olympic rower-turned-Tory candidate, alleged he had massaged his neck and discussed 'his future in the Conservative party' before changing into a bathrobe. Story described[6] him as a 'pound shop Harvey Weinstein'. Pincher was also alleged to have made advances towards Labour MP Tom Blenkinsop who told him[7] to 'fuck off'. Following the allegations of these unwanted advances, Pincher promptly resigned from the whips' office and referred himself for an official investigation.

After several months, Pincher was cleared by the Conservative party of breaking the party's code of conduct. Of the allegations, Pincher said, 'If Mr Story has ever felt offended by anything I said then I can only apologise to him.' He rejoined Theresa May's

---

* Seth Alexander Thévoz, author of *Behind Closed Doors: The Secret Life of London's Private Members' Clubs*.

government in January 2018 and was promoted to deputy chief whip[8] where his reputation as an effective party manager burgeoned during the long collapse of her government. Pincher remained in this role until Johnson became prime minister in July 2019. As a keen supporter of the prime minister's leadership bid, he was then promoted into several government departments in crucial roles: first as Europe minister, then as housing minister.

When Johnson encountered his first serious leadership turbulence in early 2022, there were widespread rumours that Pincher would gain his coveted Cabinet job of running party management, but Number 10 suspected Pincher himself was responsible for putting such stories around. Chris Heaton-Harris, chief whip, plus Nigel Adams, Johnson's closest fixer, appreciated his talents and Pincher was called upon, but returned to his old role as deputy chief whip. As an adjunct member of the Big Dog Operation and loyalist to Johnson, he was perfectly placed to help prop up support for the government. During those 'relentless' evenings in January and February, when Johnson's allies were preparing for a confidence vote at the peak of the first partygate crisis, Pincher was omnipresent along with transport secretary Grant Shapps and his intricate spreadsheet.

His appointment as deputy chief whip was not universally welcomed. One Cabinet minister said Pincher was 'obviously unsuited' to the role but 'desperate to get it', adding, 'I went to a lot of the meetings where Pincher had to shore up Boris's support. He had poor manners and was really quite rude to some of the supporters. He told somebody in the 2019 intake that he had a face for radio. That may be a funny thing to say to your closest friend, but it's not funny when you're senior and he's junior.' Craig Whittaker, another senior Tory whip, refused to serve with Pincher and quit when he heard of the appointment, although told his local paper that he left due to 'personal reasons'. But one other person involved in his appointment explained why he was chosen, saying, 'He was ruthlessly brilliant as deputy chief whip, especially his attention to detail. There was not much else in his life: politics and parliament were Pincher's life.'

Rumours about his personal conduct, however, swirled at the time of his appointment, including the chatter of further sexual harassment incidents beyond the Alex Story allegations. Steve Barclay, Number 10's chief of staff, fought for four hours against the appointment that Adams and Chris Heaton-Harris wanted to make. Meg Powell-Chandler, one of Johnson's aides, flagged his behaviour with Barclay during this debate, telling him, 'I've heard something bad about Chris Pincher, something else.' The allegation she had heard was that Pincher had acted inappropriately towards two Conservative MPs at a party conference in 2017. The new chief whip asked the Cabinet Office's propriety and ethics team whether there were any red flags about Pincher and he also spoke directly to the MP involved. The appointment was delayed for several hours, much to the confusion of the media who were widely expecting it. Yet the mandarins gave Pincher the go-ahead and did not raise any concerns.

Johnson was initially reluctant to give Pincher the job, but told colleagues, 'I don't know anybody else.' One person involved said, 'Boris gave in like he always does.' Another aide said, 'The reality was everyone agreed that he was the best man for the job.' But as with other past problems with the running of his operation, Johnson and his team seemed to be aware of rumours, or had a partial grasp of the issues, but were not aware of the full facts and did not seek to find them out. One official said, 'There were discussions about "Oh, there's an allegation about somebody who did something at a party" but no one would provide the details. Boris would never demand the information either.' It was a mixture of incuriosity and complacency that would ultimately cost him his premiership.

One Cabinet minister close to Johnson argued that the issue was the prime minister was 'too kind' towards his colleagues, adding their spin that, 'He will never give up somebody on the basis of rumours.' But they also went on to say that, 'There is a level of rumour on everybody – some of it unfair, some of them are absolute nonsense. But there comes a level of rumour where you have to say, "I just cannot take this risk as an act of self-preservation." That was what I felt on Pincher.' A close ally of Johnson admitted, 'He never should have been appointed.'

A mere six months later, the fears about appointing Pincher were realised. That June evening at the Carlton Club, he arrived at 8 p.m. to join over a hundred Conservative MPs to hear a lacklustre speech from the former environment secretary, Theresa Villiers. Over canapés of smoked duck, goat's cheese mousse and pulled pork on sourdough, the real focus of the evening was the gossip about Johnson's future and whether the prime minister could make it to the summer. Waiters were on hand to top up glasses of wine. Pincher was spotted with a flute of prosecco. One fellow whip said Pincher most likely went along for 'good intel', adding, 'When he was deputy chief whip, he would instruct colleagues to go to a drinks party, make sure we've got someone there and report back. It's perfectly good whipping.'

After the party finished around 9 p.m., Pincher took to the 'cad's corner' underneath the Carlton's staircase and settled in for further drinks with fellow MPs and hangers-on. Pincher became increasingly inebriated, according to those present, and during the course of the following couple of hours he allegedly groped two men – including grabbing a victim's left buttock and groin after buying a round of drinks. When he was spotted in the club's Macmillan Bar even later, one MP claimed he was lurching towards people and propositioning them. The *Daily Mail* reported that he was 'Clearly trying to seduce several young men', including parliamentary aides. Some urged him to drink water to sober up but he took no notice. He was eventually told to leave the club by Mark Fletcher, the Tory MP for Bolsover, a young red wall MP who had every incentive to avoid conflict with the party hierarchy. One Tory present, who was on the receiving end of Pincher's behaviour, reported him to Sarah Dines, a fellow whip, who made the situation worse by inappropriately asking the alleged victim if he was gay. She later said that she was attempting to establish exactly what happened.

Dines passed her account of that evening to the chief whip Chris Heaton-Harris. There was despair in the whips' office and among the Big Dog team at Pincher's actions. 'Our response was, "Fucking hell Chris Pincher, what have you done?"' With Johnson's position still fragile after the 41 per cent of Tory MPs had rebelled against him a few weeks before, his supporters were nervous about any further scandals. The next morning, Thursday 30 June, Heaton-Harris spoke to several MPs and staffers who had been at the Carlton. He summoned Pincher to explain himself, who confirmed his behaviour had crossed a line.

Yet no formal complaint was made and no formal action was taken against Pincher, until *The Sun* approached Downing Steet with the allegations that afternoon. Team Johnson realised Pincher would have to quit as deputy chief whip, which he did at 8 p.m. that evening as the story went public. In a short resignation letter,[9] Pincher told Johnson, 'Last night I drank far too much . . . I've embarrassed myself and other people which is the last thing I want to do and for that I apologise to you and those concerned.' The fifty-two-year-old said quitting was 'the right thing to do' and said he would continue to support the government from the backbenches. *The Sun* reported that Pincher would remain a Tory MP as those in government believed he had 'done the right thing' by falling on his sword. It was a huge misstep: as with the other botched responses to scandals, the first stage – as with grief – was always denial.

With his resignation from government, some in Downing Street hoped a line had been drawn under the situation. Several aides, however, told Johnson and Guto Harri, his director of communications who was handling the response to Pincher, 'You're going to have to suspend him.' But Harri was concerned for the MP's state of mind and resisted. In a crisis Number 10 meeting on Friday morning, Harri compared Pincher to David Kelly, the chemical weapons expert who killed himself following leaks about the Blair government's handling of the Iraq war. One official present said, 'Guto told the press office that they needed to be nice because it would be their fault if he did anything wrong. I was not happy at all about our position on someone who was an alleged predator. You can't put the onus on people like that, saying if they disagree, you might be risking Pincher's mental health.'

Another factor too was that Conservative party HQ was reluctant for yet another by-election. After the dual losses of Wakefield and Tiverton and Honiton the week before, one senior official told Number 10, 'We can't have any more.' Pincher's 19,634 majority in Tamworth would almost certainly have collapsed and the seat would have flipped to Labour, as it had in the dog days of John Major's government in 1996, when a previous iteration of the same seat fell on a huge swing. Tensions were running high throughout the day. One Johnson aide said the mood was 'frustrated and angry' because Pincher was still a Tory MP facing the most serious of allegations. 'We spent five days on the wrong side of sexual misconduct. It comes down to "Whose side are you on?" And for some reason . . . the government was seen as being on the side of the sex pest rather than the victim.'

That Friday morning, the Welsh secretary Simon Hart was given the chore of the morning media broadcast round and made it clear he thought Pincher should lose the whip. 'I know what I'd like to see happen – you can probably tell what that is by the way I'm trying to avoid answering your question . . . I think we might be having a very different conversation as the day goes on.' It was an uncharacteristic act of insubordination from an otherwise scrupulously loyal Cabinet minister that exposed just how far Johnson's stock had fallen so quickly. Only with increasing numbers of Tory MPs publicly saying he should be suspended, was it dawning on Number 10 how serious the Pincher situation was. 'Nobody thought his behaviour would be as significant as it was,' one Johnson ally said. 'The press office completely fucked it up. The David Kelly comparison was insane.' The internal anger at the mishandling of Pincher outstripped any of the previous errors. One senior aide said, 'when the incident happened at the Carlton Club, I screamed "For fuck's sake!" at people. First, it was happening again, we were defending the indefensible. And second, our response was utterly insane.'

Ahead of Downing Street's first encounter with journalists, the line of the questioning became obvious. Given all of the rumours about Pincher's behaviour: what did Johnson know and when about his misconduct? And were there other allegations he had not acted on? It had been reported that Pincher had even been assigned a minder to prevent him from drinking too much. Later that morning, Westminster's political journalists gathered in the media suite for a painful briefing where Pincher was the only topic. The prime minister's spokesperson told the media Johnson was not aware of any allegations at all about Pincher. That was not true, as Steve Barclay had flagged Meg Powell-Chandler's concerns in February when the Cabinet Office's PET team were ordered to dig into their files to see if there were any red flags.

The spokesperson realised his error and rapidly corrected the line to any 'specific' allegation against Pincher. But the civil servant would not repeat what specific allegation Johnson was supposed to be aware of. When this line became public, one senior Tory MP texted a colleague, 'What the fuck is wrong with these people? Have they learned nothing?'

When asked about any allegations surrounding Pincher's appointment in February, the spokesperson said, 'In the absence of any formal complaint it was not appropriate to stop the appointment on the basis of unsubstantiated claims.' Within Number 10, there was some doubt whether the spokesperson had all the facts about Pincher and what Johnson and his team had known. 'He was told by Guto that the PM didn't know about any specific allegations. But I'm pretty sure he didn't check that with the PM,' one government insider said. Johnson later on expressed his deep annoyance at Hari for the public statements. As the lobby briefing concluded, the official was asked over and over whether Johnson made an error in appointing Pincher. The Number 10 spokesperson stuck to a well-trodden but increasingly implausible answer: 'The prime minister always looks to appoint those who he thinks are the best fit for different positions in government, he has done that throughout his time as prime minister.'

As the Friday wore on, Johnson's aides Declan Lyons and Ben Gascoigne told the prime minister 'this is not going to hold' and warned he would have to backtrack on keeping Pincher in the Tory party. Pressure was building on all sides from MPs, the Cabinet, the civil service and the party. Caroline Nokes and Karen Brady, former ministers under Theresa May's government, wrote to Heaton-Harris to warn of 'serious reputational damage' to the party if Pincher remained an MP. The pair called for a zero-tolerance approach on sexual harassment and a 'thorough investigation' of any allegations. 'Anyone subject to such an investigation should not be allowed to sit as a Conservative MP and represent the party in any capacity,' they wrote.

With the anger swelling from MPs, Johnson realised he had made another bad call. 'The PM was open to taking the whip off him, there wasn't some sort of massive internal thing about defending him,' one ally said.

Some in Johnson's inner circle insisted they did not want to remove the whip until a complaint was made. One government insider said, 'When there are allegations of wrongdoing, it is difficult to remove the whip until there is a formal complaint.' With hindsight, almost everyone in Downing Street admitted they should have acted much sooner. One of Johnson's key advisors made it clear to the prime minister they should be more honest about the situation, that Number 10 was aware of some allegations but had not fully investigated the matter.

In a clear echo of partygate, no one in Downing Street had put together all the details of what had taken place with Pincher before the press response was formed. One ally of the prime minister said, 'Even at that stage, the work hadn't been done so Boris was making decisions with half information, without timeline explanation of what had actually taken place.' Steve Barclay, his chief of staff, and long-time confidant Lynton Crosby told Johnson directly the whip would have to be taken away, but until late in the day, the prime minister resisted.

Later that afternoon, though, the inevitable U-turn came. A formal complaint against Pincher was made by one individual present at the Carlton Club through parliament's Independent Complaints and Grievance Scheme and the Conservative whip was withdrawn. Pincher would sit as an independent MP while the allegations were investigated. But another twenty-four hours of damage had been wrought on the Johnson government. After defending the prime minister over the Owen Paterson saga, partygate, the Met police fine, the privileges committee investigation, Cabinet ministers had finally had enough. One senior member of the Cabinet said, 'I'd completely had it by this point. I didn't get into politics to defend a sex pest, which is what we were being asked to do.'

And just as with the privileges committee fiasco in May, Tory MPs were furious that they had to defend Johnson only for the rapid U-turn to come. 'This was where the anger really tipped over into ministers in the Cabinet, because Number 10 did exactly the same thing,' one senior party advisor said. 'All this time, people were asking what they knew about parties. Everyone in Westminster knew about Pincher and so the ministers saw straightaway that Number 10 was lying again. The system was not working.'

The wider implications of what had taken place were difficult to avoid for Johnson. Pincher was the fifth Tory MP to face such allegations over the past twelve months. Neil Parish, who had resigned in Tiverton and Honiton, had watched pornography in the House of Commons chamber. David Warburton, MP for Somerton and Frome, faced sexual misconduct allegations from three women. Imran Ahmad Khan, Wakefield's MP, was sent to prison for child sex abuse. Another anonymous MP was arrested on suspicion of rape. The prime minister's spokesperson denied the Conservative party had a problem. 'It's regrettable that we've seen a small number of people not meet the expectations that people would expect of MPs, which is why the prime minister is keen for everybody in parliament and across all the political parties to work together to improve that culture.' But the Pincher affair was far from over.

***

It was well over a year and a half since Dominic Cummings had left Johnson's side but he was observing the end of Johnson from afar with glee, offering up frequent contributions on social media, hauling up tales from his Number 10 past to cause further embarrassment. On Saturday 2 July, the prime minister's ex-chief aide took to Twitter[10] to highlight the mess Johnson had got himself into over Pincher: 'If [Johnson] didn't know about Pincher as he's claiming, why did he repeatedly refer to him laughingly in No10 as "Pincher by name Pincher by nature" long before appointing him . . .?' Cummings claimed Downing Street was 'lying again' over its knowledge of Pincher's behaviour. One Johnson ally admitted, 'It sounded very much like something he could have said.'

The following day, Sunday 3 July, the *Mail On Sunday* reported[11] that Johnson had told colleagues of Pincher back in 2020, 'He's handsy, that's a problem.' The paper also said that Johnson had been told of claims Pincher had made unwanted advances towards a fellow Tory MP, plus the revelation Pincher made unwanted advances towards a twenty-four-year-old in 2012. Number 10's line that Johnson was not aware of allegations before appointing him deputy chief whip was falling apart. The *Mail On Sunday* also featured disturbing details that Pincher threatened to report a Tory staffer to her superiors when she attempted to stop his 'lecherous' advances at a party conference event. Pincher denied all the allegations.

Almost every newspaper that day featured claims about Pincher's past conduct. *The Independent* spoke[12] to one Conservative MP who was groped by Pincher on two occasions – first in December 2021 and again in June 2022. 'He put his hand on my crotch and moved it around. I shook my head and said "No, I don't want that" but he [Pincher] just smiled . . . he carried on until I was able to move away,' the MP said. Pincher again firmly denied the allegations, but the damage to his party was growing. After months of sex-pest stories, the Tories were rapidly gaining the potent stench of sleaze, just as it had in the late 1990s before heading to a landslide defeat.

The most damning details came in *The Sunday Times*, which had been attempting to publish an exposé on Pincher for several months, only to encounter legal obstacles. As soon as the Number 10 press office received their inquiries, some aides urged Johnson to act immediately, before the stories were published. 'I kept saying, "Why are we not removing the whip?"' one government insider recalled. 'The end result was the end of Pincher, so why don't we do it now?' Some in Number 10 were hoping the paper would publish so they could finally remove him. 'Each week it went on without them publishing, the more difficult it was for us – about what we had known for how long. Had it all come out earlier, the Carlton Club wouldn't have happened and there wouldn't have been more victims,' one official said.

On 3 July, *The Sunday Times* published[13] what had been originally flagged to Steve Barclay in February when Pincher was appointed deputy chief whip. It reported that Pincher slid his hand down an MP's inner leg, who 'considered it an unwanted physical pass, and·quickly reached down and removed Pincher's hand'. The victim met with his whip and urged them to monitor Pincher's mental health, but did not think the incident warranted a formal complaint. Through his lawyers Pincher denied acting inappropriately. The accusers were critical of Number 10's handling of sexual harassment allegations and admitted they had not taken it any further because 'this is something that happens in Westminster'.

The poor sod put up by the government to comment on all these troubling reports was Thérèse Coffey, the serious and steady work and pensions secretary and Number 10's reliable go-to media minister whenever a dead bat response was required.

Her aim was to say as little as possible, and not further implicate the prime minister. Speaking to Sky News's *Sophy Ridge On Sunday* programme, she channelled the hapless Manuel from *Fawlty Towers* with a range of interviews that could be summed up by his catchphrase: 'I know nothing.'

When asked about the (accurate) reports that the Cabinet Office's PET team had been asked to look into Pincher, Coffey replied, 'There's an element of a bit of vetting that goes on – but ultimately the decision is that of the prime minister. I'm not part of those individual conversations.' By the time she took to the BBC to speak to Sophie Raworth on their *Sunday Morning* programme, her line had softened. Coffey said to the 'best of my understanding' Johnson had 'not been aware of specific allegations'. Coffey was then asked how she knew the prime minister was not aware of the claims against Pincher. 'I have not spoken to the prime minister,' she curtly admitted, pointing out Johnson had been abroad at the G7 and NATO summits. Once again, another scandal and another party management meltdown was taking place with the prime minister abroad. So who had told Coffey? 'Somebody from the Number 10 press office,' she stated. 'As usual, one gets briefed on a wide variety of topics when you come onto a show like this today.'

Despite almost twenty-four hours of equivocation on keeping Pincher in the Tory party, Coffey implausibly argued Number 10 had been decisive. 'What's important . . . [is] the specific allegations were made and a very proactive decision was made to remove the whip as well, as Chris had already resigned from government.' On the *Mail On Sunday* allegation in which Pincher was described by the prime minister as being 'handsy', she stated she had not spoken to anyone in Number 10 about this. Coffey did her best with the information she had been given by Downing Street, but Johnson's political team were still not clear on what exactly happened with

Pincher and another series of media responses was given without the full facts, making the scandal even worse. The prospect of an umpteenth U-turn was approaching, yet Johnson's team repeated the same error in failing to see it coming.

That evening, the Cabinet Office's PET found a formal note about an examination into Pincher's behaviour during his time as Europe minister. Number 10's insistence it had not known about any allegations was ruined. Simon Case, head of the civil service, communicated to the prime minister's office they would have to change the line.

In a brief interlude from the Pincher scandal, Johnson had dinner that Sunday with Rishi Sunak to thrash out plans for a joint economic speech about their vision for the country. In his typical manner of dismissing media storms, the prime minister did not spend the weekend figuring out a response but was focused instead on his next endeavour. Relations between Johnson and Sunak had reached their lowest ebb and Number 10 was nervous about the meeting. Only the two men were present, no aides or partners attended.

The supper did not go well. One government insider said the pair clashed because 'there was a fundamental disagreement over the direction of the government'. Johnson made the case for tax cuts more quickly which Sunak refused. Johnson argued VAT should be slashed immediately to boost growth which Sunak rejected. It was a similar debate to the one that would later take place between Sunak and Liz Truss in the summer's leadership race.

The Pincher row was, however, briefly discussed. According to one government insider, Johnson asked Sunak what he made of the row. One Johnson ally said, 'The chancellor said nothing helpful, he just didn't offer any view at all.' The prime minister was frustrated that his chancellor appeared unwilling to engage with his plight and Johnson was fearful that Sunak was disconnecting from the government.

That night, another meeting took place that would be critical in Johnson's future. Sajid Javid had watched the unfurling reports about Pincher's behaviour with dismay. The health secretary continued to harbour deep anxieties about Johnson and Javid thought he might have reached the point when he no longer had confidence in him. Javid invited two of his special advisors to his home that evening and spoke to a handful of Tory grandees to assess their views. For the first time, Javid seriously contemplated resigning. All of his confidants told him 'the time is coming', but that he should stay put for now. For the final time, he gave Johnson the benefit of the doubt and decided to see if the prime minister could make it through the summer in the hope a reshuffle would improve things. As with many others in Johnson's orbit, Javid seemed to keep on making the mistake of assuming Johnson could change the way he operated.

When Monday 4 July dawned, the Number 10 press office arrived at work early to figure out how they could reset their public position following the PET discovery that Pincher's behaviour had been formally known about. That morning, children's minister Will Quince was sent out onto the airwaves to defend the government. Despite the urgent debate in Number 10, however, he reiterated the same lines as Coffey the day before – declining to comment on 'speculation, gossip or rumour'. Quince told[14] the BBC he had asked Number 10 on both Sunday and Monday 'firmly and clearly' what had happened and what they knew; he was given a 'categorical assurance that the prime minister was not aware of any specific allegation or complaint made against the former deputy chief whip Chris Pincher.'

Just as Sajid Javid had been sent out by Number 10 earlier in the year to state there were no parties and no rules had been broken, Quince was inadvertently not telling the truth. One senior advisor said it 'wasn't so much a conspiracy as a cock-up' and there was a breakdown between the press office and a little-known team in Number 10: the briefing team. Before government ministers head off on a media round, this small team of aides provide lines to take – this usually happens around 5.30 a.m. before the first interviews start an hour later. One veteran Whitehall official said the ineptitude of this team was to blame for many of the Johnson government's failures: 'The briefing team was always terrible in this administration. They take their instructions from the press office, but they consistently messed up the lines that secretaries of state took on the [broadcast] rounds.'

In the case of Quince, the briefing team were acting on incomplete information. They had not been aware of developments over the weekend and relied on the same press lines that had been used in Friday's briefing and given to Thérèse Coffey on Sunday – unaware that a major shift had occurred. 'It wasn't so much they had deliberately withheld information from Will. They were constantly twenty-four hours behind what was happening, so they kept giving ministers the old lines,' one insider said.

At 11.30 a.m., the daily lobby briefing for political journalists commenced. The Downing Street media suite was full of reporters eager to push the prime minister's chief spokesperson on what they knew about Pincher's behaviour. Number 10 finally had to admit that:[15] 'The prime minister was aware of media reports that others had seen over the years and some allegations that were either resolved or did not progress to a formal complaint, but at the time of the deputy chief whip's appointment he was not aware of any specific allegations.' The complaint in question was the incident in the Foreign Office.

More details on what had happened in February came out, including about Pincher's appointment: 'He [Johnson] did take advice on some of the allegations that had been made, but there was no formal complaint at that time and it was deemed not appropriate to stop an appointment simply because of unsubstantiated allegations.' The sudden shift in position alarmed ministers and MPs, and lost Downing Street what little credibility it had left. If they hadn't already, from this briefing onwards, the media and the wider public stopped believing what they were being told.

And still more allegations about Pincher emerged: Mark Dabbs, a marathon runner in Pincher's Tamworth constituency, claimed on 4 July[16] the MP 'was brushing his hand across my bottom' when the pair posed for a photo in 2018. Dabbs said his behaviour was 'bordering on sexual assault' and told *ITV News*[17] that Pincher made a series of suggestive and inappropriate comments during their meeting. Pincher again denied any wrongdoing.

***

Tuesday 5 July would prove to be a momentous day in Johnson's time as prime minister. It began in the wooden and marble grandeur of Westminster Hall, where much of Britain's political class attended the National Parliamentary Prayer Breakfast. Over coffee, pastries and orange juice, hundreds listened to the Reverend Les Isaac, founder of the Street Pastors movement, who spoke on the pertinent theme of 'serving the common good'. Boris Johnson was present, along with the opposition leader Keir Starmer and dozens of senior ministers, including health secretary Sajid Javid, who had carefully heeded the Reverend Isaac's message on honesty and integrity. While the politicians were

aspiring to improve their spiritual standing, a longstanding opponent of Johnson sought to ruin his political one.

Simon McDonald was the embodiment of the Whitehall
establishment that the prime minister loathed. He joined the
Foreign Office in 1982, straight out of Cambridge University,
and served as British ambassador in Israel and Germany. After
decades of diplomatic service, he was appointed as the department's permanent undersecretary and head of the diplomatic
service in 2015. When Johnson arrived as foreign secretary the
following year, the pair clashed over Brexit – one of the prime
minister's allies described him as 'a rabid anti-Brexiteer.' When
Johnson, now prime minister, announced that the Foreign and
Commonwealth Office would merge with the Department for
International Development, Johnson informed McDonald he
would be retired early.[18]

Two years later, McDonald delivered his revenge. That
Tuesday morning at 7.30 a.m., he tweeted his letter[19] to the
parliamentary standards commissioner about Number 10's
utterances on the Pincher affair, accusing them of 'still not
telling the truth' about Pincher's behaviour. The mandarin said
a complaint had been made in the summer of 2019 about
Pincher – regarding actions similar to what happened at the
Carlton Club – and it had been discussed with the Cabinet
Office. 'An investigation upheld the complaint; Mr Pincher
apologised and promised not to repeat the inappropriate behaviour.' Critically McDonald claimed that Johnson 'was briefed in
person about the investigation and outcome of the investigation' and said this constituted a formal complaint. In six brief
paragraphs, McDonald had accused the prime minister and his
team of lying and in doing so he plunged the government into
its deepest crisis to date. Coming on the record from one of
Whitehall's most senior figures gave the claims substantial heft.

One Number 10 insider said, 'It was reported as more in sorrow than anger. He was a trusted source, while everything we said was complete bollocks.'

Dominic Raab, the deputy prime minister and justice secretary, was not at the prayer breakfast but had the unlucky job of representing the government on Tuesday's media round. He was ambushed with McDonald's letter live on *BBC Breakfast* – the country's most watched morning programme. Looking decidedly prickly, Raab said,[20] 'That is news to me, that the prime minister was briefed on the specific complaint that was made and then the outcome, precisely because it didn't lead to a formal disciplinary grievance process, let alone formal action.' Raab said he had spoken to Johnson directly, who had assured him he had not been directly told about Pincher's misconduct.

When Johnson returned to Downing Street from the breakfast, he scrambled his political and press team for a crisis meeting on how to respond. The aides gathered in the Cabinet room with a palpable sense that the situation was becoming lethal. One aide said, 'There was a long and deep personal animus between them [Johnson and McDonald] but at this stage, things felt very out of control.' Team Johnson only had a few hours to prepare a public response: as well as the 11.30 a.m. press briefing, an urgent question was granted by the House of Commons speaker on the Pincher affair. Michael Ellis, a junior Cabinet Office minister who had often seemed to be the one made to defend the indefensible in parliament, was chosen to respond.

Finally, five days into the crisis, the prime minister's inner circle sought to figure out what they knew and when about Pincher. 'We had five days of being confused about what exactly happened,' one government insider said. It emerged that Helen MacNamara, the former head of the Cabinet Office's PET team, had briefed Johnson on the investigation. One official explained:

'There's a wider problem that people are a little bit hazy with Boris because they think he doesn't do stuff formally so they can be less formal. If you're going to have that kind of discussion with the prime minister you need to provide written minutes to make sure it's done properly.' Whether Johnson forgot, or whether his press chief Guto Harri had failed to properly check with him before announcing the government's position previously, was unclear. But the public position would have to shift.

Ellis and the prime minister's spokesperson agreed they would not say he 'forgot' as it would open the prime minister up to ridicule. Although there was anger at the Cabinet Office, the finger was not pointed internally – one official present said, 'The PM did not know of any specifics about the Foreign Office incident, it was a total cock-up by the Cabinet Office.' Instead the pair agreed on the line that the Foreign Office matter was discussed in a brief chat a number of years ago. Johnson's inner circle were furious about how the McDonald letter was being reported.

As journalists gathered in the media suite for yet another packed briefing, tensions were high. Johnson's official spokesperson Max Blain wearily began setting out the prime minister's diary. But before he could take questions, Jason Groves of the *Daily Mail* asked him, 'Are you planning on telling us the truth today?' The spokesperson sheepishly responded: 'We always seek to provide the information we have at the time,' noting the facts 'take time to establish'. The spokesperson confirmed Johnson knew about the formal complaint about Pincher's inappropriate behaviour. 'The prime minister was informed but not asked to take any action as a result. As a result of that action, the minister carried on serving in that department for a number of months.' The emphasis was placed on the fact it was not a formal complaint – contrary to McDonald's letter – and it was a 'brief conversation' three years ago that was buried deep in the prime minister's memory. The briefing was the most painful of Johnson's time in government.

At the same moment, Ellis lumbered up to the Despatch Box to deliver a similar message to MPs. 'Last week, when fresh allegations arose, the prime minister did not immediately recall the conversation in late 2019 about this incident. As soon as he was reminded, the press office corrected their public line.' He went on, 'The position is that the prime minister acted with probity at all times.' He did not use the word 'forgot' but in exchanges with Labour MPs, it was clear what he meant. One Cabinet minister watching him in the Commons remarked, 'The Number 10 line was he basically forgot. When that came out, I thought "This is seriously bad and lame."' Downing Street had wanted to rebut some of McDonald's claims but, after shifting their line several times, they had lost the right to be heard. 'The ship had sailed,' one official said.

As the Number 10 team failed to mount a response, the Big Dog and Brains Trust teams were activated again to ring round MPs and defend the government's position. Johnson's inner circle were flailing around. 'By Tuesday lunchtime, the wheels were coming off,' one ally said. 'There was no strategy to deal with the crisis. Internecine warfare took hold inside Downing Street, with officials telling journalists that the operation was collapsing. 'Number 10 began briefing about people in Number 10 which made it an even worse atmosphere to work in,' one insider said. A bunker mentality began to take hold. 'We were all raging, but our position just wasn't cutting through,' one senior official recalled. 'At that point, none of us had any access to the PM so it was getting harder to formulate a response.'

Later that Tuesday, Downing Street inexplicably allowed cameras in to film footage of the weekly Cabinet meeting. Every minister around the table seemed uncomfortably glum or furious or a mixture of both. Thérèse Coffey, who had been sent out on Sunday to propagate false information on behalf of Number 10, looked especially stern. Even loyalist ministers such as Jacob Rees-Mogg and Nadine Dorries were expressionless. Levelling up secretary Michael Gove and health secretary Sajid Javid appeared haunted. Chief whip Chris Heaton-Harris stared down at his papers, while attorney general Suella Braverman resolutely focused on the wall in the middle distance. Even though Pincher was not raised at the Cabinet meeting, he was present in spirit. Simon Case, head of the civil service, had his head bowed throughout.

The ensuing discussion was scarcely more positive than their demeanour. After his inconclusive supper with Rishi Sunak the previous Sunday, Johnson wanted to define the government's overall economic strategy that could counter rising inflation, the cost of living crisis and lacklustre growth. Following his inadequate spring statement, Sunak was forced to announce a £15 billion package[21] at the end of May that almost doubled energy bill support, particularly for poorer households. All homes would be given a £400 discount on energy bills, in addition to a £150 council tax rebate for many others. The offering was highly redistributive, aiding less well-off households, but it was not well received by Tories concerned with fiscal probity.

At the start of the Cabinet meeting, Johnson told ministers he was planning to hold a regular series of 'economic press conferences' that would set out what the government was doing to help people. He drew a parallel with the frequent broadcasts during the coronavirus pandemic that were credited with effective messaging. But no one was clear what these press conferences would achieve. Michael Gove, levelling up secretary, said whereas the government had a clear message on Covid – punchy slogans such as 'stay at home, protect the NHS, save lives' – there was no agreement around the table about what the government's central economic messaging would be.

The Cabinet broke out into a debate on what the economic message should be and it was immediately apparent no one agreed. Kwasi Kwarteng, business secretary, heartily argued that the government 'must cut taxes now'. Michelle Donelan, the universities minister, readily agreed. Sajid Javid, health secretary, talked up supply-side reforms to boost growth. Sunak shot back that now was not the time to cut taxes with inflation soaring. Kwarteng tried to sum up with, 'There's no disagreement, we all believe we should cut taxes.' Gove interjected to say, 'Literally the chancellor doesn't, so we don't have a coherent message.' Johnson was having none of it and said 'no, no, no' – so incredulous that the ministers began laughing. Not a single person mentioned Pincher, the mistruths and the chaos unfurling around them.

***

After the Cabinet meeting, Johnson's inner circle bickered about whether or not he should front a televised message to apologise for Downing Street's mishandling of the Pincher saga. Johnson had almost lost confidence in Guto Harri and the press office's ability to get a message out there. One close aide said, 'He was pushing for a clip, it was really his only option at this point to try and get it done.' Other aides disagreed. 'I told him this was a bad idea,' one advisor said. 'He said, "Why?" And I said, "I'm not entirely clear what it is you are trying to get across."' Johnson dismissed these concerns and insisted he had to clear up the mess. Once again, the facts were not clear.

Preparations were duly made for the BBC's political editor Chris Mason to come to his House of Commons office that afternoon to film a short clip that would be broadcast on the 6 p.m. news bulletin. His team agreed he would say sorry for appointing Pincher deputy chief whip – another U-turn on the previous days – and explain that the Foreign Office complaint was made in passing three years before. Johnson would also apologise for not looking into the matter further.

At the same time, half a mile away across Westminster, Sajid Javid concluded after the Cabinet meeting that he had had enough. Following his unhappiness on the previous Sunday evening and the revelations from the McDonald letter, the health secretary and his team discussed whether they had reached the moment to go. One person with knowledge of the conversations said, 'We all agreed that the PM and his team lied, they had done it again. The general feeling was "How can this just continue now?"' Javid took further soundings: he texted Rishi Sunak that afternoon, but the pair never found time for a call. He also spoke to education secretary Nadhim Zahawi about the situation. Javid instructed Samuel Coates, his closest aide, to draft a resignation letter. After speaking to Michael Gove, Javid made his decision and signed the letter.

He was not the only minister contemplating their future. Next door to Johnson in Number 11 Downing Street, Rishi Sunak had reached the same conclusion. The chancellor was despairing not only at the government's Pincher response, but also at the economic incoherence of the government's policy. The Cabinet meeting had confirmed in his mind that he held irreconcilable views on the economy as to the best way forward from Johnson. As with Javid, he had taken soundings over the weekend from his advisors, supporters and family, who similarly concurred that his time in government was drawing to a close. One MP close to Sunak said, 'Rishi was properly fed up and decided that afternoon he could no longer defend the government.' But he was cautious too, fearing that quitting abruptly could endanger his leadership hopes.

Some senior Tories with contacts to both men think that Sunak and Javid coordinated their actions in some way, but aides close to the pair insist that they did not speak that Tuesday afternoon and there was no communication about their plans to resign. Johnson's inner circle also didn't believe it was a coordinated coup. 'I can't see how it would have helped Rishi to have coordinated with Saj. As you saw during the leadership contest, the narrative of being the man who sunk the knife in is not particularly helpful. If it was coordinated it was a very silly thing to do. What Sunak should have done is stayed and let Sajid do it.'

Johnson returned to the Palace of Westminster in his motorcade that afternoon to record the BBC clip. With the camera crews setting up in his suite, he practised his apology in Sunak's House of Commons office – at the very moment the chancellor was penning his resignation letter elsewhere. As the prime minister prepared to meet Chris Mason, one of his aides informed him that Javid had requested an urgent one-to-one meeting. Instantly they knew he was about to quit. One senior Number 10 figure said, 'For months when people asked what would happen with Cabinet, I'd always said Sajid was the weak link. He'd quit it before . . . he wanted to be prime minister, which is not an ignoble ambition, but he wanted to run for it.'

After the broadcast crew had left, Johnson and Javid met in the prime minister's office. Steve Barclay, Johnson's chief of staff, was floating around but the health secretary insisted he wanted to speak to Johnson alone. The pair chatted for almost half an hour, but having stated his intention Javid did not budge. One official involved said, 'He didn't want Saj to go, but he knew he'd made up his mind and understood where he was coming from.' Javid walked down the corridor to his own parliamentary office to make his resignation public.

As Johnson was conversing with his aides about handling Javid's resignation, around fifty of his closest MP supporters were gathered in the conference room of his parliamentary office for a thank you drink for their assistance during the vote of no confidence. The room was 'packed', according to those present, with the assembled Tories gossiping about the Pincher affair – unaware of what was about to happen. The prime minister and his political team watched the 6 p.m. news where his apology was the lead item. Looking red-faced, sweaty and flustered, Johnson said it was 'bad mistake' not acting on the complaint and admitted that he should not have made Pincher deputy chief whip: 'I apologise for it.' Speaking about his frustration at his Number 10 team and McDonald's letter, Johnson told the BBC he was 'fed up with people saying things on my behalf'.

Johnson put forward his explanation of what had happened: 'About two and a half years ago I got this complaint, it was something that was only raised with me very cursorily but I wish that we had, I in particular, had acted on it and that he had not continued in government because he then went on, I'm afraid, to behave, as far as we can see, according to the allegations that we have, very, very badly.' The prime minister concluded he was, 'Sorry for those who have been badly affected by it.' Yet two minutes into his apology, as it was being broadcast on the 6 p.m. news, Sajid Javid tweeted his resignation letter. Several floors above the party in the parliamentary press gallery, journalists glued to the TV screens screamed aloud at what had just happened. The BBC production team struggled to work out how to cover the moment while the prime minister was still speaking: their caption led on the prime minister's apology, then it shifted to 'BREAKING . . .

Sajid Javid resigns', while Johnson continued to fluster through the pre-recorded clip.

In his letter, Javid spoke of his longstanding private concerns about the integrity of the government he was part of – he was later to say that the sermon at the prayer breakfast had shaped his thinking. 'The British people also rightly expect integrity from their government. The tone you set as a leader, and the values you represent, reflect on your colleagues, your party and ultimately the country,' he wrote. 'Sadly, in the current circumstances, the public are concluding that we are now neither. The vote of confidence last month showed that a large number of our colleagues agree.' Javid said Johnson had not shown the 'humility, grip and new direction' required and he had concluded, 'It is clear to me that this situation will not change under your leadership – and you have therefore lost my confidence too.' Johnson and his team knew it was coming, but the drinks party were unaware. A wave of shock rippled through the room next door, as the assembled MPs balanced their glasses of wine alongside their phones to squint at his letter.

Nine minutes later, Javid's resignation was toppled from the news headlines. When his resignation was made public, a scramble took place in Number 11 to print off Rishi Sunak's resignation, and deliver it next door so he could publicly declare it. At 6.11 p.m., Sunak resigned as chancellor. It is unclear whether he alerted Johnson: Sunak's colleagues said he attempted to call the prime minister on WhatsApp and he did not pick up; Johnson's team insisted they had no idea he was resigning. What Team Johnson had feared for almost six months had come to pass.

In his letter, Sunak wrote, 'The public rightly expect government to be conducted properly, competently and seriously. I recognise this may be my last ministerial job, but I believe these standards are worth fighting for.' The chancellor said he had been loyal and supported Johnson publicly even when they had disagreed, especially on economic policy. 'I firmly believe the public are ready to hear that truth. Our people know that if something is too good to be true then it's not true. They need to know that while there is a path to a better future, it is not an easy one.' Sunak concluded, 'In preparation for our proposed joint speech on the economy next week, it has become clear to me that our approaches are fundamentally too different.'

As the news broke, Johnson exploded in front of his aides with a diatribe of four-letter words. Javid's resignation was instantly brushed away. Sunak's resignation posed a far bigger problem. After months of their disintegrating relationship, Johnson saw his departure as a 'personal betrayal' and it was universally believed by Johnson and his aides that Sunak had resigned to challenge him for the Conservative party leadership. 'Boris was very, very upset. He thought the [resignation] letter was a tissue of lies about their relationship.'

A close ally explained, 'The difference with Saj is that the PM and Rishi worked very closely. The PM did everything to involve Rishi in everything – not just economy stuff – but he was going to the Number 10 morning meetings, throughout. The PM wanted Rishi to know everything he was thinking and made so much effort to bring him in. That is why it hurt so much.'

After his outburst, Johnson faced two pressing tasks: one to shore up the rest of the Cabinet, second to fill the gaps in his government. But before any of that, he had to immediately face an increasingly agitated room of his supporters, ploughing through the complimentary wine. Johnson entered the room to raucous cheers and banging on the tables. The prime minister delivered a classic stump speech. 'I want to thank everybody, everyone has done a fantastic job. We fight on,' he shouted. He sought to cast Sunak and Javid's resignation in a positive light.

'Those of you who champion free markets and tax cuts might find in light of the very recent news that we might be able to deliver some of those now,' to greater cheers. Even his closest aides were stunned at the performance. 'His ability to turn the room around was amazing,' one MP present said. Another MP said, 'It was incredible given the fact he had just lost his health secretary and chancellor, he was just brilliant.' After the meeting, his supporters queued up to lay into Sunak, with several telling Johnson it was 'good riddance'.

After leaving the party, Johnson instructed his chief whip Chris Heaton-Harris to phone round the Cabinet to ensure no one else was quitting. One of their chief fears was Michael Gove, who Johnson's team saw as close to Sunak and Javid and who could be on the verge of quitting. The levelling up secretary was unreachable: he was at the Royal Opera House watching *Cavalleria Rusticana* (about a blood feud in Sicily) and *Pagliacci* (about the downfall of a clown). When the news of the resignations came through, Gove was chatting to Theresa May. The pair agreed no one could take on the role of chancellor with much credibility. Gove was forced to abruptly leave the opera house and publicly said he had no plans to do anything.

Johnson hopped back in his motorcade to Downing Street, where the Big Dog team was summoned to start shoring up his standing. An emergency reshuffle was required that night to find a new chancellor and health secretary. The mood was rapidly darkening. 'I thought it was bad with Saj's resignation,' one senior government insider said. 'But when Rishi went I thought it was terminal.' When Johnson arrived at Number 10, he told aides that as long as he could form a government, he would stay on and that he had absolutely no plans to quit, yet the prime minister's final twenty-four hours as undisputed leader of the country and the Tory party had begun. Both Johnson and his inner team adopted a bunker mentality to try and rebuild his government, to avoid further major resignations and to keep him in office for as long as possible. But privately, nearly all of them knew the end was almost nigh.

7. The Bunker

The education secretary, Nadhim Zahawi, was enjoying supper on Tuesday 5 July when he received an abrupt message from Boris Johnson's chief fixer, Nigel Adams: 'Get your arse over here'. With the precipitous departure of the chancellor and health secretary, Zahawi sniffed a promotion in the air. As his ministerial Jaguar wormed its way through the traffic to 10 Downing Street, Zahawi's eagerness got the better of him and he repeatedly texted Adams to ask, 'What am I getting Nige?' Either job would have been a promotion, but Zahawi sensed it might be the big one. Adams shot back it was not for him to say and that he would just have to wait.

Fifty-five-year-old Zahawi was one of the most prominent faces of Boris Johnson's government, first as the media-friendly vaccines minister during the coronavirus pandemic and latterly as education secretary. Born in Iraq, Zahawi's family moved to the UK when he was eleven years old, his story encapsulating what might be called 'the British dream'. From refugee to millionaire, he gained huge financial success as a founder of the pollster YouGov. Zahawi's parliamentary career began in 2010 and he gained junior ministerial office under Theresa May's government in 2018. As a long-term backer of Johnson since his mayor of London days, Zahawi's career took off when Johnson became prime minister. He was also frequently mooted as a potential successor.

Zahawi was one of three names that evening to be in contention to be Johnson's third chancellor of the exchequer. Leaving the drinks party for his loyalist MPs, Johnson returned to Number 10 where the Big Dog team had been scrambled to work through a Cabinet reshuffle. The usual cast of Johnson's crisis managers were present: fixer Adams, strategist Ross Kempsell, chief whip Chris Heaton-Harris, his old *Telegraph* editor and confidant Will Lewis. From the formal Downing Street team were his political advisors Declan Lyons and Ben Gascoigne, plus director of communications Guto Harri and chief of staff Steve Barclay.

One other senior aide was present at the reshuffle. David Canzini, Number 10's deputy chief of staff, had been decidedly absent from most of the inner circle crisis meetings that had taken place previously, but he found his way to the centre of the events that evening at the prime minister's request. Some in the Big Dog team were puzzled: 'Canzini got himself in the room and I do remember thinking, "What the fuck is he doing here?"' Within Number 10, opinion about Canzini, who had been brought on board in 2022, was mixed. A range of glowing media profiles had not boosted his standing internally, with suspicions he had briefed them himself.

Crammed into the prime minister's private office, the assembled aides pondered how to restack the government. Should they seek two immediate replacements for Rishi Sunak and Sajid Javid? Or should they push for a much bigger reshuffle – the sort Declan Lyons had sketched out for later in the summer? Soon, however, the room concluded that Johnson did not have the political capital and authority to undertake a major reconstruction. The task, therefore, was to prove the Johnson government was still functioning and not hand his rivals any further ammunition. 'People were saying, "There's no way he can function, he's got to go, we want him marched out of the door with his wife and kids." So we had to get a functioning and competent government,' one insider said.

The first spot to be filled was the most straightforward. In his motorcade back from parliament to Downing Street, Johnson decided Steve Barclay should replace Javid. His chief of staff (previously a junior health minister) was mooted for the role a year before when Matt Hancock was forced to resign for breaking Covid rules for embracing his aide Gina Coladangelo. The smooth and assured fifty-year-old Barclay had shown a keen interest in health policy while in Number 10: monitoring reams of official statistics behind the NHS and talking up the government's manifesto commitment to forty new hospitals. He had essentially put himself forward for the role. One senior official said, 'Steve was obsessed with data and waiting lists, he's very into the technical details of health policy. So he volunteered himself. He also obviously wanted to get the fuck out of Number 10.'

Johnson asked his chief of staff to leave the room while his fate was pondered. He soon returned; the deal was swiftly done, and the pair emerged into the Cabinet room as the prime minister declared, 'Meet our new health secretary!' Barclay looked delighted and relieved, according to those present. They shook hands and the health secretary departed for his new ministry. It may have seemed insignificant at that moment but Johnson had just lost his third Downing Street chief of staff in almost three years. There wouldn't be a fourth.

Next came chancellor. Number 10 were not blessed with a range of options for the role that would be judged as credible by the markets when they opened the next morning. The three names in contention were foreign secretary Liz Truss, police minister Kit Malthouse and Zahawi. Truss was a serious candidate, but Johnson opted to keep her at the Foreign Office given the fragile geopolitical situation. 'There was a discussion about Liz but on balance the PM decided the Ukrainian situation was sufficiently important that she should stay focused on the international stuff,' one official said. Another person close to Johnson said, 'Liz could have easily done the job. He would have liked to appoint her chancellor, but he felt if there was any road left he wanted to keep her as foreign secretary.'

Malthouse's name soon fell by the wayside and so Zahawi was the consensual choice. As Zahawi was waiting to see the prime minister, Johnson's office had rapidly asked the Cabinet Office's propriety and ethics team to do due diligence to ensure Zahawi was suitable for such a high-profile role. Their work was questioned as days later it was alleged[1] that Zahawi was under investigation by the National Crime Agency and HM Revenue and Customs, something he later denied. He was taken into the Cabinet Room by Johnson for a lengthy one-to-one chat. Johnson did not want the same schism to open up between prime minister and chancellor that had developed with Sunak.

Zahawi was sympathetic with Johnson on the need to cut taxes and implement supply-side economic reforms to boost growth. 'It felt for a brief moment we finally had a Number 10 and Number 11 team that could work well together,' one ally said. 'The mood that night was, "Actually this is a good thing, now we have a chancellor who will get stuff done."' In their discussion, Johnson and Zahawi agreed to a set-piece economic speech in the near future – a rehash of what the prime minister had sought to do with Sunak weeks before. Their bonhomie would not last long.

As Zahawi accepted the job, Johnson's team had already lined up his replacement as education secretary: Michelle Donelan, the eager universities minister. The thirty-eight-year-old arrived at Number 10 quarter of an hour after Zahawi and was desperate for a Cabinet role: while in a waiting room, she texted Nigel Adams almost directly asking for education secretary. 'She went into the Cabinet Room, where the PM was appointing ministers, begging for a Cabinet job. She was jumping up and down like a pogo stick with excitement,' one person present said. Johnson's team had no qualms about appointing her; as universities minister she had impressed Number 10 and was already primed for a promotion in the July reshuffle. 'She was impressive, she would be another woman at the top table, she was the right choice,' one minister said. Very soon, however, Donelan would earn the dubious record of being the shortest-serving Cabinet minister in British history.

While Number 10 was busy filling the three top slots, resignations from the government had continued – albeit of a more junior level than Sunak or Javid. At 7 p.m., Andrew Murrison resigned[2] as the government's trade envoy to Morocco, citing Simon McDonald's letter (his letter to the prime minister was photographed so poorly that it was likened to a notice of repossession in the window of a fried chicken restaurant, and he had to repost it twenty minutes later so the press could read and report it properly). Next came Bim Afolami, who resigned live on TalkTV[3] as vice chair of the Conservative party when the presenter guided him to the conclusion he had lost confidence in Johnson. Five junior ministerial aides from the 2019 intake of MPs followed: Jonathan Gullis, Saqib Bhatti, Nicola Richards, Virginia Crosbie and Theo Clarke. The trickle of departures, which soon turned into a torrent, suggested to Johnson that the effort to oust him was gathering unstoppable momentum.

The last departure of 5 July had been long expected in Downing Street. Alex Chalk, solicitor general, had been on resignation watch for months and had told almost any MP who would listen that he was unhappy and about to walk – not least over Johnson's partygate fine. In his letter,[4] the Cheltenham MP said he could no longer defend the culture and course of the government: 'The cumulative effect of the Owen Paterson debacle, Partygate and now the handling of the former Deputy Chief Whip's resignation, is that public confidence in the ability of Number 10 to uphold the standards of candour expected of a British Government has irretrievably broken down.'

Team Johnson mostly dismissed these resignations as ungrateful nonentities, many of whom had not supported the Johnson project to begin with. Under Guto Harri's direction, the press office pumped out a series of media briefings that heralded their two big new appointments: Zahawi was described as a 'class act', someone who would reset economic policy. 'For the next stage, we need a plan for growth and not just balancing the books. He represents the government's values and commitment.' Barclay was heralded[5] as a 'massive upgrade' on Sajid Javid: 'He has a first class forensic brain, great clarity of thought and will use data to drive improvement.' There was one final barb at Sunak from Downing Street: 'He had no real plan for growth [and was] just obsessed with balancing the books.' Johnson and his political team were exhausted and fearful of what would lie ahead. One insider said, 'We left that night with a sense that the situation was very difficult but at least we've plugged the holes. We could say that we had a functioning Cabinet.' Another senior official said, 'That night it was feeling okay.' But another said, 'I was still extremely worried.'

There was very little sleep, however, for Zahawi who had been put forward for the morning broadcast round of interviews on Wednesday 6 July. Having left Number 11 for home, the new chancellor was WhatsApping colleagues until 3 a.m., digesting his new brief and finalising how exactly he would summarise his long, rambling discussion with Johnson on the government's new economic agenda. He grabbed two hours' sleep before waking at 5.30 a.m. to travel into the studios. One government insider said,

'When you become chancellor, you get a load of briefings and he was doing his best to brief himself. Nadhim did that media round with barely any preparation or sleep.'

July 6 began with Zahawi adopting a more conciliatory tone for the Johnson government after the dual major resignations the night before. The new chancellor said the prime minister was 'right to apologise'[6] over the appointment of Chris Pincher as deputy chief whip: 'When the prime minister realised he'd made a mistake, he came out and explained that. He said with the benefit of hindsight that he made a mistake. I think that's good leadership to come out and say that, to say: "Look, you know, I don't get every decision right."'

Zahawi also made a clear break with the Sunak era on the economy. Steve Swinford, political editor of *The Times*, summarised Zahawi's broadcast round as[7] 'the most expensive in history', as he went about reversing key policies from the previous era with plans to splash cash far and wide. The new chancellor strongly hinted that a rise in corporation tax due in 2023 from 19 to 25 per cent would not take place, which would lose the government a cool £16 billion a year. Zahawi also suggested a future income tax cut, at £5 billion, and reiterated his pledge to deliver a 5 per cent pay rise for teachers. Were that to be replicated across the public sector, it would add £12–15 billion to government expenditure. Such profligate spending was exactly what Johnson had wanted in a chancellor, but there was a notable absence of a plan on how it was going to be paid for.

As the interviews took place, though, it became clear that the new chancellor would not only have to answer questions about spending plans. While he was live on Radio 4's *Today* programme, the schools minister Will Quince resigned – his anger over the mistruths he was told to propagate over the Pincher affair came to a head. One senior Tory who spoke to Quince said he felt under 'so much pressure to resign from his family and friends'. His politics were firmly on the left of the party, but he remained loyal to Johnson throughout. His resignation soured the mood in Number 10. 'He just felt Boris couldn't continue, it wasn't a move to bring Boris down,' one friend said. 'Will wanted Boris to stay, but his resignation created momentum against the PM.' Ambushed live on air with news of his departure, Zahawi mournfully said he was sorry to see Quince go. 'He was a great minister, all I would say to colleagues is people don't vote for divided teams, we have to come together,' he said.

Number 10 was relieved Zahawi had not committed any major gaffes. 'Given the pressure he was under, at least he didn't have a car crash,' one official said. 'But the situation was becoming farcical.' While Zahawi was still on the *Today* programme, Laura Trott, an aide to transport secretary Grant Shapps, also quit, so he was forced to use the same words that he had used about Quince, that he was sorry she had quit and everyone needed to pull together.

The dam had broken. At 9.43 a.m., schools minister Robin Walker quit. At 11.06 a.m., it was city minister John Glen. At 11.43 a.m., it was prisons minister Victoria Atkins, who expressed concerns that the values of 'integrity, decency, respect and professionalism' had fractured. Johnson's inner team again shrugged them off. 'None of these people were a surprise,' one ally said. The loss of faith in Johnson was also spreading to Tory MPs. Rob Halfon, chair of the education select committee and a popular blue-collar Tory, also withdrew his support that morning, stating 'the public have been misled' over both partygate and Pincher. He was joined swiftly by Lee Anderson, a former member of Arthur Scargill's National Union of Mineworkers and now Tory MP for Ashfield in Nottinghamshire, who posted on Facebook:[8] 'It is my belief that our PM has got all the big decisions right and guided us through the most difficult time in my life time and I have always backed him to the hilt. That said, integrity should always come first and sadly this has not been the case over the past few days.'

While outwardly stating that this was all manageable, a sense of foreboding took hold in Number 10. Conservative MPs had started to leave the Johnson support group on WhatsApp. One senior government insider said, 'I'm a relentless optimist and we kept going. We still had the MPs' support team, we still had good numbers, they were still there. They still want to show they were loyal.' But the situation for Johnson was soon to take another turn for the worse. As he was beavering away in his private study, ignoring the junior resignations and preparing for what was undoubtedly going to be a bruising session of prime minister's questions, he was about to receive a visit from an old university chum who had some especially grave news to deliver in a deadly soft fashion.

***

After his interrupted evening at the opera, Michael Gove had mulled over the resignations of Rishi Sunak and Sajid Javid, both close Cabinet compadres.

Gove and Johnson had an especially intertwined and turbulent past. Their political psychodrama began when Gove was Johnson's campaign manager for the Oxford Union presidency in the 1980s. Both developed careers as budding journalists on different publications in the 1990s and then became parliamentary colleagues in the 2000s. Their relationship broke down in 2016, when Gove declared Johnson was unfit to be prime minister and became responsible for sinking Johnson's first Tory leadership campaign. Even though Johnson brought him back into government as one of his most senior ministers, first at the Cabinet Office then as levelling up secretary, the prime minister's most ardent loyalists never forgave Gove.

That Wednesday morning, the levelling up secretary spoke to dozens of Tory MPs and ministers and many told him that Johnson's time as prime minister was drawing to a close. He had come to the same conclusion. Gove was concerned that Downing Street had developed a bunker mentality and that Johnson was not receiving good advice about his prospects, so he decided to do something about it. Gove contacted Simone Finn, Number 10's deputy chief of staff (and a close friend and former partner), to ask for five minutes alone with Johnson before or after the prime minister's questions' prep. Throughout the Johnson premiership, Gove had been part of the team that role-played questions, quips and quibbles for the weekly jousts with opposition leader Keir Starmer in the House of Commons (as one of parliament's strongest, most amusing debaters, he had done the same throughout David Cameron's leadership too). He arrived at 10 Downing Steet early and was told by Finn he could have a brief word before the prep session begin.

Johnson did not know he was seeing Gove. Nigel Adams, his perennial fixer, was in Johnson's office when a knock came on his door at 10.25 a.m. Finn said, 'Michael is here, he wants to see you.' Johnson responded, 'But he's going to see me in a minute because we're doing PMQs prep.' She insisted. Gove walked into the prime minister's private office and the Number 10 aides filtered out.

He looked straight at Johnson and delivered the fatal blow for the second time in six years: 'Boss, I'm really sorry to say this but I think you should announce you're standing down today.' According to those briefed on what happened, Gove went on 'it's up to you obviously how' and he explained how he saw events panning out based on his conversations that morning. 'There are going to be a slew of junior ministerial resignations, many more than you may have been told. I anticipate they will include some of the best people in the party, people who are huge fans of yours. But you will not be able to get an administration together, it will be insupportable. If you survive that, the 1922 [Committee] will change the rules and you will lose a vote of confidence. I don't want to see you go that way.'

Johnson sarcastically thanked Gove: 'You've delivered the bullet in a polite way,' and he responded with a tale about one of his uncles who had 'failed to take his meds one day'. The man was a planning officer in East Ham and ended up in a dispute with his superiors, so barricaded himself into the town hall with a shotgun. The uncle was eventually bundled out by the police. 'That is going to be me,' the prime minister said. 'I'm going to fight, they're going to have to prise me out of here.' Gove, slightly stunned, responded, 'Okay, I totally understand prime minister.' Johnson told him he disagreed with his analysis of the situation; that there was no strong alternative leader. 'I think it would be bad for Ukraine, bad for Brexit, bad for the economy.' Gove acknowledged those reasons and explained they were why he had remained in government 'under stress' in recent weeks.

According to colleagues, Gove decided to tell Johnson the game was up because he thought it was impossible for him to go on. 'Michael wasn't going to run for leadership, he wasn't in anyone's camp, so he could tell him as the most senior minister in terms of experience. He felt it was his duty to do so – not to say anything would have been colluding in an illusion.' Gove did not issue an ultimatum for Johnson or threaten to quit himself, he told the prime minister he would not discuss the meeting with anyone.

Johnson did not see Gove's intervention in such a pure or positive way. The prime minister afterwards told only a handful of his inner circle what Gove had said and was 'absolutely furious' – particularly at the timing. Many saw it as Gove's final, ultimate treachery. One close colleague said, 'It was a deliberate knife in the front before a key moment'. Another claimed that the Gove meeting 'fucked his mindset' ahead of the Commons: 'Wednesday morning is all about the psychology of the PMQs and Gove knew exactly what he was doing.' Johnson's aides were equally angry. 'Literally before he's about to do PMQs, he's stabbed him in the fucking back – again,' one said. Then, in one of the most totally bizarre moments of a tumultuous day, Gove joined the prime minister's questions preparation session at 10.30 a.m. as if nothing had happened.

Johnson's special advisor Leonora Campbell role-played Keir Starmer as normal. Gove, who had told Johnson a mere ten minutes before that he should quit, made several observations on how to deal with difficult questions about his future. One aide asked how he would respond if Rishi Sunak popped up to ask something. Guto Harri responded, 'Oh I'm sure he's living in California already' and started humming 'All I Wanna Do' by Sheryl Crow which includes the line 'Until the sun comes up over Santa Monica Boulevard'. Not everyone was willing to go along with the charade: Nigel Adams entered the PMQs prep session knowing what had happened in Johnson's meeting with Gove, saw Gove was present, and walked straight back out.

After the preparation session, Gove returned to his ministry across Westminster and told colleagues that Johnson had 'utterly lost it' and had gone 'mad'. Johnson went to the House of Commons for what would be his penultimate prime minister's questions. That lunchtime, Johnson was determined to carry on through sheer effort of will. He felt the storm would pass, as so many others had. One colleague recalled a conversation Johnson had with Geoffrey Cox, the attorney general, during the 2019

Brexit wars in parliament. The lawyer said to him at one stage, 'Prime minister, you just can't do that.' Johnson replied, 'Geoffrey all my life people have been telling me "you can't do that". And I've always proven them wrong.'

***

Prime minister's questions is one of the most divisive aspects of Westminster politics. To its detractors, it is the worst kind of ya-boo politics, where serious debate is substituted for cheap laughs, petty point scoring and childlike behaviour by MPs. For its supporters, it is a vital moment of accountability, where every week both party leaders are put under intense scrutiny for half an hour to assess their capabilities and standing. Are their policy positions coherent? Can they rival their opponent with their arguments and rhetoric? And, most crucially, does the leader have their MPs behind them? The volume of support – in cheers, the customary Tory shouts of 'yeah yeah yeah' and the 'ahhs!' at moments of surprise – can make or break a leader's momentum. It scarcely matters outside the political bubble, but has a lot of traction within it.

When Johnson slid onto the green benches that Wednesday lunchtime, the response was muted from Conservative MPs. His most loyal supporters – ministers Nadine Dorries and Jacob Rees-Mogg on the frontbench, MPs such as Conor Burns, James Duddridge further behind – attempted to muster some customary cheers. But from the moment he arrived, it was palpably clear that Johnson's political authority was rapidly draining. From the press gallery, the government benches looked glum, the opposition side of the Commons were openly laughing at Johnson, perhaps the most damaging response for a leader to be receiving.

Keir Starmer began by reading out, chapter and verse, the allegations against Chris Pincher. He wanted to 'remind people propping up this PM how serious it is'. The question he then posed to Johnson was: 'Why did the prime minister promote Chris Pincher knowing he had been guilty of predatory behaviour?' Johnson replied that Pincher was no longer whip and was under investigation over the complaints, before adding that he 'abhors' the abuse of power, in his or any other party. Having dodged the specific question, Starmer tried again asking why he was promoted. He also asked whether Johnson had used the phrase 'Pincher by name, Pincher by nature'. Once again, Johnson dodged the question and said he was not going to 'trivialise the matter' and he reiterated, 'I greatly regret that he continued in office.' His lame efforts to pivot to 'hearing about other jobs' and new employment figures fell flat.

Starmer remained lawyerly focused, noting that Johnson had not denied using the 'Pincher by name' phrase. His fire was turned back on Conservative MPs, who he claimed were acting as if the Pincher scandal 'did not matter'. Johnson responded he had acted immediately by removing the whip (this was not true, he had waited almost twenty-four hours before kicking Pincher out of the Tory party). The opposition leader moved onto the mass of resignations, describing it as 'the first instance of sinking ships fleeing the rat'. Johnson tried to rebut Starmer by stating he had no right to talk about integrity as he had campaigned for Jeremy Corbyn to be prime minister; that he voted forty times against Brexit; and that he had faced a police investigation over the beergate saga. 'Pathetic,' Starmer responded, to a torrent of jeers from the Labour benches. Such attacks had worked for Johnson six weeks ago, whipping up cheers from his backbenchers, but now they were met in almost silence.

The opposition leader summed up the Pincher affair as 'awful behaviour, unacceptable in any walk of life ... he ignored it'. Starmer said the Tories remaining in his government were 'the charge of the lightweight brigade' – a line that even Johnson found amusing. He painfully went through all of Downing Street's shifting stances on Pincher, dismissing the prime minister's team as 'a Z-list cast of nodding dogs'. Struggling to find an adequate response, all Johnson could muster was that he wanted to 'get on with our job' and focus on topics that he felt mattered to the public. Starmer wrapped up the session by referring back to his days as director of public prosecutions and listening to evidence of victims, like those alleged to have been abused by Pincher. Johnson's finale was stating that eight of Labour's shadow Cabinet ministers voted to get rid of Trident nuclear deterrent. Again, it fell flat.

The two most damaging moments came during questions from his own team. First, ex-minister Tim Loughton asked Johnson if he could think of 'any circumstances in which he should resign?' The prime minister stated that if he was unable to help the people of Ukraine or deliver on his mandate then he might go – a hint that being unable to form a government might prove to be a red line. Then Gary Sambrook, the Conservative MP for Birmingham Northfield and a member of the 1922 executive, in a truly shocking interjection, recalled an exchange in the member's tearoom when Johnson had said openly: 'There were seven people, MPs, in the Carlton Club last week and one of them should have tried to intervene to stop Chris from drinking so much.' In complete silence, Sambrook went on, 'As if that wasn't insulting enough to the people who did try and intervene that night. And then also to the victims that drink was the problem.' He called on Johnson to 'take responsibility' and quit.

And for good measure, one last senior Tory called on Johnson to quit. David Davis, the former Brexit secretary, reiterated a sentiment he had made back in January, during the peak of the first partygate crisis. Davis had reiterated one of the most iconic lines in British political history, from Leo Amery (quoting Oliver Cromwell) speaking to former prime minister Neville Chamberlain in the famous Norway debate: 'You have sat there too long for all the good you have done. In the name of God, go.' On this occasion, he was more muted: 'I ask him to do the honourable thing and put the interests of the nation before his own interests.'

Immediately after PMQs came a personal statement from Sajid Javid. Every resigning Cabinet minister is granted their moment to have a say in the House of Commons and while Rishi Sunak did not put his name forward, the outgoing health secretary took up the opportunity. Mutters among MPs that morning were that Javid was hoping to reiterate what Geoffrey Howe, the former foreign secretary, had done to Margaret Thatcher in November 1990, when his devastating critique hastened the end of her premiership. Javid did not reach those heights, but his speech was another deep blow: he recalled the prayer breakfast the morning before, where the Reverend Les Isaac spoke. 'I will never risk losing my integrity,' Javid said. 'I believe a team is only as good as a team captain and a captain is only as good as their team, so loyalty has to go both ways. Events of recent months have made it increasingly difficult to be in that team.' The former health secretary warned that 'the problem starts at the top' with the prime minister. He told MPs: 'At some point, we have to conclude that enough is enough. I believe that point is now.' Johnson was forced to sit and listen to his speech, stony-faced.

And still the ministerial resignations continued – so much so that Sky News began a rolling ticker in the corner of the screen throughout that day's news coverage. One minute into PMQs, Jo Churchill resigned[9] as a junior environment minister with a personal attack on Johnson: 'Recent events have shown integrity, competence and judgement are all essential to the role of prime minister, while a jocular self-serving approach is bound to have its limitations.' Soon after PMQs finished, housing minister Stuart Andrew was the next to go:[10] 'Our party, particularly our members and more importantly our great country, deserve better.' But the most consequential resignation came at 2.24 p.m. when five prominent ministers from the 2017 intake quit as a group: Kemi Badenoch, Lee Rowley, Neil O'Brien, Julia Lopez and Alex Burghart. These ministers were seen as central to the future of the party. When Gove told Johnson some of the best Tory MPs were due to quit, he may have had Badenoch and O'Brien in mind, both having served in his department. The MPs wrote, 'It has become increasingly clear that the government cannot function given the issues that have come to light and the way in which they have been handled. In good faith, we must ask that, for the good of the party and the country, you step aside.' Johnson was said to be 'particularly hurt' by Burghart giving his notice as he had formerly served his chief parliamentary aide. Just twenty minutes later, at 2.47 p.m., the former international trade secretary Liam Fox withdrew his support. At the exact same moment, employment minister Mims Davies also resigned.[11]

After PMQs, the Downing Street press team gathered for their usual huddle with political journalists outside the Commons chamber. They were bombarded with question after question about Johnson's future. His press secretary claimed he still maintained the support of a majority of MPs. Would Johnson fight a confidence vote? 'Yes.' Did the prime minister think he could win a confidence vote? 'Yes.' Would new ministers be appointed? 'Yes, over the coming days.' But events were overtaking Downing Street's narrative: as the press briefing took place, John Stevens of the *Daily Mail* broke the news[12] that Gove had visited Johnson that morning and told him to quit.

Back in Downing Street, the mood shifted to disbelief as it became apparent that it would be impossible to fill the widening ministerial gaps opening up in his government. 'It was absolutely insane,' one aide said. 'That feeling only got stronger and stronger as the day went by.' Another close Johnson ally said after PMQs, 'It was done by this point, it was irrelevant what happened next because the course of events was set.' After the solemn response from MPs to Johnson's lacklustre Commons performance, the mood in the Tory party whips' office was bleak. 'That lunchtime was when I started getting really anxious that this could be it,' one insider said.

Yet Johnson disregarded the chaos unfurling around him and focused on his next duty: a two-hour appearance in front of parliament's liaison committee. Roughly three times a year, the prime minister of the day appears in front of a special committee formed of select committee chairs to take evidence on any topics the senior MPs see fit. Even in happier times, for Johnson these sessions were testy affairs, where rivals would seek to take chunks out of him and he would sometimes struggle with policy detail. It was already proven to be far from his best speaking platform. Hunkered down in his House of Commons office, Johnson prepared for two hours for the approaching session with his team, seeking to ignore the resignations going on around them – a 'totally surreal' situation one person present recalled. Johnson was not on his best form either, one official present said: 'It was a dire prep session. The boss wasn't being given good enough or accurate enough information, and his answers weren't forensic enough.'

The session commenced at 3 p.m. Johnson was immediately asked whether it would be possible for his government to function with thirty resignations; he responded there was a 'wealth of talent' on the Tory benches. Stephen Crabb, the former work and pensions secretary, mooted that he might struggle to replace those who had gone. Given the unfolding background news, and the sense that the government was collapsing about him, the committee afforded a strange experience to those watching. Johnson was having to answer detailed questions about policy and world events, such as grain supply in the Bosporus and the phasing out of petrol cars by 2030, yet there was an increasing sense that unless he was able to urgently respond to the flood of resigning MPs these were issues he was unlikely to be in office to deal with. As his core political team watched the session in his House of Commons office, the mood was 'grim' as the news of more resignations came through.

Johnson was questioned as to whether he would require the Queen's permission to call an election, or whether he would inform her, an indication some MPs were becoming concerned at some of the rumours emanating from his supporters. He dodged the question and said no one wanted an election. He was asked how important the truth was. 'Very important,' Johnson responded. At the session, as well as Ukraine and partygate, Pincher was a constant topic: Johnson acknowledged what had been obvious to all of his colleagues for nearly a week, Number 10 should have immediately established a timeline about the Pincher matter and it was 'by mistake' that many of the government's public responses had been incorrect.

As the liaison committee session drew to a close, with two more ministers resigning during proceedings, Labour MP Darren Jones informed Johnson that the BBC, Sky News and *The Times* had reported that a delegation of Cabinet ministers were waiting for him back at Downing Street, likely to tell him that his position was untenable. 'So you say,' he retorted. Jones was right: over the two agonising hours of questioning, some of the most senior members of Johnson's government had gathered, demanding to see him as soon as possible. Johnson was soon back in his motorcade on his way to hear what they had to say.

***

When Johnson arrived at Downing Street the atmosphere at Number 10 was sombre, with some staff in tears realising that the end was in sight. His deputy chief of staff David Canzini confirmed that half a dozen Cabinet ministers were waiting upstairs to see him. The cabal consisted of chancellor Nadhim Zahawi and education secretary Michelle Donelan – both of whom had been appointed by Johnson less than twenty-four hours ago – with Wales secretary Simon Hart and policing minister Kit Malthouse. Some of Johnson's staunchest defenders also visited Number 10 during the Wednesday evening: transport secretary Grant Shapps, who saved Johnson several times with his spreadsheet of loyalty, international trade secretary Anne-Marie Trevelyan and home secretary Priti Patel.

Northern Ireland secretary Brandon Lewis also wanted to see him, but was flying back from Belfast, while business secretary Kwasi Kwarteng had made it known he thought Johnson should step aside. Of the most senior ministers in his Cabinet, only foreign secretary Liz Truss did not tell Number 10 that Johnson should go, but then handily she was in Indonesia for a G20 foreign ministers' summit. With such a breadth of ministers calling time on his premiership, it was difficult to see how he could continue.

But the prime minister was not giving up. During the afternoon, a team had been scrambled to a cosy but well-appointed room known as the study – Margaret Thatcher's favourite place to work, where Johnson had punched the air to celebrate his 2019 election victory. The gathering became known as 'The Bunker' and featured members of all of Johnson's support networks including the Big Dog team, the Brains Trust and his closest Number 10 advisors, assembled for one final heave to try and save his premiership.

From the Big Dog team, there was Nigel Adams, minister without portfolio and Johnson's chief fixer, Conservative party HQ's Ross Kempsell, chief whip Chris Heaton-Harris and his aide Charlotte Owen. From the Brains Trust, Tory strategist Lynton Crosby was in communication from Australia, his protégé Isaac Levido was present, plus Will Lewis, Johnson's former editor and friend. And from the Number 10 team, director of communications Guto Harri was present along with political aides Declan Lyons and Ben Gascoigne. Plenty of others attempted to join, knocking on the door to try and influence what was happening but everyone was denied entry in an effort to control the chaos. Shelley Williams-Walker, Number 10's head of operations, drew up a cast list and gave it to one of the building's custodians to keep nonessential aides away.

While the prime minister was taking questions from the liaison committee, The Bunker team had assembled a list of everyone who had not quit and remained loyal to Johnson. Will Lewis looked at the list and stated, 'This is enough, it's a lot of names we've got here.' Number 10 also asked the Cabinet Office just how small a government could be and still function. One Whitehall official said, 'We looked at whether to go for a broad reshuffle or slim it down to the bare minimum.'

But some in The Bunker had privately concluded the exercise was in vain – and perhaps for the first time this was something that Johnson himself had begun to privately moot to a select number of people when he returned to Number 10 at 5.30 p.m. 'Once he came back from liaison, he was making the decision that it was over. Boris wasn't saying it out loud to many people, but he was talking about how futile the situation was becoming.'

Before Johnson could see the waiting ministers, two other meetings took precedence. The first was with Graham Brady, chair of the 1922 Committee. The committee's official rules meant Johnson was technically safe from another challenge until June 2023. With tremendous pressures for another ballot, however, its executive committee had met that afternoon. The eighteen-strong group expected Brady to propose changing the rules for another contest, yet he was concerned about the legitimacy of such a move, given that the executive's year-long term had almost finished. He had an alternative: the 1922 would bring forward its annual elections to the following Monday, which would renew their mandate from Tory MPs, before rule change was discussed. One senior Tory said, 'Graham thought it looked dreadful that we were pushing out the dregs of our year in elected office on something so important.' His proposal was agreed.

At 6 p.m., Brady strode determinedly in his trademark royal blue suit out of the parliamentary estate and past the Red Lion pub filled with early-evening drinkers, in the direction of Downing Street. In a failed effort to avoid photographers, he circled up the right-hand side of Whitehall, crossing the road, and returning back down towards the Cabinet Office's white palace at Number 70. He avoided walking up Downing Street, conscious of the image he would create entering the famous black door. After walking through the Cabinet Office to Number 10 – through the notorious link door that physically separates the political side of government from the civil service – Brady went into the Cabinet Room to see Johnson at around 6.15 p.m.

The pair sat opposite each other, with chief whip Chris Heaton-Harris at the far end of the long table taking notes. The mood was business-like, with little of Johnson's jovial patter. The prime minister was expecting Brady to tell him that the rules had been changed and another confidence vote was happening. Instead, Brady explained the decision to elect a new 1922 executive, with the outcome due in five days. But Brady gravely told Johnson this was far from a reprieve: 'In my honest assessment, given the mood in the parliamentary party, it is inconceivable that the new executive would be more averse to changing the rules.' Brady informed Johnson it was 'almost inevitable' a vote of confidence would take place on the Tuesday. 'It is fairly obvious you would lose it,' he added.

The prospect of pushing the leadership question into the following week gave Johnson an opening to keep going. The prime minister was in a 'firm frame of mind', Downing Street insiders said, up for a fightback against MPs. He delivered Brady a robust defence of his record; speaking of 'all the great things' he still had left to do with the 2019 election mandate. 'Boris was firmly of the view that if Conservative MPs wanted to stand in his way and prevent him from fulfilling his duties to the British people, they should be made to do it. They should have a confidence vote,' one ally said. Brady politely told him, 'It would be better for the country, the party and for you personally if you didn't push it to that point.'

Johnson's allies had discussed and prepared for such an outcome and their solution was to try and rebalance the 1922 Committee in his favour, hoping they could thwart a rule change and confidence vote. The political team decided early on not to challenge Brady but to take a shot at replacing two vice chairs: William Wragg and Nus Ghani, both arch Johnson critics. They instead supported the candidacy of Sheryll Murray and Miriam Cates, MPs deeply loyal to the prime minister. One senior member of the 1922 said, 'Their assumption was they were going to heave out the disloyal people.' But the collapse of Johnson's standing in the party made such efforts futile – in fact, it risked emboldening the anti-Johnson factions.

Brady bid the prime minister farewell just before 6.30 p.m. and left Downing Street in a pre-booked car – just as he had done following his fateful meeting with Theresa May in 2019 – to avoid media attention. Brady promised the prime minister he would not speak to journalists about their meeting and a formal announcement was made that the 1922 executive elections would take place the following week. Later that evening, though, the substance of Brady's meeting leaked, much to his annoyance. James Duddridge, Johnson's parliamentary private secretary, was later heard boasting on the House of Commons terrace to MPs, 'We're calling Graham Brady's bluff.' But the chief whip told[13] Johnson that Brady was correct: he no longer had the numbers to win a confidence vote.

Before returning to The Bunker, Johnson spoke to the Queen at his weekly audience with her. Whereas most items in the prime minister's diary are flexible, the constitutional link between Downing Street and the monarch is not. 'It's a diary fixture every Wednesday evening at 6.30 p.m., he just had to do that,' one senior official said. No one except Johnson and the monarch know what was discussed on that phone call, although it seems implausible that his dire political situation was not a topic. The timing of their chat, however, stoked fears among Tory MPs that Johnson was about to make one last throw of the dice and to try and call a general election.

One of Johnson's inner circle confirmed 'every possibility' was war-gamed in The Bunker, including a snap poll. One person involved said, 'The election was mentioned because the thing that freaks out the 2019 MPs the most is the idea of an election. They're terrified because they've never been back to their patches at the ballot box.' An ally of Johnson confirmed it was 'inevitable' that the idea was discussed in the final hours. Jacob Rees-Mogg, Brexit opportunities minister, made it clear to colleagues that he thought the idea was unwise. Johnson rejected the proposal, according to those present. 'It was never going to happen,' one ally said.

However, such were the fears within Whitehall that Johnson may do something reckless if his position was threatened that secret planning had taken place in the preceding months at the most discrete and deep levels of the British state, in case he asked the Queen to dissolve parliament. In the lead-up to Johnson's final days, there was much media chatter about the Lascelles Principles: a constitutional convention from 1950 that defined the circumstances in which a monarch could reject a prime minister's request for an election. From 2011 to 2022, the sovereign's prerogative power to dissolve parliament was handed to politicians through the Fixed-term Parliament Act – a wholly destructive invention that set an election for every five years and was responsible for much of the turmoil during the Brexit wars. In one of his more welcome legacies, Johnson's government revoked the legislation and the de facto power returned to the monarch.

The Lascelles Principles were defined by Alan 'Tommy' Lascelles, King George VI's private secretary, in a pseudonymous letter[14] (under the sobriquet 'Senex') to *The Times*. He set out the three criteria when an election request could be rightly rejected:

1. The existing parliament was still vital, viable, and capable of doing its job.
2. A general election would be detrimental to the national economy.

3. He [the King] could rely on finding another prime minister who could carry on his Government, for a reasonable
period, with a working majority in the House of Commons.

Even during the chaos of Johnson's final days, all three of those
conditions would have surely been met. Parliament was still
viable, thanks to the Conservative party's eighty-seat majority
and there was no danger it would lose a confidence vote – MPs
were terrified of being wiped out by Labour. Soaring inflation
and the cost of living crisis would mean that a six-week campaign
would harm the economy. And there were plenty of viable interim
Tory leadership contenders who could have commanded a majority in the House of Commons.

How would this have been communicated to Johnson? For the
Queen to reject an election request outright would have prompted
a full-blown constitutional crisis and have put the monarch in the
most perilous position of her reign. One senior Whitehall figure
said, 'It was a question that couldn't be put to the Queen because
the Queen would have to say "yes". The PM cannot ask the question to which she ought to say "no" by the convention.' Instead, a
'magic triangle' of senior establishment figures had ensured it
would never reach that point. Graham Brady, representing the
parliamentary Conservative party, Simon Case heading up the
civil service, and the Queen's chief courtier Edward Young had
private channels of communication to ensure safeguards were in
place. This scenario had been discussed previously between
Brady, Case and Young when Theresa May's premiership hit the
buffers in 2019. During that time, Brady worked with Buckingham Palace to ensure the leadership timetable would minimise
inconvenience for the Queen.

As Johnson's grip on power became more precarious, one
senior Whitehall insider said of the moment, 'If there was an

effort to call an election, Tory MPs would have expected Brady to communicate to the Palace that we would be holding a vote of confidence in the very near future and that it might make sense for Her Majesty to be unavailable for a day.' Another senior official confirmed it would be politely communicated to Downing Street that Her Majesty 'couldn't come to the phone' had Johnson requested a call with the intention of dissolving parliament. One senior government figure said the 'magic triangle' had such a scenario mapped out. 'The Queen would never be asked a question to which she will say "no" to, because the magic triangle will ensure that the prime minister doesn't ask.' One Johnson ally said he knew it was a fruitless idea too, that 'the Palace would have wanted to see if there were others who could command confidence instead of accepting his call'.

At this juncture, Brady would have been politely asked by the Palace if his party could decide on another leader who would have parliament's confidence. All the guidance was informal and never tested, as Johnson opted not to push the election button.

Aside from a snap election, another idea mooted in The Bunker was whether a rule change by the 1922 Committee could be legally challenged. That again was swiftly ruled out, given that past legal opinion confirmed the Conservative party does not have locus on the committee and how it operates – the '22 is a members' association without a constitution that is run on convention. The only formal element is its chair, who has a place on the Tory party board. 'It would be like standing outside a golf club, of which you are not a member, and dictating its new constitution,' one senior Tory said.

The last bold move discussed in The Bunker was another major apology outside Downing Street by Johnson for his handling of the Pincher affair. 'That was quickly rejected because we'd already done about fifty of them,' one official said.

While Johnson spoke to Brady and then the Queen, The Bunker was preparing options to form a new government. Yet the resignations were totting up: by 7 p.m., thirty-nine ministers had quit government. At one point, Scotland secretary Alister Jack entered the study to ask whether Ruth Edwards, his parliamentary private secretary, was on the list. One official responded, 'I don't think she's loyal anymore.' Jack insisted she was – 'No, no she's still viable.' A few ministers later, he returned to the room, asked for Ruth Edwards's name, and tore the paper in half. She had just resigned from the government.

But it seemed the only option left for Johnson was to try and rebuild his government. Before that, though, he would have to see the ministers who had been waiting several tedious hours for a private audience with him. He returned to his study to prepare to see these colleagues, or the 'self-appointed death squad' as one of his aides called them.

***

The small dining room can be found on the second floor of Downing Street, above the prime minister's office and the Cabinet Room, and a couple of corridors along from the study, which had become The Bunker. Stewing in and around this wood-panelled room for nearly three hours, with increasingly cold pots of tea, were Nadhim Zahawi, Anne-Marie Trevelyan, Grant Shapps, Simon Hart, Michelle Donelan and Kit Malthouse. After separately voicing their disquiet to Chris Heaton-Harris over the events engulfing Johnson, Heaton-Harris had invited them all to Downing Street. The security convention that phones should be left at the entrance of Number 10 had been abandoned, as the ministers oscillated between watching Johnson's liaison committee appearance, looking at social media, reading the news, and

WhatsApping MPs and their private offices with thoughts about when the government would collapse.

Number 10 aides were sent to mind the ministers, trying to ensure they did not work themselves up into more of a frenzy. Simone Finn, deputy chief of staff, took turns with Charlotte Owen, an aide to Johnson and the chief whip. One official who witnessed the scene said, 'There was the most awkward silence, it was like a tea party. We kept pouring more and more cold tea because we had to do something. Because the aides were there, they didn't want to talk amongst themselves.' The ministers and officials tried to make light conversation. There was frustration in The Bunker team that the ministers refused to leave.

David Canzini, deputy chief of staff, popped into the dining room on a number of occasions and according to those present he pulled ministers aside and muttered that he too privately felt the PM needed to resign. The Downing Street team had begun to split: the likes of Canzini wanted to focus on a handover time-table while the Big Dog team wanted to fight till the very end. Others who felt he must stay on included Andrew Griffith, head of the Number 10 policy unit, director of communications Guto Harri, and Ben Elliot, Tory party chairman (who popped into the dining room). As Wednesday afternoon drifted into the evening, the scene became more fraught; no one was sure exactly why they were being made to wait so long and what the prime minister was doing. News of his discussion with Brady had not made it up the staircase.

Those present assumed they would be seeing Johnson as a group. Along with Johnson's strategist Ross Kempsell, the chief whip Chris Heaton-Harris decided, however, that they should go in and see Johnson one by one – an echo of the Cabinet proces-sion which went in and saw Margaret Thatcher individually as she questioned their loyalty. 'By going in one by one, he was able to make slightly different pitches to everybody,' one Cabinet minister said. 'Had we all gone in as Chris Heaton-Harris had originally planned, it would have been over by 6 p.m. on Wednesday evening. The PM would have gracefully left, but they rolled the dice another time.'

Before the ministerial meetings began, the consensus in the small dining room was that it was over for Johnson and the chats would be about persuading him to exit gracefully. One minister said, 'There was not a single person in the [dining] room, not one, who suggested that the PM should stay, with the possible exception of Ben Elliot.' The person added that even firm loyalists such as Anne-Marie Trevelyan and Priti Patel had concluded it was done. 'There was no dissent between any of us that the number was up.' Before the audiences took place, though, Johnson told his aides he was not rolling over. 'His view was "I'm not going, if they want me gone, they're going to need to dip their hands in blood and do it themselves,"' one aide said. The meetings may have slowed down Johnson's exit, but did not stave it off. Having lost the support of the Cabinet, his public bullishness did not tally with the reality of the situation.

One of the ministers insisted to Johnson that even if he survived this crisis, there were many others ahead. One told him, 'We're going to be going through this agony over Christmas and the New Year, a little more than a year out from the 2024 election.' The calculation of those gathered was that they needed to cooperate quickly 'in order to give as much opportunity as they could to repair the situation, bed down a new regime, and put all of this behind them so they had a possibility of a compelling argument'. Johnson's base within the party had been almost entirely transactional, based on his election appeal. With that gone, his closest colleagues turned on him.

The first minister to see Johnson was Nadhim Zahawi.

According to those who waited with the newly appointed chancellor, he was the most emphatic that Johnson should quit, and that despite his patronage he was the 'leading advocate for instant resignation' as one colleague said. Facing Johnson and with his fixer Nigel Adams present, Zahawi was full of brio and confidently told Johnson that it was over. Yet the prime minister persuaded him that there remained a path through. The pair returned to their favoured topic of economic reform and agreed to a joint major speech in the coming days. 'By the end of the meeting they were shaking hands, hugging, and saying they were going to launch a new financial strategy,' one insider said.

Zahawi was not seen again by the ministerial delegation and returned straight to the Treasury. The first the delegation heard of how it had gone was when it emerged that the chancellor was planning a joint press conference with the prime minister. 'We were a little bit surprised, given Nadhim Zahawi's vociferous position on all of this,' a minister said. Next in to see Johnson was Grant Shapps, transport secretary, who was 'reasonable' and did not say he should go, but argued the situation was problematic. When news filtered through to The Bunker that Shapps was part of the group, the aides were particularly dispirited. 'The moment that killed me was when Grant came in,' one official said. 'I thought, if Grant thinks it's done, it's done.'

Two of the meetings were particularly long and did not reach a firm conclusion. Education secretary Michelle Donelan was in with Johnson for 'absolutely ages' and caused much chagrin. 'She fucking U-turned massively and went in saying she wanted to give up the education job,' one official said. Johnson responded in disbelief saying, 'You were only just appointed to it twenty-four hours ago!' She rapidly climbed down and remained in post for that evening. Policing minister Kit Malthouse was in with Johnson for the longest period, almost an hour. 'He was waffling on and on about whether he did or didn't support him. He obviously didn't but it was going around the houses,' one aide said. Another person said Malthouse, who had been a deputy mayor during Johnson's stint in City Hall, went in to tell him that it was over but was convinced otherwise. Meanwhile, The Bunker became increasingly irritated by David Canzini, who, as one person there recalled, 'was talking with these secretaries of state, talking bollocks . . . saying "He's a goner" while we're downstairs convincing them to stay'.

Priti Patel, home secretary, became upset during her audience. She did not tell Johnson to go but said she concluded it was over. 'She didn't put the knife in,' one insider said. More Cabinet ministers arrived for informal chats with Johnson, including the deputy prime minister, Dominic Raab. Raab awkwardly told Number 10 staffers he had to attend a white-tie dinner at Mansion House that evening, but required assistance with the outfit. An attendant was found with the skills to fix his bow tie. After he was dressed he saw Johnson, who found his outfit highly amusing. One insider said Raab offered a rare moment of levity: 'Are you actually going to walk out of the front door to the world's media in white tie?' Johnson asked, and Raab responded, 'You're finding this far too funny.' He ended up exiting the building by a side entrance.

Throughout the meetings, culture secretary and Johnson loyalist to the end, Nadine Dorries, was ever-present in the corridors of Number 10 together with his policy chief Andrew Griffith, drumming up enthusiasm and discussing how to keep the PM in place. Not everyone appreciated their efforts. 'It was blind loyalty to the PM. They were nodding dogs, completely lacking any sort of common sense,' one senior official said. Later that evening, one of the last ministers to see Johnson was Wales secretary Simon Hart, who had waited close to five hours in the upstairs dining room. Their meeting was to prove one of the more consequential that evening.

When Hart eventually saw Johnson, the prime minister told him: 'I've got a plan, just give me till Tuesday. I can turn this around. We owe it to the fourteen million people who voted for us.' The minister responded, 'I love your optimism but I don't think we're there anymore. That was an argument that might have worked six weeks or six months ago. But I think we're past that point.' Hart told Johnson that if the 1922 Committee didn't move against him soon, they would find a way to 'nail you to the floor one way or another'. He then pointed to the privileges committee investigation in the autumn. 'Every time we do this, we lose more ground, we lose more credibility and we're getting ever closer to an election. I think the game is up,' Hart said.

By now, it was dawning on Johnson that his hopes were shrinking. 'I realise I've only got a tiny chance of survival but it's one I prefer to take,' the prime minister said. As Hart left Downing Street, he pulled Heaton-Harris aside and handed him his resignation letter. 'If circumstances have altered overnight and he comes to the view this is unsustainable, chuck my letter in the bin and we'll say no more about it. But if this thing is still raging in the morning, I will have to step aside.' Heaton-Harris thanked him for not quitting that night and Hart left for the pub for a much-needed pint with his special advisor.

The press office briefed that evening[15] that Johnson had told ministers, 'It was a choice between a summer focused on economic growth, or chaos of a leadership contest followed by massive pressure for a general election' that would mean[16] 'almost certain defeat.' Journalists were also briefed that Johnson believed a lost general election would break up Britain, thanks to a potential Labour–Scottish nationalist coalition. 'He's not going to resign and he has a lot of things he wants to say this weekend before we even get to any [confidence] vote,'[17] one ally said. But the ministers had uniformly delivered the same message: his political authority was shot and regaining it would be impossible. If he did not go, some (like Simon Hart) hinted they would have to quit. Just as with Thatcher, the ministerial delegation had made the decisive difference. He would fight on for a few more hours, but Johnson realised there was likely no way out. He returned to The Bunker to see if it still might be possible to form a new government.

***

Upstairs in the study, The Bunker officials had wheeled out the reshuffle whiteboard and had begun planning to fill the empty slots within the government. The number of resignations had risen above forty and, although no further Cabinet ministers had quit, they needed to find new secretaries of state for Wales and Northern Ireland (the prime minister had not seen Brandon Lewis but anticipated he would quit). The Bunker team spoke to James Cleverly, a Johnson stalwart at the Foreign Office, who agreed he would take education. Shailesh Vara, who had previously served as a junior Northern Ireland minister, was lined up to take over the secretary of state role if Lewis went. 'Boris popped in to say "yes" and sign off all these roles,' one official said. 'We had to have a functioning Cabinet that night, whatever happened.' After Steve Barclay had moved to health secretary, a new Cabinet Office minister was also required.

There was one other Cabinet-level change Johnson was adamant to pursue immediately. Johnson had festered throughout the day about Michael Gove's pre-PMQs intervention and decided he wanted revenge. With the events of 2016 back in his mind, Johnson decided to boot out his levelling up secretary.

'That was his decision alone,' one ally said. 'It was the pre-PMQs meeting: the PM felt he was very treacherous, an unnecessary personal blow on a day that was clearly terminal. Boris felt he really didn't need to do that.' A rumour had arrived at The Bunker that Gove was to resign that evening, fuelling Johnson's ire. The prime minister was urged, 'Don't let him do this, you need to fire him.' So he left the study with Guto Harri and Nigel Adams to call up Gove.

Gove had spent the rest of Wednesday in his department, avoiding a Commons vote at 7 p.m. 'He didn't think he would be a welcome presence in the voting lobbies,' one colleague said. He had returned to his official residence at One Carlton Gardens just off Pall Mall. He invited several friends, including Theodore Agnew, a Tory peer who had resigned from Johnson's government over its failure to address Covid fraud, for drinks and to chew over the day's trauma. Gove noticed a missed call from Johnson on his phone at around 9.20 p.m. and several with no caller ID, which he assumed to be the Downing Street switchboard.

He returned the calls and asked Johnson if he was resigning. 'No Mikey mate, I'm afraid you are. I'm going to have to ask you to step back from your role as levelling up secretary. I'm reconstructing the government.' In shock, Gove replied, 'So you're not resigning?' Johnson said, 'No, you are.' Gove told him, 'No, I think it should be you. I think you have lost the confidence of the party.' Johnson disagreed and told him, 'I'm sure you can understand after our conversation this morning.' He wrapped up the call by thanking him for his service. Gove, bewildered, told his colleagues Johnson had lost it: 'Poor Boris is going to be gone tomorrow, so there's no particular point me doing anything.'

Number 10 took glee in the sacking, telling[18] the media, 'You cannot have a snake who is not with you on any of the big arguments who then gleefully briefs the press that he has called for the leader to go.' Gove's aides strongly denied leaking his meeting with the prime minister that morning. Johnson's allies also briefed out they believed Gove had been plotting for weeks previously. The 'snake' comment, though, was unpopular among some senior figures in Number 10, who wondered if Guto Harri had acted alone. 'I thought the whole affair was uncivilised, especially the aggressive briefings. Whether you like him or not, Gove has contributed massively to Conservative politics over the last decade.'

Johnson returned to The Bunker and to reconstructing his government. Eventually, Brandon Lewis arrived at Downing Street. Johnson ducked out to perform the same turnaround job on the Northern Ireland secretary that had worked on Kit Malthouse, Nadhim Zahawi and Michelle Donelan. Not only did Lewis maintain his job, but he was able to blag a promotion. Despite the tight security in the study, Lewis breezed into the room and took a look at the reshuffle board. Sensing the weakness of the team that was being assembled, Lewis argued he should get a grander job and was offered Chancellor of the Duchy of Lancaster and Cabinet Office minister. He initially accepted and went home.

With the 10 p.m. news bulletin approaching, Team Johnson wanted to have new ministers to announce and to stabilise his standing. Die-hard supporter Nadine Dorries took to social media to state Johnson was going to carry on:[19] 'The PM's priority is to stabilise the government, set a clear direction for the country and continue to deliver on the promises he made and the British public voted for.' James Duddridge, Johnson's parliamentary aide, gave an interview to Sky News, fresh from the House of Commons terrace, where he insisted new ministers including 'major appointments' would be announced that night. The Number 10 press team, however, had gone home. 'There was no point hanging around for something that was never going to happen. We were ready to announce stuff but it transpired rapidly, there was nothing to announce,' one official said.

As the minutes ticked down, the phone calls became increasingly frantic. The Cabinet secretary Simon Case advised The Bunker that Buckingham Palace would soon be unable to approve the appointments that night. Johnson faced the prospect of further ministers resigning and the nation waking up on Thursday 7 July to a half-empty government. Johnson's team were struggling to persuade MPs to take up the jobs; it was reaching the point where he could not form a credible government. Greg Hands, energy minister, was apparently dragged into Downing Street from a dinner in Chelsea to be offered the post of party chairman. He refused. And still the resignations continued, reaching forty-three by 10 p.m.

The Bunker made a major misstep at this point, which resulted in an immediate Cabinet resignation. Simon Hart received a call from his chum David TC Davies, the junior Welsh office minister, who said he had been asked to go to Number 10 to succeed him as secretary of state. 'I didn't think you'd resigned,' Davies told Hart, who responded, 'I haven't.' Davies said he would not take the role and thought it was 'disgraceful' they were trying to ease him out. Hart thanked him and said, 'You go do whatever, you're not obliged to show me any loyalty.' Number 10 assumed Hart would quit in the morning but among all the chaos they had acted too soon.

Hart left the pub and called up Chris Heaton-Harris, fuming 'You've already offered my job to someone else, so we might as well call it quits now.' The chief whip profusely apologised and said it should not have happened. Hart sat on a park bench to tweet his resignation letter, when a Tory apparition appeared in the form of Charles Moore, Johnson's former *Telegraph* editor who had organised the Garrick Club dinner the previous October. Moore asked Hart, 'Oh Simon, what are you up to this evening?' He responded, 'If you wait fifteen seconds, I'm literally resigning.' Hart's letter on Twitter said:[20] 'Colleagues have done their utmost in private and public to help you turn the ship around, but it is with sadness that I feel we have passed the point where this is possible.'

With Brandon Lewis having talked himself into leading the Cabinet Office, the team needed to find a new Northern Ireland secretary, as well as a levelling up secretary to replace Gove. For the latter, officials scrambled to get hold of Simon Clarke, chief secretary to the Treasury and another fervent Johnson supporter. Around 10.30 p.m., he did not immediately answer his phone. When Number 10 reached him, Clarke 'ummed and ahhed' and said he would prefer to stay in the Treasury rather than take a promotion to a full Cabinet role. One aide in The Bunker said, 'I thought even him, Simon, the super-loyal guy, was showing a bit of reticence. He must have been thinking "shit, they might not even be able to get through to tomorrow."'

And at this moment, Johnson finally realised it was over. When Clarke refused to take levelling up secretary, other names were mooted in the study, including one close Johnson ally who had served him loyally as a minister several times. After hearing the name of the minister being seriously suggested, Johnson told the room, 'It's not fair on the nation to give them a D-list government.' Levelling up was his *Grand Projet*; if he could not find someone willing and able enough to see it through, the prime minister concluded he had finally, after months of struggling on, reached the end of the road.

Team Johnson concluded they had failed on a basic constitutional principle: they could not form a viable Cabinet to run the country. Advice had been taken on just how slimline it could be. 'We could have probably fudged it, it's not like it's some hard and fast thing. If you have an attorney general you're okay basically,' one senior official said. In 1834, the Duke of Wellington occupied the role of prime minister, sole secretary of state and leader of the House of Lords for a month, with only a lord chancellor for support. Being in the House of Lords, he did not occupy the office of chancellor of the exchequer, which was left vacant and filled pro tempore by the lord chief justice.

Johnson left The Bunker with a departing message: a plan for a Cabinet would have to be ready for the following morning, the government would still have to function. But it would not be with him at the head. 'I can't do this, it's all too ghastly, it's not me,' he announced. After weeks and months of fighting, Johnson had finally given up.

At 11 p.m., The Bunker dissolved. The aides went home. Chris Heaton-Harris and Nigel Adams, who shared a flat in Westminster, collapsed on their sofa while trying to speak to attorney general, Suella Braverman. They realised she had just announced on ITV's *Peston* programme that she would run for the Tory party leadership – but was not resigning from the government. Heaton-Harris was furious and gave her a piece of his mind down the phone. That night, Heaton-Harris and Adams, who had done more than any other minister to shore up Johnson's position, realised the end was nigh and no further politicking could save him. One Tory whip said, 'Chris reached the conclusion that evening that it was coming to an end, that we couldn't stop the fucking tide.' Instead the best they could hope for was to secure a functioning government the next morning and ensure Johnson left on his own terms.

Johnson returned to the Downing Street flat after his aides had gone home. He spoke with his wife Carrie, who was supportive and did not offer advice either way; she told him, 'Do whatever you think is right.' He phoned Lynton Crosby, his closest and longest-serving advisor, to ask for his advice from Australia. 'Mate, I've been thinking about it, what do you think? I think this is unsustainable,' Johnson said. 'I don't want to destroy the Conservative party.' Crosby responded, 'I think you're right. My advice, based on everything I know, is that it's irrecoverable.' Crosby told him he would be better focusing on his exit terms rather than facing the indignity of being heaved out by the 1922 Committee. One of The Bunker team said, 'That night, by the time he'd gone up to the flat, I think he'd made that decision. It wasn't that he wanted to go, it was a case of "the fuckers are not going to throw me out the door."'

The Bunker team had told Johnson they would support him until he personally decided it was over. 'We were always going to fight to the end for him because we owed it to him,' one close ally said. Even if a government could have been formed that Wednesday night, the aides knew it would not last long. 'We couldn't sustain any more attacks. People were still resigning, people weren't answering the phone. People were refusing jobs. We couldn't do it. Boris told us, "The country deserves better."'

Throughout the day, the prime minister had told aides that he owed the fourteen million who had voted for him in the 2019 election to deliver on their priorities. His pledge would only be partially complete: Johnson had taken the UK out of the EU, seen it through the coronavirus pandemic, taken a world-leading role in the Ukrainian war, but his administration had collapsed. Johnson slept on his decision to leave the job he had dreamt of since childhood.

8. Hasta la vista, baby

On Thursday 7 July, Boris Johnson got up and decided that the decision of the previous night still stood. As with all his previous major speeches, the prime minister began drafting his resignation address on his own before meeting with The Bunker team to talk through the details of his departure. Most of the team arrived back in the study around 7 a.m. His most inner circle did not want the news of his resignation to leak, so The Bunker team locked the door when everyone had arrived. Nigel Adams, his chief fixer, called Graham Brady at 7.30 a.m. to let him know that he should expect a call from the prime minister 'fairly soon' about his departure. Brady told Adams he thought it was 'the right decision' adding, 'It is a sad day when the prime minister goes.'

Over strong coffee and bacon sandwiches, the first draft of the speech was read out to the room before editing began in haste. Johnson's fixer Adams and strategist Ross Kempsell were present, along with the chief whip Chris Heaton-Harris, political advisor Ben Gascoigne, Tory party chairman Ben Elliot, his friendly outside advisor Will Lewis and Number 10's director of communications, Guto Harri. After the dreary sombreness and despair of the past evening, the mood in The Bunker had lightened. 'He was pretty jovial at that stage because the decision had been made. He was joking around much more,' one person present said. But in an odd way, Johnson's core team had yet to fully comprehend he was actually leaving. 'It was surreal,' one said, although another

Number 10 aide added, 'It had to end on Thursday morning. It was obviously incredibly sad, but also a relief.'

Several insiders who saw the first draft of Johnson's speech said it was originally 'far punchier' than the version he went on deliver outside Number 10. 'It shone through that he was very angry,' one ally said. Early drafts contained references to MPs and ministers 'going to beaches and sun loungers' as if to suggest that if he could have got through the summer their attitudes on his longer-term prospects would have changed. His aides suggested it struck the wrong tone.

While The Bunker was preparing for his departure, the ministerial resignations continued. Brandon Lewis, having first accepted then rejected the offer of Cabinet Office minister, quit the Cabinet at 6.47 a.m.,[1] telling Johnson that his government was 'past the point of no return'. Junior Treasury minister Helen Whately followed him out of the door two minutes later[2] stating, 'There are only so many times you can apologise and move on.' At 7.30 a.m., the security minister Damian Hinds also resigned,[3] stating there had been a 'serious erosion' of standards and 'we must have a change of leadership', followed swiftly by science minister George Freeman who said the UK had reached a 'constitutional crisis'. David Frost, the former Brexit minister, popped up to argue[4] that Johnson should go immediately with an interim leader installed until a leadership contest was finished. Even though the prime minister had not announced his decision to quit yet, his position had become wholly untenable.

Johnson made the call to Brady at 8.30 a.m. and told the chair of the 1922 Committee, 'I've reflected on our conversation yesterday and I've changed my mind.' Brady thanked him and they discussed the timetable of how the forthcoming leadership contest would play out. Both agreed that a new leader should in place by the Tory party conference in early October and the prime minister would have a graceful path out of Downing Street. Although he had technically resigned as Tory leader at that moment, there was no discussion with Brady about exiting Number 10 immediately or about an interim prime minister being installed. Johnson also made a courtesy call to Windsor Castle to inform the Queen he would be stepping down.

Publicly, there was no knowledge of his departure and the pressure continued to grow. Nadhim Zahawi, who had been health secretary on Monday 4 July, appointed chancellor by Johnson on the Tuesday, called for him to go and then on Wednesday changed his mind, U-turned one final time. In a letter on Treasury notepaper at 8.43 a.m.,[5] Zahawi said he was 'heartbroken' that Johnson had not heeded his advice and 'you must do the right thing and go now'. Johnson's inner circle were scornful of his decision. 'Nadhim made one of the greatest political miscalculations and misjudgements in history,' an ally said. 'But for that letter he could have been a serious contender in the leadership race.' Another Johnson aide said, 'Being prime minister is 95 per cent judgement. He showed a catastrophic failure of it.'

Another Cabinet U-turn came at 8.51 a.m., when Michelle Donelan announced[6] 'with great sadness' she was also quitting after less than forty-eight hours in the role. The Bunker team agreed that Johnson's departure would need to be announced immediately to avoid any further embarrassment. 'We needed to get it out there otherwise the parliamentary party was going to try and remove him that day – the chief whip and others thought that's where it was going,' one senior government insider said. 'We needed to make it clear to the world that he wasn't going to stay.' Chris Mason, the BBC's political editor was live on an extended Radio 4 *Today* programme when he received the call from Guto Harri. After taking a brief moment off air, at 9.10 a.m.

Mason announced 'the prime minister has agreed to stand down' and that he would be making a speech at lunchtime.

Immediately, pressure mounted on Johnson to leave straight away. The timetable had not been agreed, but the prospect of the prime minister remaining in office until October was met with a backlash after the traumatic events of the previous forty-eight hours. Kwasi Kwarteng, business secretary, tweeted, 'What a depressing state of affairs. So much needless damage caused.' He called for a new leader to be installed 'as soon as practicable'. Former education minister Nick Gibb called[7] for him to go immediately: 'After losing so many ministers, he has lost the trust and authority required to continue. We need an acting PM who is not a candidate for leader to stabilise the government while a new leader is elected.'

One senior member of the '22 committee said deputy prime minister Dominic Raab would have been the obvious choice. 'It would have constitutionally straightforward, made easier by the fact that Raab wasn't planning to stand for leadership,' the MP said. But Johnson's allies in The Bunker team moved quickly to ensure this did not happen. One insider said, 'We needed to show there had never been a precedent for a caretaker prime minister. We were running around the building trying to find Simon Case to put out some kind of statement saying it's not going to happen.' Ultimately there was no need for Case's letter; much of the parliamentary party was unhappy with Johnson staying on but such were the speed of events that the focus was already moving on to who would be the next prime minister.

The Bunker team discussed whether his speech should be delivered in the Downing Street garden or outside the Number 10 black door. Shelley Williams-Walker, head of operations, was keen for it to happen on the street with a lectern and Johnson agreed.

With the announcement having been made and the speech ready to go, the Bunker team worked to form a new functioning government. 'As soon as that briefing went out, people started accepting Cabinet jobs and picking up the phone,' one aide said. The whiteboard from the previous night was refreshed. 'We had to ensure there was a Cabinet and working government by the time he went out on the steps. Otherwise if the government collapsed, it would have given Labour the chance to say you need to call an election,' an insider said.

The new Cabinet was proclaimed before the statement. Greg Clark was the first shock name[8] to be made public. The dry but competent former business secretary, who was one of the twenty-one MPs Johnson had booted out of the party in 2019 for voting against leaving the EU without a deal, replaced Michael Gove as levelling up secretary. James Cleverly, the junior Foreign Office minister and close Johnson ally, was promoted to education secretary. Kit Malthouse was elevated to Cabinet Office minister. Robert Buckland returned to government as Welsh secretary, while Shailesh Vara was named as the new Northern Ireland secretary. There was relief when the gaps were filled.

Andrew Stephenson, who worked with the Big Dog support group, was made Conservative party chairman. Later, scores of junior ministers were announced, including many who had resigned such as Will Quince, returning as education minister. The appointments were a mixture of Johnson loyalists and figures from the centre of the party – with a dollop of implausible MPs who would never normally be ministers. One Johnson ally remarked, 'He may have finally ended up with the Cabinet he should have had all along.'

At midday, a message went out around the Downing Street offices that anyone available was welcome to gather outside to hear the speech. Officials beyond Johnson's core team were torn as to whether to appear. 'I thought "fuck that" because I was so fucked off about how undignified his demise was,' one official said. But another said, 'I was really proud of some of the things that we achieved with Covid and Ukraine. It was a moment of history so I decided I might as well go out.' A notice also went out to Johnson's support network of MPs and around a dozen MPs turned up including Conor Burns and Andrea Jenkyns (who was photographed sticking her middle finger up at a crowd of protesters outside the Downing Street gates). Carrie Johnson, together with their baby girl Romy, joined the crowd with Tory chairman Ben Elliot. 'It wasn't perfect, we were absolutely exhausted and had about an hour to invite everybody. But it was better than him standing alone,' one insider said.

At 12.30 p.m., Johnson bounded out of Number 10's black door and met the wall of cameras with a cheery 'good afternoon'. The prime minister said it had become clear that the will of the Conservative parliamentary party was that there should be a new leader and prime minister, with a temporary Cabinet in place. He heralded his electoral gains, the biggest Conservative party majority since 1987 and rattled through his achievements, from Brexit to Ukraine, to the Covid vaccine rollout. The tone throughout was upbeat, if testy. Given all of those achievements, Johnson set out why he was off:

'In the last few days, I tried to persuade my colleagues that it would be eccentric to change governments when we're delivering so much and when we have such a vast mandate and when we're actually only a handful of points behind in the polls, even in midterm after quite a few months of pretty relentless sledging and when the economic scene is so difficult domestically and internationally. I regret not to have been successful in those arguments and of course it's painful not to be able to see through so many ideas and projects myself. But as we've seen, at Westminster the herd instinct is powerful, when the herd moves, it moves.'

Johnson's anger at the ousting was palpable, despite the toning down of the original speech. He referenced the 'vast mandate' his party had and noted the Tories were merely 'a handful of points behind in the polls'. He accepted Westminster life would go on without him: 'My friends in politics, no one is remotely indispensable and our brilliant and Darwinian system will produce another leader, equally committed to taking this country forward through tough times.' He concluded, 'I know there will be many people who are relieved and perhaps quite a few who will also be disappointed. And I want you to know how sad I am to be giving up the best job in the world.' With a final Johnsonian flourish, he finished with 'but thems the breaks'.

His speech was not wholly well received. Many commentators noted there was no apology for his mishandling of partygate and the Chris Pincher affair, and that instead it was a valedictory for his achievements in office. Some judged it as proof he privately harboured hopes of returning to high office in the future. Soon after the address, the foreign secretary Liz Truss took to social media to say he had 'made the right decision' and echoed his core message. 'The government under Boris's leadership had many achievements – delivering Brexit, vaccines and backing Ukraine. We need calmness and unity now and to keep governing while a new leader is found.' That process began immediately; the herd had moved on.

***

Johnson's leadership had been in so much trouble for so long that the proto-leadership campaigns of his successors were in a chaotic state. From the end of 2021 and throughout 2022, furtive conversations had taken place between potential contenders and Conservative MPs. The questions asked in private were always the same: would you back me if I stood? Should I stand? Do you think I have a chance? Are you taking soundings too? Do you have any good donors I could tap up? Who is good in the media to speak to?

The structure of the race was the same as the 2019 contest that had elected Johnson and consisted of two distinct stages. All campaigns would have to meet a threshold of support among MPs to make it onto the ballot paper. A rapid series of shortlisting rounds would take place among the parliamentary Conservative party. When the field was narrowed to two contenders, the contest would move out to the wider Tory party with televised and regional hustings for members. Getting a basic campaign running, with slick communications, and targeting MPs was all that mattered in the first stage of the race.

The abrupt end of Johnson's premiership meant that none of the major contenders had fully fledged campaigns, slogans or policies in place – although informal networks of MP supporters had been built up over months, if not years. This explained why the first two candidates to publicly declare were lesser known. First was the attorney general Suella Braverman, who announced her intention to stand on ITV's *Peston* programme before Johnson had even resigned. As one of the most hardline Brexiters in the Tory party, Braverman made an early pitch for the right bloc. Second came Tom Tugendhat, chair of the foreign affairs select committee and a long-time Johnson critic. In an article[9] for the *Telegraph*, Tugendhat talked up his military experience and said it was a moment for renewal: 'I have served before, now I hope to answer the call as prime minister.'

Having witnessed the brutal sacking of Michael Gove the previous Wednesday evening, Rishi Sunak realised the end was nigh for Johnson, that a leadership contest was finally inevitable and that he would run. 'When Gove was fired, it looked mental from the outside, it was like *King Lear* in there,' one Sunak ally said. On Thursday 7 July, the day Johnson resigned, Team Sunak scrabbled around to find a discreet venue to crank up their nascent campaign. A suite was booked at the luxury Conrad Hotel opposite St James's Park Tube station. Mel Stride, chair of the Treasury select committee, began working through MPs, along with Rupert Yorke, one of Sunak's special advisors. Oliver Dowden, the former Tory party chair, assumed a chairman-like role, while Liam Booth-Smith, Sunak's chief of staff at the Treasury, took on the same role for the campaign.

In the temporary 'Ready for Rishi' headquarters, his team crammed into the hotel suite to script and film a launch video, which they planned to post as soon as possible. Contrary to the perception that a sophisticated video had been in the works for months it only came together at this point, with Sunak's wife Akshata spending much of the day digging through old family photos. The first take of his video was filmed against an upturned mattress in the suite. His team credited Cass Horowitz, Sunak's social media manager, for pulling it together. 'It's a tribute to Cass on his social media team, who were fabulous, in how quickly they turned the whole thing around,' one insider said.

That Thursday also marked the highlight of Westminster's social calendar: *The Spectator's* summer party. Hundreds of politicos, journalists, advisors, senior civil servants and hangers-on poured into the magazine's clammy bijou garden at 22 Old Queen Street for hours of free-flowing champagne and biting intrigue. With Johnson's resignation earlier that day, the party became the first major event of the leadership contest. Sunak was persuaded to attend the party by Nerissa Chesterfield, his long-time media advisor, who chaperoned him. Dressed in a well-fitted suit and open-collar white shirt, Sunak worked his easy charm on the guests with a glass of juice in hand (he is one of politics' rare teetotallers).

Guests could hardly move without bumping into a confirmed or likely leadership contender. Chancellor Nadhim Zahawi was present, guided to the key faces by his parliamentary aide David Johnston. Tom Tugendhat attended alone, hobnobbing for a brief period, as did Kemi Badenoch, the recently departed local government minister. All corners of the Tory establishment were present, including recently sacked minister Michael Gove, Graham Brady and former Cabinet ministers David Davis and Matt Hancock. Gove's aide Josh Grimstone had a full-blown row with Guto Harri in the middle of the garden over Gove's sacking, calling out Number 10's behaviour[10] as a 'fucking disgrace'. The talk of the party was that the race could be Sunak's to lose, but many guests remarked that there was a notable absentee – a Cabinet minister who had long been a fixture of the party circuit.

Almost 8,000 miles away in Indonesia, Liz Truss was attending a G20 foreign leaders' summit. The foreign secretary had jetted off on Wednesday 6 July after much debate among her team about whether being physically absent from Westminster would damage her chances if Johnson fell, or whether she would be criticised for putting ambition over duty. 'It was a really difficult call. Even at that point, we thought the PM might be fucked. But similarly, he could have made it through to conference,' one ally said. 'As soon as she landed, I knew we'd fucked up. We told Liz to get home as soon as possible.' Being out of the country showed she was loyal to Johnson, which was to prove hugely beneficial later in the race. Truss was privately clear she had to go but when Johnson did quit on the Thursday lunchtime, she returned.

As Truss was travelling back on an official government plane, she was notionally forbidden from undertaking any party political work. The foreign secretary's (relatively) small aircraft had to refuel in Dubai, giving Truss a useful four-hour window to start calling her key allies and MPs, rapidly kickstarting her campaign from the deserted airport lounge. She spoke initially to Thérèse Coffey, her close friend and ally in building parliamentary support, who was assisted by Iain Duncan Smith, the former party leader. When she landed back at Stansted Airport on the Friday evening, the calls started again. Having missed the *Spectator* party, her campaign was already forty-eight hours behind her rivals.

On Friday 8 July, with the odd sore head, Sunak's campaign team gathered at their new office on Smith Square, opposite the Conservative party's historic former central office. From 7.30 a.m., two final takes of his launch video were shot and rapidly edited. Sunak's campaign decided he would be the first major candidate to declare. 'We thought just go early, be the first out, pick up some momentum,' one insider said. From the off, however, his advisors warned him it was going to be an 'uphill fight'. Few chancellors make the journey from Number 11 to Number 10 Downing Street, as they face the difficult task of defending an economic record; Sunak would be no different. He would have to contend with his having raised taxes to their highest level in seven decades – plus his prominent role in the defenestration of Boris Johnson (who remained popular among activists).

Sunak's launch video went live that afternoon,[11] playing heavily on his family backstory. 'Let me tell you a story. About a young woman, almost a lifetime ago, who boarded a plane armed with hope for a better life and the love of her family,' it began. The former chancellor made a coded attack on Johnson's economic record. 'Do we confront this moment with honesty, seriousness and determination?' he asked. 'Or do we tell ourselves comforting fairy tales that might make us feel better in the moment but will leave our children worse off tomorrow?' Johnson's allies retaliated, accusing Sunak of treachery. One told the *Financial Times*,[12] 'Rishi will get everything he deserves for leading the charge in bringing down the prime minister.' The prediction turned out to be more prescient than even Johnson's most vindictive allies could have hoped.

That weekend, several other contenders announced bids, but one expected candidate opted out. Ben Wallace, the defence secretary who had played a vital role in the Ukraine war, said on Saturday 9 July he would not stand 'after careful consideration'. He added, 'It has not been an easy choice to make, but my focus is on my current job and keeping this great country safe.' Had Wallace stood, he would have likely been the favourite to gain the feted status of Johnson's anointed successor. In a succession of surveys by ConservativeHome, a highly influential website edited by former MP Paul Goodman, he was the clear pick[13] of the party's grassroots.

As Wallace opted out, a surprise contender opted in with a bid that would capture the Tory party's imagination. Kemi Badenoch, who was present at the *Spectator* party, set out her plans[14] in the Saturday edition of *The Times*. She argued forcefully against 'relative decline' and called for hard truths and discipline. Her pitch leaned heavily on cultural issues, including free speech, combined with fiscal discipline. Badenoch summarised her decision to stand: 'I'm putting myself forward in this leadership election because I want to tell the truth. It's the truth that will set us free.'

Having recovered from her delayed entry to the race, Truss's campaign team gathered in the kitchen of her Greenwich home on the Saturday morning – including work and pensions secretary Thérèse Coffey and trade minister Ranil Jayawardena, alongside strategists Jason Stein and Ruth Porter, press secretary Adam Jones and close advisor Sophie Jarvis. Her house became a revolving door of supporters – local neighbours Kwasi Kwarteng and James Cleverly visited and pledged their support, neither insisting on jobs in return. Greville Howard, a Tory peer, and Jon Moynihan were appointed as the campaign's treasurer and chairman to use their longstanding networks to raise the necessary funds.

Team Truss spread out around her house to make call after call to MPs to regain lost time – at one point, Truss was perched on a tiny chair in her daughter's bedroom. One campaign insider described the first days of her bid as chaotic. 'We were so far behind, we had nothing because Liz would not let the campaign get up and running before Boris had gone. There was no policy, no people, no MPs.' During that Saturday, Truss dictated the framing for her campaign. She told the assembled aides in Greenwich, 'It's going to be me versus Rishi. Rishi is not cutting taxes. I don't need to go nuts, but I need to cut a bit to set the parameters. We're going to scrap the NI rise, scrap the corporation tax rise, and we're going to scrap the green levies.'

The race rapidly became crowded with candidates who had little chance of winning. Grant Shapps, the number-crunching transport secretary, launched his bid with a piece in *The Sunday Times*[15] on Sunday 10 July, a staunch defence of Johnson. The same day, former health secretary Jeremy Hunt launched his campaign with a pledge to cancel the corporation tax rise due to take place in April 2023. The oddest entry came from Rehman Chishti, previously Johnson's special envoy on religious freedom. In a low-key video[16] that seemed to have been taken by himself in his garden, he explained, 'For me it's about aspirational conservatism, fresh ideas, fresh team for a fresh start taking our great country forward.'

Monday 11 July marked the formal start of the contest when the rules were confirmed after negotiations between the 1922

Committee and the Conservative party's board. Graham Brady wanted a quick process, but representatives of the voluntary wing of the party hoped for as many regional hustings as possible. 'They thought having twenty-five-odd events was more important than having a new prime minister and Cabinet in place for the next prime minister's questions in September,' one senior Tory said. Brady argued for the process to be wrapped up by mid-August, the voluntary party wanted to push it out until October. A compromise was reached with a dozen hustings and the result being announced on 5 September. The threshold to make it onto the ballot paper was twenty MPs in the first round, up from eight in the 2019 contest, and rising to thirty in subsequent rounds.

Two campaigns launched that day. As a scorching heatwave hit London, the former health secretary Sajid Javid set out his bid in a tiny corner of the Cinnamon Club, an upmarket Indian restaurant at the heart of Westminster, with a message focused on values, 'Over the last couple of years, our reputation on values and policies has slid away.' The other was more notable: Liz Truss's launch video was published that Monday, shot in her Greenwich back garden with a much lower-key feel than Sunak's slickly produced offering. Her core message was about delivery, referencing her five Cabinet positions and her record in striking trade deals and navigating the Ukraine crisis. 'To win the next election we need to deliver, deliver and deliver for the British people,' she said. Truss simultaneously published an article in the *Telegraph* setting out her trio of tax-cutting policies 'from day one' in Downing Street.

MPs' nominations opened and closed on Tuesday 12 July, with eight candidates on the ballot: Kemi Badenoch, Suella Braverman, Jeremy Hunt, Penny Mordaunt, Rishi Sunak, Liz Truss, Tom Tugendhat and Nadhim Zahawi. Three early contenders were out: Grant Shapps, Sajid Javid and Rehman Chishti, the last of whom failed to gain the backing of a single MP. There was speculation that Zahawi would struggle to get onto the ballot, especially as his launch speech had a similar social mobility pitch to Sunak: 'From the little boy who spoke no English to a husband, father, self-made businessman, vaccines minister, education secretary, and now chancellor of the exchequer. With a plan to deliver, and a track record of success, I am running to be your next leader.'

Wednesday 13 July brought the first round of voting, along with Penny Mordaunt's campaign launch. Jammed back into the tiny room at the Cinnamon Club on one of the hottest days of the year, the trade minister pledged a return to core Conservative values with a heavy dollop of patriotism. She likened the Tory party's plight to Paul McCartney's triumphant performance at the recent Glastonbury Festival. 'We liked hearing those new tunes but we really wanted to hear the old favourites.' Combining social liberalism with a pro-Brexit stance found much favour with MPs and party members.

A pair of critical endorsements also came that day. As they exited Downing Street following one of Johnson's final Cabinet meetings, Brexit opportunities minister Jacob Rees-Mogg and culture secretary Nadine Dorries endorsed[17] Liz Truss – granting her the semi-official status as the continuity Johnson candidate. With the backing of the Tory party's most ardent pro-Boris ministers, any questions on Truss's loyalty to the outgoing leader were quashed. One senior figure in Truss's campaign said, 'That was the first moment when I thought "Fuck, we might actually do this."'

In the first shortlisting round, Sunak came top as widely expected with the endorsement of eighty-eight MPs. But a shock second place came with Penny Mordaunt, who garnered sixty-seven supporters, usurping Liz Truss who came third on fifty. Kemi Badenoch put in a strong showing with forty MPs, followed by Tom Tugendhat on thirty-seven. Suella Braverman came third from last with thirty-two, followed by Nadhim Zahawi on twenty-five and Jeremy Hunt last on eighteen. The former health secretary, who had been the first to call on Johnson to quit back in June, was out of the running, as was Nadhim Zahawi – quite the fall for a contender who was widely expected to be a frontrunner to succeed Johnson had it not been for his flip-flopping.

Mordaunt had established herself as the insurgent: the pollster YouGov said 27 per cent of members backed her to be the next prime minister. ConservativeHome reported she was the top choice of activists. In a series of head-to-head run-offs, the survey also predicted Mordaunt would beat every other candidate – including thrashing Sunak 67 per cent to 28 per cent. The Truss campaign were taken aback by Mordaunt; one ally put her success down to being a 'blank canvas' for other senior Tories. 'She was a fresh start and everyone was able to project onto her what they wanted the prime minister to be,' an insider said.

The contest picked up pace on Thursday 14 July when Liz Truss formally launched her campaign event. Her speech echoed the core messages of her launch video, serving up red meat to the party's low-tax pro-Brexit wing. The foreign secretary pledged to slash the tax burden, shrink the state and take a tough line with Brussels over the Northern Ireland Protocol dispute. Truss praised Boris Johnson and said she would take up his mantle with the war in Ukraine. However, it was an awkward event, as Truss's delivery was robotic and stilted, and when leaving the stage, she turned the wrong way and struggled to find the exit. That night, the second round of MPs' shortlisting took place. Sunak came top again, with 101 supporters, and Penny Mordaunt came second with eighty-three backers. Truss made gains with sixty-four MPs now behind her campaign. Tom Tugendhat and Suella Braverman trailed last with thirty-two and twenty-seven backers respectively. Failing to meet the required threshold of thirty supporters, Braverman was out, handing the right flank of Tory MPs an opportunity to unite around one candidate. When Braverman endorsed Truss, she delivered the party's substantial Brexit bloc — including the European Research Group of ardent Brexiters.

Mordaunt's momentum still perplexed and troubled Truss's camp, who feared the trade minister could pick up more supporters in the coming rounds that would make it impossible for Truss to catch up. Facing the real prospect of not making the final two shortlist, Team Truss dispatched David Frost to take chunks out of Mordaunt. Speaking to TalkTV,[18] the former Brexit minister expressed surprise she was a viable candidate: 'I'm sorry to say this, I felt she did not master the detail that was necessary when we were in negotiations.' Frost also took a swipe at her pro-Brexit credentials: 'She wouldn't always deliver tough messages to the EU when that was necessary.'

Friday 15 July marked the first week of the race with a televised debate on Channel 4. The surprise winner was Tom Tugendhat, the only candidate to decline to say Boris Johnson was an honest man. He called on the Tory party to fix the collapsing trust in politics:[19] 'I've been holding a mirror to many of our actions and asking those in our party, those in our leadership positions, to ask themselves, "Is that what the public really expects?"' A snap poll found 36 per cent of viewers thought he performed best, followed by Sunak on 24 per cent and Penny Mordaunt on 12 per cent. Liz Truss came last on 7 per cent.

Truss's campaign put her bad performance down to a (misguided) assumption that the debate would not take place. Conservative party HQ had mediated discussions with the broadcasters and the Truss team thought Sunak would not participate, so giving them a proviso to opt out. But when the former chancellor announced he would be attending, they had no choice; they did not have the momentum or supporters for victory to be assured. Truss was simply not ready for a prime-time debate. 'She was nervous. We had done no prep,' one ally said. Over at Sunak's campaign headquarters, his team were confidant in their core message: 'Our plan was keep it simple, keep it to the economy because we've got the best plan,' one insider said. With their MP's lead growing in every shortlisting round, they did not have Truss's concerns. Some MPs wondered if he was lending votes to help Mordaunt and damage Truss, but his campaign strongly denied it.

Two days later, on Sunday 17 July, a slew of attacks appeared against Mordaunt in the *Mail On Sunday* and *The Sunday Times*, the result of some dark arts. The rival campaigns had combed through her past statements, particularly her post-Brexit manifesto book *Greater* and comments on trans issues she had made. 'We thought she was fucked then,' one opposing campaign official said. 'The trans stuff was toxic, so we just had to deploy it at the right moment.' That night was the second televised debate, this time on ITV. The so-called 'blue-on-blue' attacks between the candidates increased significantly. Sunak was repeatedly lambasted for raising taxes, while he in turn attacked Truss for 'fantasy economics of unfunded promises'. He also suggested that Mordaunt was more radical than Labour under its former leader Jeremy Corbyn. Sunak did better and was crowned the winner of the debate by a snap poll, coming first with 24 per cent. Tugendhat also put in a good performance and came second, but failed to reclaim the magic of his first turn. Truss put in a significantly better performance on 15 per cent. After a full day of prep, she was calmer and more confident.

In the third round of voting on Monday 18, Tugendhat was eliminated. But Team Truss remained concerned that they had yet to see a clear path to challenging Sunak in the final two. Kemi Badenoch was still gaining momentum, picking up nine supporters from Suella Braverman, putting her total of fifty-eight within touching distance of the foreign secretary's seventy-one backers. But Mordaunt's tally dropped back by one, suggesting that the attacks had stalled her momentum. 'Penny was still fifteen MPs ahead of us but losing one vote. That was it, she was done for. You can't ever go backwards,' one Truss ally said.

On the fourth shortlisting round the following day, it was Badenoch who was out. With Truss and Mordaunt bunched together, it was not at all clear who would go up against Sunak in the final two. Truss had gained fifteen supporters and was closing the gap with Mordaunt – yet she remained in third place. The night before the final vote, Truss's allies thought it was going to be 'on the wire' if she made it through. Come Wednesday 20 July and the final shortlisting vote, Truss gained twenty-seven new supporters from Badenoch's backers and jumped ahead of Mordaunt. The Truss campaign credited Thérèse Coffey and Iain Duncan Smith's whipping operation for getting her over the line, combined with the efforts of her close advisor Sophie Jarvis. The final race was set: the next prime minister would either be Johnson's foe Rishi Sunak or his anointed acolyte Liz Truss.

Johnson was entirely absent from the race, making few public utterances and no comment on the contest. On 18 July, he spoke at the Farnborough Airshow[20] about a recent flight he had taken in an RAF Typhoon – a video later emerged showing Johnson living out his *Top Gun* fantasies somewhere over the North Sea. At his last prime minister's questions on Wednesday 21 July, he told the House of Commons it had been 'mission largely accomplished' and he offered some advice for his successor,[21] 'Number

241

one, stay close to the Americans, stick up for the Ukrainians, stick up for freedom and democracy everywhere. Cut taxes and deregulation wherever you can and make this the greatest place to live and invest, which it is ... focus on the road ahead, but always remember to check the rear-view mirror. And remember above all it's not Twitter that counts, it's the people who sent us here.' In his last words as prime minister from the Despatch Box, he thanked his staff and the speaker. In a way no other previous prime minister could get away with, he signed off by channelling Arnold Schwarzenegger: 'Hasta la vista, baby.'

***

If Rishi Sunak triumphed in his first televised clash with Liz Truss, the dynamic flipped when the pair went head-to-head for the BBC debate on 25 July. The former chancellor may have come first in the MP shortlisting stage but, as his campaign team anticipated, the party's 170,000-odd members would prove more difficult to convince. From the start of the second stage of the contest, all available data suggested he was on course to lose. Days before the debate, YouGov put Truss twenty-four points[22] ahead of Sunak. Sensing that the momentum was slipping away, the former chancellor chose to take a markedly more aggressive approach on primetime national television to stir up the race's dynamics.

In the run-up to the BBC debate in Stoke-on-Trent, one of the former Labour heartlands won by the Tories for the first time in the 2019 election, Truss was incredibly nervous once again. Senior officials on her leadership campaign acknowledged 'she doesn't like debating' so a whole day had been blocked off for pre-preparations – with her advisor Jason Stein role-playing Sunak and Rob Butler, the MP for Aylesbury and a former TV presenter, tasked with improving her presentation. She knew the stakes were high: a solid performance would affirm her standing as the leading candidate to be prime minister. Yet if she did badly, it would raise questions about whether she could withstand the pressures of Number 10. When she left her Greenwich home for the debate, confronted with a full camera pack at her front door, one aide said, 'It almost felt like she was going off for war.'

Before the debate, Team Truss decamped to the Port Vale football club for further preparations with Stein, Butler and her policy aide, Jamie Hope. The room was so cold that at times Truss had to wrap herself in a blanket. Her team reckoned they did a total of twenty-four hours of preparation for one hour of television, a sign of how seriously she took the occasion. Truss's team arrived at the venue late to ensure there was minimal time for her to stew on the daunting task. Before she left her green room for the stage, the sounds of Bruce Springsteen's 'Dancing in the Dark' were heard, followed by Mark Ronson's 'Uptown Funk'. As one campaign insider put it, 'Liz went on in the optimum state of mind and Rishi fucked it.'

The exchanges between the two were the testiest to date. As in the first parliamentary stage of the race, it was the economy that dominated. Sunak posed a question to Truss about why she sought to 'cause misery to ordinary people' by risking higher inflation by borrowing billions to fund her tax cuts. She hit back that he was 'scaremongering' with 'Project Fear', a reference to the Remain campaign during the 2016 Brexit referendum. Sunak used the opportunity to remind the audience he had voted to Leave and she had not: 'I remember the referendum campaign and there was only one of us on the side of Remain and Project Fear and that was you.' But despite this moment on the attack, Sunak spent most of the evening on the back foot. He was even forced to defend his dress sense, following an attack earlier in the day by

Nadine Dorries who had compared his supremely tailored suits to Truss's '£4.50 earrings'.

Any hope that the blue-on-blue attacks would cease had disappeared. Many commentators noted that Sunak frequently spoke over Truss. In the green room, her campaign team grew increasingly furious with his attitude, resulting in a campaign comment reported by Steve Swinford of *The Times*:[23] 'Rishi Sunak has tonight proven he is not fit for office. His aggressive mansplaining and shouty private school behaviour is desperate, unbecoming and is a gift to Labour.' The Truss campaign believed Sunak made a fatal error that evening in the way in which he aggressively debated, and which would define the rest of the race. 'They'll know what a massive mistake they made because for days, people would come up to Liz, it was always a woman over fifty-five, a core Tory voter who had seen golf club sexism. They watched Rishi and thought, "He's every fucking knobhead who has ever shouted at me in my life,"' one insider said.

Sunak now appeared to be floundering, whereas Truss was improving. The next ConservativeHome leadership survey put Truss thirty-two points[24] ahead of Sunak. Over the next six weeks of the campaign, he never came anywhere near to closing the gap.

One final TV clash took place on Tuesday 26 July, hosted by TalkTV. The event was marred when halfway through the debate itself, co-host Kate McCann dramatically fainted (to the extreme horror of Truss,[25] which was captured on camera) and the event was called off. It was not rearranged and neither Sunak nor Truss would debate each other directly again.

The rest of the Tory leadership contest was dominated by a dozen hustings organised by Conservative party HQ. Across the UK – from Perth to London, Belfast to Norwich – Sunak and Truss were interviewed by a range of journalists, including this author in Exeter. Each event took the same format: Truss and

Sunak were introduced by a prominent MP supporter, delivered a ten-minute stump speech and were interviewed individually with an audience Q&A. Although they continued to take lumps out of each other's policy positions, Teams Sunak and Truss agreed through backchannels that further blue-on-blue attacks were bad for the Tory party's wider standing and further personal conflict should be avoided.

August brought a handful of notable policy interventions, followed by trip-ups from both contenders. On 27 July, Sunak sharply reversed his position on no tax cuts and announced he would scrap VAT on energy bills to ease the cost of living crisis – the very policy he had blocked while serving as Boris Johnson's chancellor. Business secretary Kwasi Kwarteng, who went on to become Truss's chancellor, described[26] it as a 'screeching U-turn'. The policy gave Sunak a talking point, but it shredded his fiscal credibility pitch. He had conceded the argument on the need for tax cuts to Truss but left an opening for her larger and better developed offering.

From the last weekend of July, Truss's team rolled out what was termed 'Operational Rolling Thunder' to announce a series of prominent backers. Masterminded by Mark Fullbrook, a Tory strategist since Margaret Thatcher's days in power who worked on Nadhim Zahawi and Penny Mordaunt's bids before going on to be Truss's chief of staff, a new prominent name was lined up each day. On Saturday 30 July, Tom Tugendhat was splashed in *The Times* as backing Truss[27] – citing her tough stance on China and foreign policy. On Sunday 31, it was former Northern Ireland secretary Brandon Lewis. Chancellor Nadhim Zahawi soon followed, as did former health secretary Sajid Javid. Tugendhat, Lewis and Javid were more natural Sunak supporters, coming from the left of the party, and yet each affirmed Truss as the frontrunner.

Penny Mordaunt, however, was the endorsement Truss's team were happiest with. The trade minister texted Truss on Friday 28 July, while Rishi Sunak was taking a pasting by Channel 4's Andrew Neil and while Truss was hosting a pizza dinner in Deptford with her husband, two daughters and core campaign team. Team Truss suggested Mordaunt could be the surprise guest at the Exeter hustings on 1 August. She was sneaked into the venue without the organisers or Sunak's team realising what was coming. There was one endorsement, however, that Truss failed to bag. Priti Patel had taken soundings early in the contest had decided not to run. She had a proto-campaign ready to go but it never happened. After the BBC debate, Truss called and texted the home secretary but never heard back. 'That was a sad one,' a campaign insider said. In an early draft of Truss's first Cabinet, Patel was lined up to be justice secretary, but she would ultimately end up returning to the backbenches.

It was not all smooth going for Truss. Her campaign posted a press release on 1 August proposing regional pay boards for the public sector to 'tailor pay to the cost of living where civil servants actually work'. In effect, her proposals would slash pay for millions of teachers, nurses and armed forces. Outside the south-east of England, the average cut would be about £1,500 per person. By midday on 2 August, the plan was ditched and the Truss campaign admitted she had not intended to cut pay. Internally, the blame game was visceral. 'A policy was made up and sent out. Liz went fucking tonto,' one insider said. 'At least it was easy to U-turn on a policy that she didn't know existed.' Truss told her team to U-turn immediately because she did not believe in it: 'My whole brand is that I don't say things I'm not going to do.' Her campaign moved the agenda on when the *Daily Mail* endorsed Truss[28] after weeks of positive front pages. She was also endorsed by *The Daily Telegraph*,[29] brokered by Nadhim Zahawi who arranged a breakfast between

Truss and the Barclay family, who owned the paper. Sunak's only major media endorsement came from *The Times*.

Truss's next major campaign intervention landed on Saturday 6 August, when she told the *Financial Times*[30] she rejected 'handouts' to ease the cost of living crisis, preferring instead to focus on tax cuts and radical economic reform. 'Of course I will look at what more can be done. But the way I would do things is in a Conservative way of lowering the tax burden, not giving out handouts.' Her team said they felt 'very confident' about the announcement, but Truss's campaign was forced in later weeks to soften the stance after widespread alarm among MPs. Penny Mordaunt claimed[31] she was 'misinterpreted' and was making a general point about preferring cuts to further spending. At the Norwich hustings on 25 August, Truss was similarly criticised for saying 'the jury is out' on whether France's Emmanuel Macron was a friend or foe. 'If I become prime minister I'll judge him on deeds not words,' she told the audience. Yet these weak moments failed to dent Truss's standing. From the BBC debate onwards, she was seemingly destined for Downing Street and thrived at the members' events. One Truss ally said the hustings were akin to 'a giant garden party'. 'It's just her talking to Tory members, these are her people. The TV debates were just not her comfort zone at all.'

Despite pressure to wrap up his campaign early, Sunak continued to fight all the way through to 5 September. He picked up a prominent endorsement from Michael Gove,[32] but lost Welsh secretary Robert Buckland[33] and his predecessor Alun Cairns who flipped to Truss. Losing endorsements publicly was without precedent in recent Tory leadership races and only served to reinforce Westminster's consensus that the race was a done deal. At every hustings, he was quizzed about his role in Boris Johnson's downfall and struggled to combat the sense he had acted ignobly – speaking to the cliché of Michael Heseltine who said of his part in Margaret Thatcher's downfall, 'He who wields the knife never wears the crown.' He sought some final momentum with a long interview with *The Spectator* magazine speaking about the pandemic response, claiming it was 'wrong to scare people' and that the government's advice on Covid had come from too narrow a pool of advisors. In his final campaign interview, Sunak told the *FT*[34] he had 'won the argument' and warned that he 'struggled' to see how Truss's sums would add up. The global financial markets, if not the Tory membership, would agree with him.

Sunak's campaign were phlegmatic about their failure. 'History will be very kind very quickly to Rishi,' one ally said. 'As the economic crisis bites, the party will realise he was right.' Despite their failure, one senior Sunak official concluded, 'I don't think there's anything that we did wrong. We could have taken on the Boris treachery argument head on.' But after the betrayal narrative set in from the parliamentary stage of the campaign, and having almost no support from the Tory press, Sunak's campaign never showed any momentum. 'We didn't get much of a channel to make our argument,' one insider sighed.

***

And where was Boris Johnson? Despite his aides forcefully arguing he should stay as prime minister until September, he did surprisingly little during his final weeks in office. On 30 July, the prime minister and his wife Carrie hosted a wedding party in the Cotswolds, having been forced to move it from Chequers after his defenestration. On the vast property of Anthony Bamford, Tory donor and tycoon of construction equipment giant JCB, whose diggers provided the most memorable visual representation of

Johnson's 2019 landslide by smashing a 'Get Brexit Done' wall, guests enjoyed drinks on hay bales and South African street food.[35] Despite the trauma of his departure, several close political allies attended, including Jacob Rees-Mogg, defence secretary Ben Wallace and his long-time fixer Nigel Adams. A leaked video on social media showed Johnson joyfully cavorting around the dance floor to Neil Diamond's 'Sweet Caroline' with his wife and son Wilfred.

Throughout August the country was gripped by fears about the cost of living crisis and energy bills, but Johnson was bound by convention not to make any major new policies. He was criticised by his political opponents for taking two holidays, in Slovenia and Greece, while the leadership contest was rumbling on. In the last weeks of his premiership, he made one final visit to Ukraine to see President Volodymyr Zelenskyy and toured the country for a series of photo opportunities and speeches. The only substantial announcement came with his decision to sign off the construction of Sizewell C nuclear power station in Suffolk.

Johnson's allies remained concerned that he could soon be out of parliament as well as Downing Street. With the privileges committee investigation looking into whether he lied to parliament ramping up in early September, his allies argued it was a sham process. On 7 August, culture secretary Nadine Dorries mused, 'If this witch hunt continues, it will be the most egregious abuse of power witnessed in Westminster. It will cast serious doubt not only on the reputation of individual MPs sitting on the committee, but on the processes of parliament and democracy itself.' Such attacks were decried by senior Tories, who argued it was an apolitical parliamentary process that must take place. The Truss campaign dodged whether they would back a serious punishment for Johnson that could lead to a by-election, arguing it was 'not a row we want to have'.

Relations between Johnson and Truss were cordial. Johnson spoke to the foreign secretary in the last week of July where in effect the pair discussed a job swap and his potential return to the Foreign Office to concentrate on the Ukraine war. But ultimately, Johnson and Truss agreed it would be too complicated. They had breakfast on 29 July in his Downing Street flat – Truss was surprised to find there was no gold wallpaper, contrary to all the stories about the expensive redecoration of his residence. Johnson gave her plenty of 'good advice', according to her allies, which was followed up by a later visit to Chequers with political thoughts on the campaign, as well as setting in motion the handover of power. Such invitations were not extended to Sunak.

Team Truss were only too aware that she was succeeding in the contest thanks to her predecessor's patronage. Johnson made it clear he would not be leaving public life and would continue to speak up on topics that mattered to him. One Truss ally drew an analogy that Johnson would be the Margaret Thatcher to her John Major, where the early years of his premiership were blighted by her backseat driving. Their fears were heightened when polls throughout August suggested the Tory party had 'sellers' remorse' about what had happened to Johnson, while he continued to refuse to rule out a political comeback. Their hope was the political caravan would move swiftly on and policy delivery would establish her position. One senior Truss ally said her team was confident he would soon come to terms with losing office. 'Once he leaves parliament, his mind will wander and he'll give less of a fuck about coming back. Once he leaves the bubble of being PM, and starts earning money, he'll start to think, "This is not such a bad life."'

At 12.30 p.m. on Monday 5 September, the results of the contest were announced at the Queen Elizabeth II conference centre in Westminster. In the very same room Johnson was crowned Tory party leader three years earlier, Truss was confirmed as his successor after beating Sunak with 57 per cent to 43 per cent – a smaller margin than her team had hoped. In her victory speech, the fourth Tory prime minister in six years pledged to deliver a 'great victory' for the Tories at the 2024 election. She stated, 'we will deliver, we will deliver, we deliver', albeit on a markedly different platform to Johnson. Whereas he was focused on investment and levelling up, Truss pivoted to the liberty-inspired message that dominated her leadership bid: 'I know that our beliefs resonate with the British people: our beliefs in freedom, in the ability to control your own life, in low taxes, in personal responsibility.'

The next morning, 6 September, Johnson stood outside Number 10 for the final time as the storm clouds literally gathered above Downing Street. Before he jetted off to tender his resignation to the Queen at Balmoral, he offered some parting words to the Tory party. 'Well, this is it folks,' he surmised, with a last pop at MPs for ending his leadership earlier than he hoped. 'The baton will be handed over in what has unexpectedly turned out to be a relay race. They changed the rules halfway through.' After rattling through his policy achievements, he left the country with a final metaphor for his future hopes. 'I am now like one of those booster rockets that has fulfilled its function and I will now be gently re-entering the atmosphere and splashing down invisibly in some remote and obscure corner of the Pacific. And like Cincinnatus I am returning to my plough.' It was missed on absolutely no one that Johnson had keenly likened himself to a fifth-century statesman who left Rome for his farm, only to be called up to return to the capital for a second time, albeit as a dictator. A subtle hint for his future it was not. Few other departing prime ministers left Number 10 with their eye already on a comeback.

Epilogue –
Was it always going to end this way?

'All political careers end in failure,' so goes the trope of the infamous Conservative MP Enoch Powell. Be it failure at the ballot box by losing an election, or failure through scandal, few recent British prime ministers have quit Downing Street at a time of their choosing. Boris Johnson certainly had no intention of leaving Number 10 when he did: as recently as April 2021, he was plotting a decade in power with aspirations to beat Tony Blair and Margaret Thatcher's three election victories. Just over a year later, his dream was over.

Through the forty hours of interviews with Cabinet ministers, senior civil servants and Johnson's closest confidants I conducted throughout July and August 2022, I posed the same question to each one: was it always going to end this way? Was it inevitable that his premiership was going to come to a crash, ending in outrage and scandal? Or was there an alternative universe where different decisions were made, with a more capable set of advisors, where his vision of a decade in power could have been fulfilled? Were Johnson's flaws too deep to offset his abilities? Was he ill-suited to the immense role that being prime minister has become?

Johnson was well known as a celebrity politician before he became prime minister; he was chosen by the Conservative party precisely because he did not fit the norms and would break convention to deliver Brexit. It was no surprise that he did not govern in a conventional sense, but few anticipated just how chaotic it would be. Through three Downing Street operations, he failed to make the job fit with his personality. During the last nine months of his government, he found great success in tackling the Ukraine war but spent most of his time fire-fighting internal blow-ups. The fatal flaw had been allowing a fissure to develop with Tory MPs, which eventually and inevitably spread to the Cabinet. The fact that his personal poll ratings tanked – along with those of the Tory party – led to his party losing faith in the prime reason he was elected leader in 2019.

One senior Conservative MP said it was 'no surprise' among the parliamentary party that Johnson's premiership ended with scandal, not least as he had failed to cultivate a support base. 'He was always living on his wits, close to the edge, taking risks, blagging his way through, and relying on personality rather than preparation. It is a recipe for the wheels falling off.'

Johnson's critics focus on his relationship with the truth, which led to the privileges committee investigation into whether he was in contempt of parliament. Politicians were lying and bending reality with rhetoric long before he became a frontline figure, yet he took a more cavalier approach than his predecessors. But again, that was well known before he became prime minister. In power, those who detested him had their fears confirmed; those who worshipped him were happy to accept his highly pragmatic approach.

Then there is attention to detail. Before he was elected Tory party leader, it was widely agreed among MPs that his best hope would be for a chairman-like role, where he would be supported by a crack team of top advisors and ministers who would oversee the day-to-day details of governing. Mark I of Johnson's Downing Street team under Dominic Cummings failed because Johnson was unwilling to let him have the power and total control he desired (the court also split as the Vote Leave supporters railed against the prime minister and Carrie). Mark II under Dan Rosenfield collapsed because he did not have Johnson's ear, or the know-how to rebuild the Downing Street operation during the partygate scandal.

And Mark III under Steve Barclay buckled due to the weight of further scandals, the contradictions of having MPs running the government, plus the collapse in relations with Tory MPs. Each of the teams had some successes – the Covid vaccine programme under Cummings and the Ukraine response under Rosenfield and Barclay – but they all failed to contend with the myriad of challenges that face a typical government every day. The evidence suggests there was no variant that could have ably supported Johnson, yet his closest allies envisaged a Mark IV that was successful, but never able to be tested. Throughout the upheaval, staff morale crumbled in Number 10 and was never rebuilt.

After their success in propping up Johnson throughout the final difficult months of 2022, the Big Dog and Brains Trust teams mooted that had they been in charge, it could have turned out differently. Johnson's outriders delivered six extra months in office from the start of the partygate scandal, but it is not at all certain they could have staved off a chaotic end to his premiership.

Within those three operations, miscommunication and chaos reigned. The policy successes of the Johnson government were thanks to small teams that were well led and empowered to take fast decisions. Whether it was the vaccine taskforce under Kate Bingham, the vaccine booster programme led by Emily Lawson or the Ukraine response under John Bew, this model worked for specific issues, but Johnson failed to replicate this successful model elsewhere in Downing Street.

One politico who worked closely with Johnson mused that by the time he reached Number 10, he had run out of officials willing and competent enough to work at the top of government. 'He never quite got the team in the way that he did when he was mayor. Boris, with all the iterations of his career, burned people. So by the time he became prime minister, the pool of people he could draw from was just getting smaller and smaller.' Some of Johnson's supporters believe he was temperamentally ill-suited to be prime minister in the twenty-first century, with the always-on demands so high.

The most strikingly consistent theme to the crises that engulfed his government was Johnson's absence at key moments. For Owen Paterson, he was in Glasgow. For the privileges committee vote, he was in India. For the by-elections and Oliver Dowden's resignation he was in Rwanda. It may have been fate or a coincidence, but too often communications broke down between Downing Street and the prime minister's travelling pack, while he was undoubtedly distracted by his travel engagements. His physical distance from Westminster added to the alienation from the parliamentary party; Johnson's preference (and indeed talent) for playing statesman on the world stage meant he neglected parliamentary politics, to which he had never really been suited.

Based on his flaws, the natural conclusion to the question as to whether it was always going to end this way then is 'yes', it was always going to come to a premature and sticky end. One senior Downing Street advisor said, 'The situation that we found ourselves in was exactly what I expected this prime ministerial tenure to look like. He was actually ten times better than I expected.' Another senior government official who worked closely with Johnson said, 'I remember Dom Cummings saying to me, "He got in there because he was the guy that could get Brexit done," but no one ever really thought about it as the Boris Johnson premiership. It was probably always going to happen because of the character flaws everyone knew he had.'

Johnson's younger allies, who had devoted less of their lives to being in his orbit, gave a more emphatic 'no' as to whether it was always going to end this way, arguing that the prime minister could have survived if the Cabinet had held their nerve. One senior ally said, 'If we had got to the summer and [Chris] Pincher had not done what he did, we'd have had a reshuffle, we'd have brought some people back, we would have had a fresh start into conference. I do think that would have been a likely scenario.' But his inner circle were also aware that his enemies would keep gunning for him, particularly those associated with the Vote Leave campaign who had lost faith in his leadership.

Within those who have worked closely with Johnson in government, there is little consensus on whether it was his personality that was responsible for the collapse of his government. One of Johnson's close political aides argued strongly there was no 'fatal flaw' in Johnson's personality that made him ill-suited to be prime minister. 'Those of us who served him made mistakes, it's always fundamentally going to happen in a building like Number 10. We were in such a defensive crouch for so long, we could never get back on the front foot in this period and start scoring runs.' With this way of thinking, had the pandemic never happened, had the errors of Owen Paterson and partygate been avoided, his tenure would have been much lengthier.

But even those who worked closely with him and insisted he got the big calls right, acknowledged he was never a details leader, that he was unable to show much interest in the mechanics of running a government. 'It is true, the great cliché of getting the big calls right, but he just couldn't get the smaller stuff, you have to sweat the small stuff in these jobs,' one aide said.

One of the senior officials drafted into Johnson's support network concluded, 'All administrations end in some form of disappointment and varying levels of crisis' but argued Johnson's did not have to end in such a brutal manner. 'There was a catastrophic series of misjudgements, mainly around communications and parliamentary handling, that led to the outcome that we got to. There was never a sufficient grip on either of those crucial elements. Everybody shares a bit of the blame – there were outstanding individual performances by people who did a great job under a lot of pressure.'

Then there is the role of Rishi Sunak. Johnson's loyalists believed his arrival in the Treasury was critical in his downfall. One close ally painted a scenario in which he survived: 'If Saj [Javid] had stayed as chancellor and people who had genuine affection and loyalty to the PM had been in Number 10, he could have been alright. The cardinal sin was the loss of the Treasury; that created Sunak as a problem. It created economic policy as a problem that could never be managed.' From the partygate scandal onwards, the chancellor decoupled from the prime minister and began to pursue his own agenda, seen through the series of wobbles that culminated in his resignation and leadership bid. There was paranoia among Team Johnson about his manoeuvres, which was not entirely misplaced.

If the fall of Boris Johnson is to be pinned on the individual, his character judgement has to be called into question. Too often, Johnson put trust in those who did not have the skills to deliver on his best interests and instead spent much of their time protecting themselves instead of the prime minister. Whether it was the ruse to save Owen Paterson, or giving Chris Pincher the benefit of the doubt, it is hard to dispute that Johnson failed because he followed ill-conceived, often politically naive advice. A minister close to Johnson said, 'You have to question some of the people he put huge trust in. He finds it hard to discipline and fire people, especially when others see as clear as day that person's in the wrong job. He just doesn't like confrontation. He likes to be liked.' One of Johnson's most ardent supporters in the Conservative parliamentary party was more direct and remarked to a colleague the week after his resignation, 'There's only one person responsible for Boris falling and that is Boris himself.'

Reflecting on the three Ps that brought down the prime minister – Paterson, partygate and Pincher – all of these crises suggested Johnson and his advisors had a difficult relationship with conventions and norms. To his critics, Johnson has debased the office of prime minister (and political discourse generally) by pushing the boundaries of truth, lying more obviously than any other politician in Britain. 'Shock news, politician lies! Do you think voters really care?' one Tory strategist said. But those who worked with Johnson throughout his career said he has a particular view on probity. 'The charitable interpretation is that he has a pragmatic view of things like honesty and the truth – that we're all in the gutter and all of us are misleading in one way or another. And we all just need to get on with it,' the aide said. 'In some respects, he was right about the hypocrisy of parliamentarians and of government. But obviously, it just goes to say, you get a drip-drip of scandals and it just reached a tipping point.'

Throughout the interviews, one consistent theme emerged, and that was that Johnson resists the idea that he has to bother with the consequences for his actions that normal people have to contend with. 'It may be there is something deep in his personality that resists the idea that he has to face up to the same reality as the rest of us,' one colleague said. Some point to his school and university days, when Johnson was rewarded for being exceptional. When the consequences of his decisions on partygate, Owen Paterson and Pincher came to a head, he refused to engage with them. But one long-term Johnson supporter dismissed the idea he was a politician who broke the boundaries of conventional politics: 'Some people say he's a Teflon politician but I've got a Teflon frying pan. It's smooth to start with but after a few years, you use it a bit, you get a little scratch and sometimes it sticks and then you get another scratch because you used the metal utensil instead of a plastic one. Then every time you cook an omelette, it sticks. Then you bin it. No one is 100 per cent Teflon, just like no frying pan lasts forever.'

Even in his final hours as prime minister, Johnson was bartering with his Cabinet ministers for one last chance. 'That was always his view: buy more time,' a colleague said. 'There was a world in which Ukraine plus the economy turns in 2024 and suddenly it looks very different.' Johnson won the 2019 election in part by pledging to end political games and focus on priorities seemingly more important to ordinary people. But from October 2021 onwards, his administration was also entirely focused on firefighting, as one Cabinet minister said: 'This is why Owen Paterson and the handling of partygate were so significant, because it was people playing politics. It looked like your bog-standard politicians messing about with politician issues.'

Johnson will be remembered as a consequential prime minister. To his supporters, he was the champion of Brexit; the leader who saw the country through the pandemic and led the world during the Ukraine war. To his enemies, he was a populist cad who debased moral standards. But neither would dispute Johnson mattered, more so than any leader since Tony Blair. His policy achievements were small but substantial. He may have only lasted three years in Downing Street, but his actions will have consequences for decades to come. His allies believe that the 'sellers' remorse' that has settled in among Tory MPs will become more pronounced in the years ahead: 'I do think in a decade's time, even sooner, they'll see they replaced an enormous figure in British politics for what people will come to regard as slightly trivial reasons.'

One of the most intriguing notions put forward by a colleague of Johnson's is that his view of politics is shaped by his adoration of the classics. Whereas most budding British politicians take to dry biographies of Disraeli and Gladstone, his cultural touch-points go much further back. 'He's a more Greek or Roman leader, than he is Judeo-Christian leader – he likes big things, big symbols,' the friend said. Such an attitude explained why he constantly ignored details and the small issues, focusing instead on the grand historical sweep, which simply does not work in a modern democracy. Enoch Powell, who made that famous elegy for political careers, was similarly a classical scholar.

Johnson once told a colleague he left the media for politics 'because they don't put up statues for journalists'. During his time as mayor of London, Johnson half-jokingly suggested a statue of himself on the M4 as it enters the city 'so they know when they're coming to London'. No statues of Johnson currently exist, so he will have to take heart that dozens of streets across Ukraine are now named after him. Long after he exits politics, the rights and wrongs of the last six months of Johnson's time in office – along with his abrupt departure – will still be debated. As the most mercurial prime minister in a generation, it was always likely his time in office was going to end this way. But as Johnson himself proved, it did not have to be.

Johnson was far from at ease about the end of his premiership and harboured hopes he would return; that the Tory party would see the error of its ways and come calling when it needed a proven election winner. But far greater events would conspire to make any yearning for the past fanciful. At lunchtime on Thursday 8 September, forty-eight hours after Johnson had tendered his resignation, Buckingham Palace issued a rare statement on the monarch's health: 'Following further evaluation this morning, The Queen's doctors are concerned for Her Majesty's health and have recommended she remain under medical supervision. The Queen remains comfortable and at Balmoral.' At 6.30 p.m., the Palace announced that she had died and King Charles III had ascended to the throne.

Her death prompted a wave of grief, mourning and national unity that most Britons had never experienced. Liz Truss was thrust onto the international stage, leading the nation's tributes to the Queen and welcoming in a new era. Emoting was not her natural arena; the prime minister's initial remarks outside Number 10 were likened by one commentator to 'reading the Queen's Wikipedia page'. But her tribute in the House of Commons fared much better, when Truss reminded MPs, 'It was just three days ago at Balmoral that she invited me to form a government and become her fifteenth prime minister.'

Johnson would have longed to be the omega to Winston Churchill's alpha, the bookend to the second Elizabethan age. Instead that honour went to his successor. One of his close allies said, 'it felt all so unfair, that moment was made for Boris'. Had the Queen's health taken a different turn, or had Johnson struggled on through the summer, he would have paid tribute to her as 'Elizabeth the Great', praising her service, humility, work ethic and sense of history. The tribute would have gone: 'so unvarying in her polestar radiance that we have perhaps been lulled into thinking she might be in some way eternal – but I think our shock is keener today because we are coming to understand in her death the full magnitude of what she did for us all.' We know this because these very words were delivered by Johnson, albeit in the House of Commons as a backbench Tory MP, not as prime minister outside Downing Street.

Epilogue – Was it always going to end this way?

At Elizabeth II's funeral, which demonstrated all the pomp and grandeur of the British state at its best, six of the Queen's prime ministers were present – four Tory, two Labour. Johnson arrived at Westminster Abbey with his wife Carrie, but there was a slight mix-up in the ordering as he came to the doors before his two predecessors, David Cameron and Theresa May. Instead of taking his pew, he was ushered to step aside and join the end of the queue for an exclusive club that no one wants to be a member of, and from which there is no escape. Johnson was now visibly an ex-prime minister, in the same category as John Major, Tony Blair and Gordon Brown. The Tory party may still turn back to its former leader – far stranger things have certainly happened in Westminster – but his departure, coinciding with the dawn of the third Carolean age, suggested he may belong to Britain's past.

Notes

Introduction – Drinks at the Garrick Club

1 www.thetimes.co.uk/article/tory-grandee-owen-pattersons-allies-plot-to-slash-his-suspension-th2t3zt8d

2 lordslibrary.parliament.uk/new-lords-appointments-in-july-2020/

3 www.telegraph.co.uk/news/2021/10/29/hounding-owen-paterson-sets-dangerous-precedent-parliament/

4 www.bbc.co.uk/news/uk-politics-48299424

5 www.theguardian.com/politics/ng-interactive/2019/jun/13/conservative-leadership-election-full-results

6 www.bbc.co.uk/news/uk-england-49132477

7 commonslibrary.parliament.uk/decision-of-the-supreme-court-on-the-prorogation-of-parliament/

8 www.bbc.co.uk/news/uk-politics-49563357

9 www.ft.com/content/cdb2dadc-ec40-11e9-a240-3b065ef5fc55

10 www.bbc.co.uk/news/election-2019-50765773

11 www.theguardian.com/uk-news/2020/feb/11/hs2-to-go-ahead-boris-johnson-tells-mps

12 www.ft.com/content/a15c78ec-4e3f-11ea-95a0-43d18ec715f5

13 www.gov.uk/government/speeches/pm-address-to-the-nation-on-coronavirus-23-march-2020

14 www.bbc.co.uk/news/uk-52192604

15 www.bbc.co.uk/news/av/uk-52801667

16 www.gov.uk/government/news/coronavirus-covid-19-what-has-changed-9-september

17 www.bbc.co.uk/news/uk-54763956

18 www.ft.com/content/6f0fc7a4-becc-474a-9924-57d9c8419551

19 www.gov.uk/government/publications/regulatory-approval-of-pfizer-biontech-vaccine-for-covid-19

20 www.gov.uk/government/speeches/prime-ministers-address-to-the-nation-4-january-2021

21 www.standard.co.uk/news/uk/dominic-raab-foreign-secretary-kabul-taliban-sky-news-b952228.html

22 www.ft.com/content/271fe3a6-58c7-4633-a05f-c4ac3c1b54f0

23 www.thesun.co.uk/news/16343362/boris-michael-gove-belting-total-eclipse-heart/

24 www.thetimes.co.uk/article/boris-johnson-is-enjoying-his-party-but-may-soon-be-facing-a-hangover-0wsclsm9l

25 twitter.com/shippersunbound/status/1445711840378511360

26 www.bbc.co.uk/news/uk-england-24459424

27 www.dailymail.co.uk/news/article-10173141/Rose-Paterson-told-article-linking-corruption-allegations-hours-taking-life.html

28 committees.parliament.uk/committee/290/committee-on-standards/news/156428/report-on-the-conduct-of-rt-hon-boris-johnson-mp-published/

29 news.sky.com/story/owen-paterson-former-minister-saved-from-suspension-as-tory-mps-back-standards-process-overhaul-12458870

30 news.sky.com/story/owen-paterson-labour-leader-sir-keir-starmer-accuses-boris-johnsons-government-of-corruption-after-vote-to-protect-mp-from-being-suspended-12459400

31 www.thetimes.co.uk/article/will-boris-johnson-get-away-with-sleaze-scandal-7qdqvwpwf

1. Partygate and an Omicron Christmas

1 www.gov.uk/government/speeches/pm-opening-statement-at-covid-19-press-conference-27-november-2021

2 www.glasgowtimes.co.uk/news/national/19753733.boris-johnson-facing-scrutiny-omicrons-spread-festive-concerns-flagged/

3 www.mirror.co.uk/news/politics/boris-johnson-broke-covid-lockdown-25585238

4 hansard.parliament.uk/commons/2021-12-01/debates/A0E282CF-039D-4F26-8F16-946B8C6E2ABC/Engagements

5 www.itv.com/news/2021-12-07/no-10-staff-joke-in-leaked-recording-about-christmas-party-they-later-denied

6   www.thetimes.co.uk/article/how-calm-ellie-was-dumped-in-favour-of-risky-allegra-on-carries-orders-00jtjskjg

7   www.theguardian.com/politics/video/2021/oct/12/a-joke-prime-minister-cummings-slams-johnson-over-handling-of-covid-video

8   www.theguardian.com/politics/2021/dec/06/dominic-cummings-very-unwise-for-no-10-to-lie-about-christmas-parties

9   www.theguardian.com/uk-news/2021/dec/08/met-police-say-they-will-not-investigate-downing-street-christmas-party

10 news.sky.com/story/covid-19-pm-facing-major-revolt-over-coronavirus-curbs-amid-authoritarianism-warning-12493843

11 www.ft.com/content/eb35a108-6186-42a4-b401-5e1df0e2c64a

12 www.reuters.com/world/uk/uk-brexit-supremo-frost-resigns-blow-johnson-mail-sunday-2021-12-18/

13 www.thetimes.co.uk/article/boris-johnson-must-sack-downing-streets-woke-crowd-says-lord-frost-dhs2jwz2r

14 www.dailymail.co.uk/news/article-10455739/How-Cabinet-stopped-Boris-insane-plan-cancel-Christmas.html

15 www.thetimes.co.uk/article/problems-mount-as-boris-johnson-ponders-next-move-on-covid-7bvm69971

16 www.standard.co.uk/news/uk/boris-johnson-kate-bingham-prime-minister-lawson-oxford-b922775.html

2. Sue Gray

1   twitter.com/Tony_Diver/status/1519209812512358401

2   www.thetimes.co.uk/article/what-your-coffee-says-about-you-are-you-a-sue-gray-americano-or-a-taylor-swift-latte-m8kt69cqv

3   www.bbc.com/news/uk-northern-ireland-57173404

4   dominiccummings.substack.com/p/parties-photos-trolleys-variants

5   www.itv.com/news/2022-01-10/email-proves-downing-street-staff-held-drinks-party-at-height-of-lockdown

6   www.telegraph.co.uk/politics/2022/01/13/two-parties-held-downing-street-queen-country-mourned-death/?

7   www.indy100.com/politics/sue-gray-downing-street-memes

8   www.thetimes.co.uk/article/dominic-cummings-boris-johnson-lied-to-parliament-about-lockdown-party-cwzhk2kcc

9   twitter.com/Nigella_Lawson/status/1486092328867663877

10 www.ft.com/content/8f849ae3-d8d0-4460-bf1e-43a35acb2ec1

11 www.thetimes.co.uk/article/paralysed-in-no-10-are-the-pm-and-his-wife-ready-to-let-it-go-2kdcnrhss

12 www.thetimes.co.uk/article/downing-street-party-crisis-johnsons-lion-king-pep-talk-fails-to-rally-aides-or-mps-in-survival-battle-fpqszmmgj

13 www.bbc.co.uk/news/uk-politics-60289339

3. Putin's Move

1   www.itv.com/news/2022-02-24/boris-johnsons-address-to-nation-in-full-after-russia-invades-ukraine

2   www.theguardian.com/politics/live/2022/feb/24/uk-politics-live-boris-johnson-sanctions-russia-invasion-ukraine-latest-updates?page=with:block-6217a3758f0814262e7ca129#block-6217a3758f0814262e7ca129

3   web.archive.org/web/20110123065155/http://www.independent.co.uk/news/media/the-blond-bombshell-540261.html

4   researchbriefings.files.parliament.uk/documents/SN07135/SN07135.pdf

5   www.gov.uk/government/news/pm-meeting-with-president-zelenskyy-8-october-2020

6   www.atlanticcouncil.org/blogs/ukrainealert/britain-and-ukraine-unveil-new-strategic-partnership/

7   twitter.com/AmySpiro/status/1498085663786344452

8   www.washingtonpost.com/national-security/interactive/2022/ukraine-road-to-war/

9   www.theguardian.com/politics/2021/nov/15/west-must-choose-between-russian-gas-and-supporting-ukraine-pm-warns

10 www.washingtonpost.com/national-security/interactive/2022/ukraine-road-to-war/

11 www.washingtonpost.com/politics/biden-putin-to-discuss-ukraine-in-video-call-amid-growing-tensions/2021/12/06/e089e36a-5707-11ec-a219-9b4ae96da3b7_story.html?

12 www.independent.co.uk/news/uk/boris-johnson-ukraine-bernard-jenkin-prime-minister-mps-b1976852.html

13 www.gov.uk/government/news/g7-foreign-ministers-statement-on-russia-and-ukraine

14 www.dailymail.co.uk/news/article-10420277/Britain-send-weapons-Ukraine-Defence-Secretary-Ben-Wallace-pledges-support.html

15 www.gov.uk/government/publications/british-energy-security-strategy/british-energy-security-strategy

16 www.theguardian.com/world/2022/jan/24/johnson-warns-of-painful-and-violent-ukraine-lightning-war

17 www.gov.uk/government/speeches/pm-statement-on-ukraine-25-january-2022

18 www.itv.com/news/2022-02-17/pm-russian-attack-on-ukraine-nursery-was-false-flag-operation

19 ukdefencejournal.org.uk/britain-sending-anti-aircraft-and-javelin-missiles-to-ukraine/

20 www.ft.com/content/35b3fdf0-6ed6-444f-849e-4076d0139d4b

21 www.nytimes.com/2022/03/06/opinion/boris-johnson-russia-putin-ukraine-war.html

22 www.spectator.co.uk/article/sunak-treasury-predicted-energy-price-hitting-5-000

23 reaction.life/boris-johnsons-popularity-in-ukraine-is-rubbing-off-at-home/

4. Operation Hillman

1 www.watfordobserver.co.uk/news/18528913.boris-johnson-visits-bovingdon-primary-academy/

2 assets.publishing.service.gov.uk/government/uploads/system/uploads/attachment_data/file/1078404/2022-05-25_FINAL_FINDINGS_OF_SECOND_PERMANENT_SECRETARY_INTO_ALLEGED_GATHERINGS.pdf

3 www.gov.uk/government/speeches/pm-statement-12-april-2022

4 www.bbc.co.uk/news/uk-politics-61083402

5 www.ft.com/content/b685482a-82f3-4602-bd02-41bb561161d7

6 www.itv.com/news/2022-02-22/revealed-itv-news-obtains-leaked-police-partygate-questionnaire

7 www.bbc.co.uk/news/uk-politics-60983517

8 twitter.com/BBCPolitics/status/1516449510679064590

9 www.thetimes.co.uk/article/rishi-sunak-apologises-after-agonising-over-future-rpf33tvdr

10 www.thetimes.co.uk/article/7c67289e-ac7e-11ec-b5dd-c16e85f55725?shareToken=b77c2d8db690a30878715486c9e137c3

11 www.independent.co.uk/news/uk/politics/rishi-sunak-akshata-murthy-non-dom-wife-tax-b2052251.html?r=68930

12 www.theguardian.com/politics/2022/apr/07/rishi-sunaks-wife-says-its-not-relevant-to-say-where-she-pays-tax-overseas

13 news.sky.com/story/rishi-sunak-says-his-wife-is-being-smeared-and-has-done-nothing-wrong-in-row-over-her-non-dom-tax-status-12584832

14 www.politicshome.com/news/article/rishi-sunak-cleared-over-us-green-card-by-independent-adviser

15 commonsbusiness.parliament.uk/document/56344/html#_idTextAnchor005

16 www.theguardian.com/politics/2022/apr/21/how-senior-tories-frantic-efforts-failed-to-block-boris-johnson-inquiry

17 redfieldandwiltonstrategies.com/latest-gb-voting-intention-8-december-2021/

18 www.telegraph.co.uk/politics/2022/05/07/keir-starmer-beergate-event-planned-leaked-memo-appears-show/

19 www.politico.eu/newsletter/london-playbook/scoops-drunk-staff-at-keir-curry-loto-xmas-party-invite-khan-dont-quit/

20 www.theguardian.com/politics/2022/jul/08/keir-starmer-cleared-durham-police-breaking-lockdown-rules-beer

21 www.bbc.co.uk/news/uk-politics-62095955

22 www.thetimes.co.uk/article/met-police-end-partygate-inquiry-with-126-fines-handed-out-f0rnpjh6c

23 www.thetimes.co.uk/article/sue-gray-report-on-downing-street-lockdown-parties-frustrated-by-police-secrecy-sxrllvrgd

24 news.sky.com/story/sue-gray-and-boris-johnson-had-private-meeting-to-discuss-handling-of-partygate-report-sky-news-understands-12617829

25 www.itv.com/news/2022-05-23/exclusive-pm-pictured-drinking-at-downing-street-party-during-lockdown

5. The 41 per cent

1   www.gov.uk/government/speeches/pm-statement-to-the-house-of-commons-25-may-2022

2   www.theguardian.com/politics/2022/feb/04/nick-gibb-becomes-latest-conservative-mp-to-call-for-boris-johnson-to-resign

3   www.bbc.co.uk/news/av/uk-politics-61100346

4   www.reuters.com/world/uk/influential-uk-lawmaker-tells-pm-johnson-gigs-up-2022-04-21/

5   www.londonworld.com/news/politics/wimbledon-mp-stephen-hammond-prime-minister-boris-johnson-quit-3710810

6   news.sky.com/story/partygate-three-more-tory-mps-urge-boris-johnson-to-quit-how-many-now-want-him-to-resign-12624248

7   www.bbc.co.uk/news/uk-politics-61636151

8   www.thetimes.co.uk/article/more-tories-challenge-boris-johnson-in-revolt-over-parties-d33gh6qj6

9   twitter.com/vicderbyshire/status/1532660093489119233

10 twitter.com/NadineDorries/status/1532778456072732672

11 twitter.com/jesse_norman/status/1533699235417403393

12 twitter.com/nadinedorries/status/1533763409627566080?lang=en

13 www.thetimes.co.uk/article/lord-geidt-threatens-to-resign-as-boris-johnsons-ethics-chief-over-parties-99gcp9fbq

14 yougov.co.uk/topics/politics/trackers/boris-johnson-approval-rating

15 www.ft.com/content/9d8b3793-7953-4f12-896e-9cb60069545a

16 www.middevon.gov.uk/your-council/voting-elections/2022-elections/tiverton-and-honiton-parliamentary-election-2022/the-results/

17 www.wakefield.gov.uk/elections/wakefield-constituency-parliamentary-by-election

18 www.theguardian.com/politics/2022/jun/24/oliver-dowden-resigns-as-conservative-party-chair-in-wake-of-byelection-losses

6. Drinks at the Carlton Club

1   www.theguardian.com/politics/2022/jul/01/cads-corner-and-mark-francois-holding-court-inside-the-carlton-club
2   www.alistairlexden.org.uk/news/conservative-party-and-carlton-club-partnership-nearly-200-years
3   twitter.com/eyespymp/status/1483552752106156036
4   www.dailymail.co.uk/news/article-10974593/How-night-Carlton-Club-ended-Chris-Pincher-frogmarched-door.html
5   policymogul.com/stakeholders/10401/christopher-pincher
6   www.mirror.co.uk/news/uk-news/like-pound-shop-harvey-weinstein-11469572
7   www.thesun.co.uk/news/4844822/bathrobe-wearing-tory-whip-chris-pincher-made-pass-at-ex-olympic-rower-and-touched-up-labour-mp-tom-blenkinsop/
8   web.archive.org/web/20180129140433/http://www.tamworthinformed.co.uk/chris-pincher-promoted-re-joins-government/
9   www.thesun.co.uk/news/politics/19054116/tory-whip-resigns-following-groping-allegations/
10   twitter.com/dominic2306/status/1543208854325977088?lang=en-GB
11   www.dailymail.co.uk/news/article-10976589/Boris-knew-Tory-MP-faced-lurid-allegations-TWO-YEARS-appointing-senior-post.html
12   www.independent.co.uk/news/uk/politics/chris-pincher-mp-grope-allegations-b2114382.html
13   www.thetimes.co.uk/article/tories-rallied-round-pincher-by-name-pincher-by-nature-in-spite-of-warnings-99r5gj5lm
14   www.bbc.co.uk/news/av/uk-politics-62049610
15   news.sky.com/story/politics-live-shocking-allegations-againt-chris-pincher-damage-reputation-of-parliament-boris-johnson-not-aware-of-serious-specific-allegations-12593360?postid=4116461#liveblog-body
16   www.mirror.co.uk/news/politics/marathon-runner-claims-tory-chris-27393078

17 www.itv.com/news/2022-07-04/bordering-on-sexual-assault-pincher-accuser-on-horrific-experience-with-mp

18 news.sky.com/story/foreign-office-boss-sir-simon-mcdonald-to-step-down-early-after-department-merger-plan-12010313

19 twitter.com/SimonMcDonaldUK/status/1544206976820854784

20 www.telegraph.co.uk/politics/2022/07/05/dominic-raab-boris-johnson-not-told-complaint-against-chris/

21 www.ft.com/content/8a56a22e-bcbe-4d7f-82ca-ebf2c8350a6e

7. The Bunker

1 www.ft.com/content/a57b6f7d-003f-4651-a6b8-3e880293efc1

2 www.andrewmurrison.co.uk/news/andrew-resigns-pms-trade-envoy

3 www.youtube.com/watch?v=gJ5Lq3eBkkc

4 www.gloucestershirelive.co.uk/news/cheltenham-news/cheltenham-mp-alex-chalk-resigns-7297122

5 www.ft.com/content/0ea7c729-b095-4796-8f34-e8cd49ba5747

6 www.theguardian.com/politics/2022/jul/06/boris-johnson-resignations-nadhim-zahawi-will-quince-laura-trott

7 twitter.com/Steven_Swinford/status/1544624832360357888?s=20&t=PIPmfNSExISEczZAAThYcw

8 www.facebook.com/LeeAndersoninAshfieldEastwood/posts/pfbid0bXnAhUrpoYy6urRn3svhdSYYVP4s1TzQUSf8ucJqFtxEHzHeB8ShCsXqjntAfSJ1l

9 twitter.com/Jochurchill_MP/status/1544637770169307137

10 www.leeds-live.co.uk/news/yorkshire-news/pudsey-mp-stuart-andrew-quits-24414405

11 twitter.com/mimsdavies/status/1544674148080910338

12 www.mailplus.co.uk/edition/news/politics/199324/exclusive-michael-gove-tells-pm-its-time-to-go

13 www.bloomberg.com/news/features/2022-07-08/boris-johnson-s-downfall-the-inside-story-of-how-his-government-collapsed

14 Turpin, Colin and Adam Tomkins, *British Government and the Constitution: Text and Materials*, p. 364. (Cambridge University Press: 2007)

15 twitter.com/AnushkaAsthana/status/1544752417757138949
16 twitter.com/JasonGroves1/status/1544757157089902594
17 twitter.com/MrHarryCole/status/1544759456088850432
18 twitter.com/ChrisMasonBBC/status/1544778322973949953
19 twitter.com/NadineDorries/status/1544780226307264512
20 twitter.com/Simonhartmp/status/1544796759645454342

8. Hasta la vista, baby

1   twitter.com/BrandonLewis/status/1544921034368901122
2   twitter.com/Helen_Whately/status/1544921576449183745
3   twitter.com/DamianHinds/status/1544928142854340608?
4   twitter.com/DavidGHFrost/status/1544930119461965824
5   twitter.com/nadhimzahawi/status/1544950219657330688
6   twitter.com/michelledonelan/status/1544952139549708288
7   twitter.com/NickGibbUK/status/544968333333876737
8   twitter.com/Steven_Swinford/status/1544987569733214209
9   www.telegraph.co.uk/politics/2022/07/07/tom-tugendhat-have-served-now-hope-answer-call-prime-minister/
10 order-order.com/2022/07/08/it-kicked-off-between-goves-spad-boriss-spin-doctor-at-the-spectators-party/
11 twitter.com/RishiSunak/status/1545426650032111616
12 www.ft.com/content/ea706ae0-284c-43f3-adb8-55c3ad8bc250
13 conservativehome.com/2022/07/03/our-survey-next-tory-leader-wallace-leads-mordaunt-by-two-votes-in-over-seven-hundred/
14 www.thetimes.co.uk/article/kemi-badenoch-i-want-to-set-us-free-by-telling-people-the-truth-85sk8prm9
15 www.thetimes.co.uk/article/tory-leadership-race-next-prime-minister-contenders-candidates-gglrzntp3
16 twitter.com/Rehman_Chishti/status/1546240922043695107
17 www.theguardian.com/politics/2022/jul/12/jacob-rees-mogg-and-nadine-dorries-back-liz-truss-for-tory-leadership
18 www.independent.co.uk/news/uk/politics/penny-mordaunt-brexit-lord-frost-b2122877.html
19 www.dailymail.co.uk/news/article-11018717/And-social-medias-debate-winner-Tom-Tugendhat-Tory-MP-makes-audience-laugh-quoting-Dumbledore.html

20 www.itv.com/news/meridian/2022-07-18/boris-johnson-attends-farnborough-air-show-in-hampshire

21 news.sky.com/story/terminated-boris-johnson-signs-off-with-hasta-la-vista-baby-in-final-pmqs-12655569

22 yougov.co.uk/topics/politics/articles-reports/2022/07/21/liz-truss-holds-24-point-lead-over-rishi-sunak-amo

23 twitter.com/Steven_Swinford/status/1551671228808708103

24 conservativehome.com/2022/08/04/conhomes-tory-leadership-election-survey-truss-58-per-cent-sunak-26-per-cent-12-per-cent-undecided/

25 www.mirror.co.uk/news/politics/liz-truss-looks-shocked-loud-27584139

26 www.theguardian.com/politics/2022/jul/27/rishi-sunak-vat-energy-bills-screeching-u-turn-kwasi-kwarteng-liz-truss

27 www.thetimes.co.uk/article/rishi-sunak-suffers-new-blow-as-tom-tugendhat-backs-liz-truss-for-leadership-wndbd8xqg

28 www.mailplus.co.uk/edition/news/politics/208330/mail-backs-truss-for-pm

29 www.telegraph.co.uk/opinion/2022/08/01/liz-truss-right-choice-tories/

30 www.ft.com/content/0d4e8e8c-a9f5-409b-86b8-884304ce0568

31 news.sky.com/story/liz-truss-misinterpreted-over-no-handouts-remark-her-supporters-say-12667655

32 www.thetimes.co.uk/article/michael-gove-liz-truss-rishi-sunak-pz67ggl9z

33 inews.co.uk/news/robert-buckland-becomes-first-Cabinet-minister-to-switch-support-from-rishi-sunak-to-liz-truss-1794189

34 www.ft.com/content/dd35044a-c568-41bc-bcdf-adf659c485d6

35 www.telegraph.co.uk/politics/2022/08/06/inside-boris-carrie-johnsons-secret-wedding-party/

Acknowledgements

When Pan Macmillan half-jestingly suggested that my second book could be on the fall of Boris Johnson, my response was that he would not be going anywhere anytime soon. But, when events rapidly conspired against my prediction, I returned to my writing desk sooner than expected.

The Fall of Boris Johnson is chiefly thanks to two superb mentors: Matthew Cole, my steadfast and patient editor at Pan Mac, and David Evans, as trustworthy and wise of an agent as anyone could ask for. With such a quick turnaround, Mike Jones made sense of the early drafts. Many thanks also to James Annal for the fine cover, Josie Turner and Hannah Corbett for their publicity prowess, and Becky Lushey for her marketing efforts.

Two comrades have contributed more than anyone else. Nathan Boroda has been a supreme researcher: his eye for detail and accuracy, combined with an overwhelming keenness for the project, was beyond reproach. Patrick Maguire was generous with his advice, proffering pints with encouragement and sage words.

I was fortunate to have several manuscript readers who helped polish the politics and the prose. Thank you to Matthew Elliott, Paul Goodman, Robert Shrimsley and Alex Wickham, plus my fantastic boss George Parker for their learned thoughts. My colleagues at the *Financial Times* were all fantastically understanding; with thanks to Roula Khalaf and Tobias Buck for allowing me to write it.

Acknowledgements

The back of this book was broken in the gorgeous Devon village of Brixham, with enormous gratitude to Emily Warburton-Brown and Sam, Michael and Fiona Roseveare for their hospitality over the warm summer. Christian May and Eliza Filby's hospitality was also much appreciated at a crucial moment.

I am fortunate in having the very best of friends. Thank you to Liz Ames and Chris Murray, Adam Atashzai, Katy Balls, Toby Coaker, James Kanagasooriam, Lucy Fisher, Charlotte Ivers, Ed Leech, Ed Macdonald, Luke McGee, Matt McGrath, Duncan Robinson, Laura Trott, Tom Tugendhat, Rhiannon Williams, Hugo Wiseman and Nicky Woolf for their unyielding support. A special thanks also to Sophia Gaston for all her patience, understanding and kindness.

My family have been as loving and supportive as anyone could ask. Bronwen Payne, to whom this book is dedicated, has given unwavering faith and kindness to the project, along with the keenest reading eyes. Dan Jackson provided some very good times on Tyneside.

Above all, this book owes a huge debt to Greg Callus, who has been a personal rock and judicious guide throughout the researching and writing. Without his steadfast support, friendship and counsel, it simply would not have been completed.

And finally, thank you to all those politicos who kindly gave me their time. Many of Boris Johnson's team had to contend with losing their jobs alongside my pesky requests. As a first draft of recent history, not everything can be exact. But I have sought to accurately portray events as the interviewees narrated them, so I hope all feel it fairly reflects a most unruly period in British politics.

Sebastian Payne, October 2022
London

Picture Credits

Page 1 top © Tim Anderson/Daily Mirror via Mirrorpix

Page 1 middle © House of Commons/PA Archive/PA Images

Page 1 bottom © Hollie Adams/Stringer via Getty Images

Page 2 top © Jonathan Buckmaster/Daily Express via Mirrorpix

Page 2 bottom and page 7 bottom right © Ian Davidson/Alamy Stock Photo

Page 3 top and page 4 middle © ZUMA Press, Inc./Alamy Stock Photo

Page 3 bottom left and right and page 6 top and bottom left © PA Images/Alamy Stock Photo

Page 4 top © Pool/Pool via Getty Images News

Page 4 bottom left © Photo Handout/UK Government via Getty Images

Page 4 bottom right © Dan Kitwood/Getty Images

Page 5 top left and page 8 middle © REUTERS/Alamy Stock Photo

Page 5 top right and page 8 bottom © MARTIN DALTON/Alamy Stock Photo

Page 5 middle left © Tayfun Salci/ZUMA Press Wire

Page 5 middle right courtesy of Ross Kempsell

Page 5 bottom © ANDY RAIN/EPA-EFE/Shutterstock

Page 6 bottom right © Sajid Javid/Twitter

Page 7 top © Allstar Picture Library Ltd/Alamy Stock Photo

Page 7 bottom left © photo-fox/Alamy Stock Photo

Page 8 top © Guy Bell/Alamy Stock Photo